World Food

ITALY

Matthew Evans

WORLD FOOD Italy
1st edition

Published by
Lonely Planet Publications Pty Ltd A.C.N. 005 607 983
192 Burwood Rd, Hawthorn, Victoria 3122, Australia

Lonely Planet Offices
Australia PO Box 617, Hawthorn, Victoria 3122
USA 150 Linden Street, Oakland CA 94607
UK 10a Spring Place, London NW5 3BH
France 1 rue du Dahomey, 75011 Paris

Photography
All of the images in this guide are available
for licensing from Lonely Planet Images.
email: lpi@lonelyplanet.com.au

Published
March 2000

Although the author and publisher have tried to make the information as accurate as
possible, they accept no responsibility for any loss, injury or inconvenience sustained by
any person using this book

ISBN 1 86450 022 0

Printed by
The Bookmaker Pty. Ltd.
Printed in China.

Combe (Florence)

About the Author
Matthew Evans is a self described taste junkie who feeds his habit by feeding himself. And then writing about it. A qualified chef by trade, he now makes a living from the less honourable profession of freelance restaurant critic, food writer and recipe columnist. He was chosen as Australia's best new food writer in 1999. Matthew writes regularly for Australian publications *The Sydney Morning Herald* and *The Age*, Melbourne. His words appear each month in *Australian Gourmet Traveller*, and on occasion in *Vogue Entertaining & Travel* and *Conde Naste Traveller*.

About the Photographer
Alan Benson is a food & lifestyle photographer. Born in Manchester, he trained as a chef in London and now lives in Australia. He is a regular contributor to *Australian Gourmet Traveller* among other publications.

About the Linguist
The language sections were compiled by members of Italy's Slow Food Organisation, with help from Peter D'Onghia of Lonely Planet. The Slow Food contributors were Gabriella Cossi, Alberto Crinella, Carmela Rita Abagnale, Davide Dellarosa, Enrico Azzolin, Enzo Massaro, Fausto Natta, Francesco Colonnesi, Franco Turaglio, Gianni Vercellotti, Lorenza Masetti, Marco Bechi, Matteo Rugghia, Oretta Zanini De Vita, Renzo Pari, Pier Luigi Botta', Piero Arnaudo, Pino Antonini, Roberto Redaelli, Salvatore Pirro, Sandro Defilippi, Valentino Gostoli, Vincenzo Nava and Walter Bordo.

From the Publisher
This first edition of *World Food Italy* was edited by Foong Ling Kong and Martin Hughes of Lonely Planet's Melbourne office. Brendan Dempsey designed, Paul Piaia mapped with finishing touches provided by Natasha Vellelley. Tim Uden and Andrew Tudor provided technical know-how. Lara Morcombe indexed. Valerie Tellini, Lonely Planet Images, co-ordinated the supply of photographs. Peter D'Onghia oversaw the production of the language section, and Kerrie Hicken assisted.

Sally Steward, publisher, developed the series and Martin Hughes, series editor, nurtured each book from the seeds of ideas through to fruition, with inimitable flair.

Acknowledgements
Matthew and Alan would like to thank all those hundreds who helped as they researched and travelled around Italy. In particular, thanks must go to Gino Di Santo and the staff at Enoteca Sileno for the contacts and advice; the Mensurati family of Norcia for the meal, the truffles and the accommodation; the staff at Dei Fabbri restaurant in Padova; Sally McGill from FD&C Wines; the Pedroni family for a meal out of hours and the

balsamico tour; Sally Webb for the market tip-offs; Giovanna Giamo for showing us a side of Sicilia we'd have never found ourselves; Megan Kriewaldt-Rialti and Lino Rialti for the fabulous meal and room as well as slipping us more than our fair share of digestivi; Vincenza Saladino for just being lovely; Marcello Fondi and family; Luisa Sale and family for the bread making; & Gabriella Cossi for the language sections and showing us yet another wonderful side of Lombardia.

Matthew also thanks Nick Haddow and Will Studd for the information on cheeses and Mallory Wall at Cafe Di Stasio for letting him drink more aperitivi than is good for him, all in the name of research. Huge heartfelt thanks to Alan Benson for the humour and support, and helping to make the travelling so much more fun. Special gratitude to Rosemary Lobban for proof reading, researching, translating and for understanding that both our lives really, honestly, truly would get back to normal one day.

Alan thanks Kimm Wilson for generously (and uncomplainingly) relaying messages, checking mail and playing the one-woman support crew for his business. He's particularly thankful for the long distance hugs, and above all for being allowed to leave home for so long at one time.

Warning & Request

Things change; markets give way to supermarkets, prices go up, good places go bad and not much stays the same. Please tell us if you've discovered changes and help make the next edition even more useful. We value all your feedback, and strive to improve our books accordingly. We have a well-travelled, well-fed team that reads and acknowledges every letter, postcard and email and ensures that every morsel of information finds its way to the appropriate people.

Each correspondent will receive the latest issue of Planet Talk, our quarterly printed newsletter, or Comet, our monthly email newsletter. Subscriptions to both are free. The newsletters might even feature your letter so let us know if you don't want it published.

If you have an interesting anecdote or story to do with your culinary travels, we'd love to hear it. If we publish it in the next edition, we'll send you a free Lonely Planet book of your choice.

Send your correspondence to the nearest Lonely Planet office:
Australia: PO Box 617, Hawthorn, Victoria 3122
UK: 10a Spring Place, London NW5 3BH
USA: 150 Linden St, Oakland CA 94607
France: 1 rue du Dahomey, Paris 75011

Or email us at: talk2us@lonelyplanet.com

contents

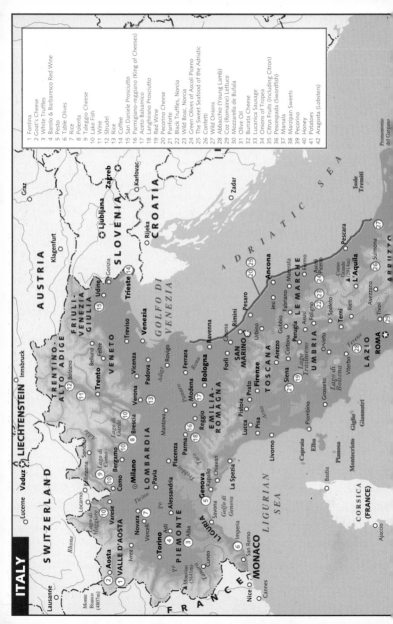

ITALY

1 Fontina
2 Goat's Cheese
3 White Truffles
4 Barolo & Barbaresco Red Wine
5 Pesto
6 Table Olives
7 Rice
8 Polenta
9 Taleggio Cheese
10 Lake Fish
11 Wine
12 Strudel
13 Rice
14 Coffee
15 San Daniele Prosciutto
16 Parmigiano-reggiano (King of Cheeses)
17 Aceto Balsamico
18 Langhirano Prosciutto
19 Red Wine
20 Pecorino Cheese
21 Panforte
22 Black Truffles, Norcia
23 Wild Boar, Norcia
24 Green Olives of Ascoli Piceno
25 The Sweet Seafood of the Adriatic
26 Confetti
27 Wild Onions
28 Abbacchio (Young Lamb)
29 Coz (Romaine) Lettuce
30 Mozzarella de Bufala
31 Olive Oil
32 Burrata Cheese
33 Lucanica Sausage
34 Onions of Tropea
35 Citrus Fruits (Including Citron)
36 Pescespada (Swordfish)
37 Marsala
38 Marzipan Sweets
39 Pecorino
40 Honey
41 Potatoes
42 Aragosta (Lobsters)

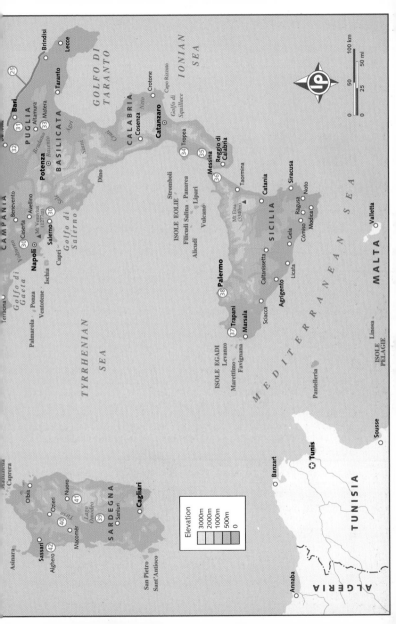

Eating in Italy is a revelation. To sit at a dinner with an Italian is to understand where their heart is at, what is important to them. To savour hand-made pork sausages under the Pugliese sun is to see, finally, how important eating is for a happy life. And to watch the fluid movements and charming manner of a Neapolitan pizza maker is to see that food isn't just part of Italian culture, it is a creative and fulfilling essence in their life.

The country that has exported its food culture around the world (think pizza, pasta) is a surprising place. It's only within the last 150 years that Italy as we know it came into being, and even today, it feels like a collection of 20 separate countries rather than a united nation. So while the people are linked under one government, differences abound. Nowhere can that be seen more than in the food. Where else can you eat couscous or strudel, over 200 types of pasta, nearly 500 types of cheese and drink wine made in over 1000 styles?

Italy is graced not only with several dialects and wildly differing geography, but it's also blessed with clever cooks. A veritable roller-coaster ride of affluence and poverty has led to a cucina (cuisine) that is one of the most regional in the world. Add to this a sense of local pride, hospitality and recognition of the seasons' bounty, and you end up with food that has a sense of its place, its time and its origins. Not only does Italian cucina have a sense of those things, but it's a life-affirming celebration of them.

Italian food is something to be enjoyed, as part of embracing the moment, as part of life. This cultural enjoyment and immersion in food is for everybody. So, while there are world-class, fine-dining restaurants in Italy, you're just as likely to have a fantastic experience watching someone make ravioli in their kitchen, as you would have eating out.

No book can list with authority every single dish authentically from every village because the subject is simply way too big. The variations on every theme are seemingly endless. Anyway, with an encyclopaedia like that, what would there be to discover?

This guide is a primer to help you get a feel for the joy of Italian food and navigate through an Italian menu. We explain the commonly found dishes and many of the obscure, regional specialities. The array of experiences that Italy holds could fill more than one lifetime. It is the differences between the regions, between one village and the next, one city and the next, even between one group of people and the next, that set the heart racing. As you will find, the only things Italians like to agree on is their differences.

the
culture
of italian cuisine

Italian **cucina** (cuisine) doesn't exist. Spend any time among the people of, say, Umbria or Puglia and you'll hear an awful lot about Umbrian cucina and Pugliese cucina. But Italian cucina? Well, that's not something they know about. The geography makes for many micro-climates and the history for plenty of micro-cultures. The result is a cucina that is one of the most diverse, unexpected and intriguing imaginable.

This diversity is due partly to the relatively recent unification of Italy, and partly to the dramatic differences in geography. The narrow band of land now called Italy covers 20 regions. Some nudge the Austrian and Swiss Alps; on a clear day Sicilia is within sight of northern Africa; Milano is closer to London than it is to parts of Sicilia; while in Valle d'Aosta, they speak French as fluently as Italian. The food in each of these places registers the geographic variances.

The Italian peninsula is dominated by rolling hills or fiercely steep mountain ranges dotted with fertile flat plains, all of which affect the way Italians eat. A corrugated mountain range, the Appennini (Appenines), runs north–south through the centre of the country, providing snow-capped peaks through much of the year, while the large water mass of the Mediterranean tempers what would otherwise be very harsh winters.

AN INTOXICATION OF THE SENSES

Italian food can be exported but the cucina can only be experienced in Italy itself. To eat with passion isn't the preserve of the well-off or well-heeled. Food and its enjoyment are embedded in the national psyche.

So you may see taxi drivers on their lunch-break eating a **panino** (bread roll) at the bar of one of the city's best ristorante next to surgeons from the local hospital. You'll see men in overalls seeking out the finest freshwater fish at a lakeside restaurant near Como. Couples dressed in Versace eat pizza from the same pizzeria in Napoli as the waterside workers, all of them folding the pizza neatly into four before hoeing in. Everyone indulges their senses whenever they can.

Just as they dress well, Italians like to eat well – not just at the flash restaurant, or at the anniversary or birthday. Even a simple pasta is cooked with the passion of an artist, and consumed with the appetite of the connoisseur. All bakers think of themselves as a Dante of the oven, every cheesemaker is a Pavarotti of the palate, and every market has its own Roberto Benigni pulling faces and making people laugh.

Food isn't the event, but it's always part of the event. Life is what happens while you're doing other things, and food is what happens as part of life. A bar is a meeting place, the coffee maker is the person you spend more breakfasts with than anyone else; the local trattoria owner can become a family friend over the years. That joke they share with you, that kiss on the cheek when you walk in the door ... that is what makes it Italy. That said, Italians wouldn't patronise these places unless the food was good.

History

While tribe after tribe, then empire after empire dominated part or all of the Italian peninsula, there is one common denominator to Italian cucina – everyone seems to have arrived, seen the food that was here, liked it and added their own bit of pizzazz to make it even better.

Take the Etruscans, the first really organised group to run the show, from about the 12th century BC. They saw the local grain, **farro** (a form of spelt), and cultivated it. The Romans added wheat and spices such as pepper and ginger. The Moors' influence can be seen today in the use of couscous and fragrant citrus along with the use of almonds in sweets. The Spanish brought the Grenache grape to Sardegna, where it became known as **Cannonau**. And in between, such home-grown empires as the Genoans and Venetians, who were zealous traders, embellished the cucina with ingredients brought back from travels to the near and Far East.

The Venetian Marco Polo did his bit to open up the minds and palates of what now forms Italy. Accompanying his father, he left Venice in 1271 bound for China, returning with a bounty including sugar, rice and spices (although rice was already introduced to the south by the Arabs).

But the real coup for cucina came when the former pirate from Genova, Cristoforo Colombo, made an epic journey to find a quicker, less perilous route to India and found the rich bounty of the Americas. Of all

---

SIGHS, KISSES AND LIES

As you eat your way across Italy, you may find some names of the dishes not translating as you'd expect. That may be because Italians use real-life expressions to describe food. You may see pasta called **stringozzi**, which is named for the leather cord once used to strangle tax collectors in Umbria; **strangolapreti** and **strozzapreti** both refer to 'priest-stranglers', and are usually a round pasta or gnocchi. **Coglioni di mulo** are **salsicce** (sausages) from Umbria that are shaped like the private part of a mule, and **le palle del nonno** ('granddad's testicles') are crinkly-looking pork sausages. **Sciatt** (dialect for 'toad' from Valtellina) are cheese-stuffed buckwheat pastries; **ossi di morti** ('bones of the dead') are little sugar-coated biscuits shaped like bones; **brutti ma buoni** are 'ugly, but good' hazelnut macaroons. Other pastries are called **sospiri** (sighs), **baci** (kisses), **bugie** (lies) and **chiacchiere** (gossip). While often the names are whimsical, there's sometimes a practical reason. For instance, **pagadebit**, a prolific grape variety from Friuli and Romagna, means 'pay a debt'.

events, this has founded what we now know as Italian cucina. Before his return, **peperoni** (capsicum), **peperoncini** (chillies), **pomodori** (tomatoes), **patate** (potatoes) and **granturco** (maize) were unknown to Europe. Who can imagine Italian food without tomatoes?

Over time, everyone who visited has added and embellished what we know as Italian cucina, always with an eye to what was good before.

Baroncello tomatoes from Pachino, Sicilia

How Italians Eat

Italians eat with gusto; they eat fast, they eat a lot, and they like to lubricate the meal with local wine.

The main meal of the day is traditionally **pranzo** (lunch), and while this is changing gradually because of modern work practices (such as the abolition of the **siesta** or afternoon nap in some cities), the big pranzo is still very much alive, thanks to the nature of the **prima colazione** (breakfast) which usually consists of no more than a cappuccino or espresso. For the few who do eat, the prima colazione of choice is a **brioche** (a pastry). The most popular brioche is **cornetto**, basically like a less flaky croissant, often filled with **cioccolata** (chocolate), **marmellata** (marmalade) or **crema** (cream). The combination of a **cornetto con crema** with a lukewarm cappuccino is positively life-affirming, and you could do far worse than spend your Italian mornings finding the perfect bar for colazione.

Pranzo can be a huge meal (after all, most people skip breakfast) and was typically eaten at home in days of yore. It was at least two courses – pasta and a **secondo,** second course – although it could be as many as 10. These days, office workers may simply grab a panino or **pizza a taglio** (piece of pizza) to eat while they work, particularly in the larger cities.

The evening meal, **cena,** is traditionally smaller than pranzo, but this, too, is changing. It used to be – and still is, to many – one course, perhaps pizza a taglio, maybe a pasta, or a plate of veal with some vegetables. Because of this, many **trattorie** (restaurants) that also operate as pizza houses only light the woodfire for the evening trade.

Stall holder at the market in Matera, Basilicata

FARE LA PASSEGGIATA

To **fare la passeggiata** is to take a stroll, but you've never seen a stroll like this. Every evening the streets in virtually all corners of Italy come alive as the locals participate in a great communal stroll, called **la passeggiata.** Whole families dress up and parade up and down certain streets. Traffic can come to a standstill as the entire population tries to get to the most beautiful parts of town for this important cultural event.

In most towns the focus for the passeggiata is the historic centre. Cobbled, car-free streets are favoured, but there should always be some shopping. While youthful eyes try to catch and hold the gaze of the opposite sex, cousins, neighbours or old friends meet and chat, and all the while a lot of window-shopping is done. What you see in most shop windows is what is in the store, and you only enter when you see what you like. Otherwise you just keep strolling, chatting, holding your mother's hand, showing off your new boyfriend or arguing with an old war buddy about politics.

The passeggiata is a tremendously civilised occasion, and starts at the end of work during the week, a little earlier in the afternoon on Saturday, and finishes at the start of dinner. Piazzas fill with old men deep in conversation. Gelato is licked, crotches are furtively scratched, arms are entwined and new babies admired.

To become a part of the passeggiata, dress well (though men won't need a tie), polish your shoes and follow the crowds. The talking is more important than the walking, and the shopping is incidental. As you talk, stop occasionally to gesture madly and reinforce your point. If you see anyone you know well, pounce on them with unbridled enthusiasm, as though you haven't seen them for years (even if you saw them during yesterday's passeggiata) and kiss them on both cheeks.

To live like an Italian, each daily evening stroll should be grasped as if it were your last. You can use the passeggiata on your way to a bar for a drink or to stimulate the appetite.

The most fascinating places to fare la passeggiata are: in the World Heritage-listed town Matera in Basilicata; on the island Siracusa in Sicilia; or through the centre of any of the demure old towns such as Reggio Emilia. In fact, the best place to stroll elegantly and talk passionately is in just about any town in Italy. And the best day to do it is always today.

Taormina, Sicilia

Etiquette

Just as an Italian at our table would make only a few *faux pas*, most guests to an Italian table get it pretty right. We simply aren't that different. That's the good news.

The bad news is that what constitutes 'good manners' alters – as it does everywhere – depending not only on whom you're with, but where you are eating, and the part of the country you're in.

The *really* good news is that Italians are so inherently hospitable that they will forgive virtually anything you do unwittingly.

Home Etiquette

You've heard that old myth about the Italian mamma who keeps feeding you until you're just about to burst? Well it's hardly a myth. Generosity at a meal is a sign of hospitality, so refuse at your own peril. Hearty eaters tend to be looked upon more favourably, particularly by older Italians, who show genuine concern for those who are noticeably thin. You may not hear things like "Come on, eat up, you'll get your figure back," but it's not far from the surface. Italian women, in particular the younger ones, are often diet fanatics, but they can still put away a fair bit of food at the right occasion.

The table setting will be the same at home as at most restaurants. There will be two forks and one knife, and a spoon if you're eating soup. You won't be given a bread plate and it's perfectly normal to break the bread over the cloth and lay it there while you eat.

There will also be more than one course at virtually any meal to which you're invited (see the Understanding the Menu chapter). Many families will bring out the **prosciutto** (cured ham) to carve at the table. **Salame** (cured sausages), often homemade, will be sliced and offered. A great steaming bowl of pasta is almost a certainty, then a small serve of meat or fish, to be followed by salad and fruit. Large meals may also contain a soup, a second pasta course, a **dolce** (dessert), or all three.

The rules of eating change depending on the family's economic situation, but the rules are all fairly similar. You should place your knife and fork back on the table after each course until after the salad or vegetables. If there are two forks, the first can be left in your emptied pasta bowl to be cleared away.

You could well only be offered one glass for both water and wine. You drink a glass of one, followed by a glass of the other. If you're used to drinking large volumes of water, it may be a good idea to slurp a lot of water just before the meal or end up incredibly drunk, especially if the host is pouring the wine.

At someone's home you can and should **fare la scarpetta** (make a shoe) with your bread and wipe plates clean of sauces – a sign you've really enjoyed the meal, and one that won't go unnoticed. Cutlet bones can be handled with the fingers, which can be surreptitiously licked, and small groans of enjoyment are positively welcomed. Serviettes aren't generally tucked into collars, but it's more acceptable to do so at home than out.

When eating pasta, don't be afraid to shovel it in. If you don't, the rest of the table will probably be finished well before you. Long strands of pasta are twirled around the fork, using the pasta bowl as the base to make bite-sized morsels. Any bits hanging down are bitten through and *not* slurped up as is done in parts of Asia. It's okay to lower your head towards the bowl and eat energetically. You will probably never be offered a spoon to eat your pasta with, as locals consider this practice quite rude.

Italians don't like people who eat with their mouth open or talk when their mouth is full. In contrast to the way they wolf down pasta, they find the North American habit of cutting the meat and then switching the fork to the right hand intriguing. They tend to understand the difference but don't consider it particularly civilised.

Restaurant Etiquette

Your behaviour should be a little more refined when dining out. The flashier the place, the more sophisticated the etiquette. It's common sense, really. So, while you may pick up a bone in a trattoria, you can't lick your fingers afterwards. In a fancy restaurant you may hesitate to pick it up at all.

Italians tend to dress with impeccable style at most meals, so try to look smart-casual, although a jacket and tie is often seen as excessive except for doing business.

DATING

Italians are the first to admit that you can't live on food alone. There's also the human side to life. So, if you've just met someone charming, you may invite him or her for a coffee 'Ti offro caffè?'. Because a caffè is such a hasty event, the interlude will be very brief. Or invite your new-found friend out for pizza. People of all ages and all over the country love the humble pizza. It's the easiest meal to eat, the most relaxed and is always suitably priced. Besides conversation, price – and the question of who should pay – are worth thinking about. Women may offer to pay, and in modern Italy we've been told it is POSSIBLE for the woman to pay. Possible yes, but in reality, it simply doesn't happen.

Ristorante, Orvieto

When young men eat with one another, the standards of etiquette drop, as they seem to everywhere. Men also tend to become louder, and have an eye out for shapely women, about whom they will pass comment, usually within earshot of the women concerned. Such behaviour is not considered particularly appropriate by some younger Italians, but many still consider it suitably lusty and flirtatious rather than meaning to give offence. The best strategy, if they're commenting about you, is to ignore them.

Women, on the other hand, tend to maintain the same social graces when dining away from their menfolk as they would in a mixed group. They may flirt but it will be more of the passing-glance-and-smile style rather than a bawdy comment.

SMOKED OUT

Apparently there is a law in Italy that requires all restaurants to provide a non-smoking area. We say 'apparently' because you will be very hard pressed to find a non-smoking section except in the most expensive of ristoranti. Smoking is a way of life – locals puff energetically on cigarettes and even cigars just as your meal hits the table. You can request a non-smoking table when you book but don't be surprised if you don't get it.

Business Etiquette

The business lunch is not only alive and well, in Italy it's an artform. Taking clients out for a meal is not just considered a friendly gesture, it is almost mandatory. So don't expect a late morning meeting to finish until after the caffè has been drunk that afternoon.

The most fantastic thing about the business lunch is that if you're the guest, usually the lunch is purely social. Little work is done and hosts are more interested in your family, how you came to be in the job, and if you miss your kids. The lunch is pure hospitality rather than hard-sell.

Italians love to show off their regional or local specialities and a business lunch is no exception. Prepare yourself for large quantities – bliss to some, an insurmountable challenge to others.

Many businesses have prior arrangements with restaurants and no money appears to change hands. This very civilised arrangement removes the inevitable bill-paying tussle. Alternatively, one of the group may fix the bill while you're still distracted, perhaps by being force-fed that last dolce.

staples
& specialities

For all their culinary distinctions, Italians are actually united by many of the staples which make up their **cucina** (cuisine). Despite the mind-boggling number of variations which exist, the regions of Italy are bound by the common use of bread, pasta, cheese, salumi, pizza, seafood, gelati and dolci, as well as the myriad vegetables and meats Italians draw on to create their favourite dishes.

Produce sold at markets and shops is often marked with its place of origin, including the prideful **nostrano** ('local' or 'homemade'). Locals always know the regions that produce the best **pomodori** (tomatoes, the best being from Pachino in Sicilia), **mozzarella di bufala** (buffalo-milk cheese, from Battipaglia or Caserta in Campania) and **aragosta** (crayfish, from Alghero in Sardegna). And while many foods are available throughout Italy, or even around the world, it's so much more relevant when you have the opportunity to try them at the source. (Many more predominantly local specialities are discussed in the Regional Variations chapter.)

The trick to good food, as any proud Italian will tell you, is in the execution. And theirs is, without question, the best in the country.

Exterior of Salumeria (Norcineria) Norcia, Umbria

Bread

Il pane, bread, is served at every meal apart from breakfast. You'll be given a basket of it in restaurants, and freshly cut chunks in Italian homes. You'll be expected to use it to moderate the richness of meals, and most of the time it will be white.

Often – and perhaps surprisingly – the bread you'll find is crusty, light and airy inside, and not as satisfying as it could be. Sadly, much of it is fairly ordinary; bread seems to be one of the first things to have suffered under the moves Italy has made towards faster and simpler food production. It's only about half a century since white bread was the preserve of the well-off. In those days, most bread was baked in community-based, wood-fired ovens.

But brilliant breads do exist if you know where to look. There are the paper-thin breads of the Sardinian interior (see Pane Fresa in this chapter), the hard-crusted, deliciously chewy loaves from those masters of the loaf in Puglia, and the heavy, German-influenced breads of Alto Adige. There's even **pane toscano**, crumbly, unsalted bread from Toscana (there's a similar version in Umbria), a somewhat acquired taste, but essential for the

Hand-made grissini on restaurant table

bread-thickened soups of the area. In Liguria and around you'll find **focaccia**, thin, yeast-risen breads usually sprinkled with salt or herbs, sliced in half and filled.

Wholemeal bread lovers should look for **pane integrale**, the general term for bread made with at least some proportion of wholemeal flour. For those who like dark rye, **pane di segale** can be found in Italy's far north.

On restaurant tables you'll see **grissini**, thin sticks of crispy bread made from a yeast-risen dough. While they usually come in packets the really good ones are **fatto a mano** (made by hand) and are served loose in the bread basket.

PANE FRESA

Chiarina Dore pulls the bread from the oven. It's puffed up like the lightest of goose-down pillows, the blistering steam inside straining to escape. It's no wonder, with the oven set at 500°C (932°F)! The loaf looks like it will sail up to the ceiling like a yeast-propelled zeppelin.

She lays the already deflating bread down on the table, allows it to settle, then presses it to remove all the air. Luisa, Chiarina's daughter, swiftly cuts through the edges with a knife, separates the top and bottom sheets, and stacks them with a weight on top.

Chiarina's family are baking **pane fresa**, the local name for **carta di musica** (music sheets), very similar to **pane carasau**, sometimes known as **sas corrias**. Confusing, isn't it! Whatever the variations, it's the same famous flatbread (really, really flat, crispy bread) that has fuelled the **pastori** (shepherds) of Sardegna for centuries.

This is a modern Sardinian bakery in the hills near Nuoro. Where there were once wood-fired ovens, most are now fired by gas. Luisa

and Chiarina work about 12 hours a day, six days a week to make the bread along with the rest of the family; shoulder to shoulder, side by side, seemingly in good humour.

Basically it's just a flour, water, salt and yeast dough that is slowly proved, rolled out to wafer-thin sheets and baked twice. The first baking is the dramatic one, as the two outside layers separate to make the air-filled pillow. The second baking is less visually arresting, but more difficult to perfect. The oven temperature is dropped to 475°C (890°F), and the thin sheets placed within for 3–4 seconds to crisp without browning too much.

The finished parchment-like sheets are sent to Cagliari, a few hours' drive south, and some even end up in Milano or Roma, such is its fame.

To serve, pane fresa is brushed with olive oil, sprinkled with salt and baked again. Or it could be dipped in stock, then doused with **sugo** (sauce), topped with shaved **pecorino** (ewe's milk cheese) and a fried egg to make **pane frattau**, a delicious meal that generations of pastori virtually lived on while out on the road.

Pizza Margherita

Pizza

Everybody eats pizza in Italy. You'll see this staple in the curiously Germanic Alto Adige region, and it is sold in slices at Taormina in Sicilia, where you can eat it within sight of a still-rumbling Monte Etna. In Napoli, where the modern pizza was born, the passion for eating it is only surpassed by its high quality. In Roma they've made it the best fast food in the nation.

You'll find pizza everywhere you go. Many of the **pizzaioli** (pizza makers) that you may encounter actually come from Napoli. These are proud and professional people who like to be considered artisans. But only because they are.

Pizza in Italy isn't the same as it is in New York or London, or anywhere else for that matter. And pizza in Napoli isn't like pizza from just about anywhere else within Italy. Taste it for what it is, rather than comparing it to the impostors that call themselves pizza all around the globe and you will be amazed at how something so simple can be so good.

There are basically two types of pizza: round pizza which is baked to order, and **pizza a(l) taglio** baked in large rectangular trays and sold in slices. Don't be afraid to ask for them **caldo** (hot) as they are always reheated in grills or ovens, and never in that insult to reheated pizza, the microwave.

TYPES OF PIZZA

Margherita	Tomato and mozzarella with a hint of fresh basil. It's named after Queen Margherita, who declared that this pizza pleased her after a visit to Napoli in 1889.
Prosciutto	The best is similar to a margherita, topped with **prosciutto crudo** (raw ham) as it is taken from the oven. Lesser versions use **prosciutto cotto** (cooked ham).
Capricciosa	Depending on the capriciousness of the pizzaiolo, this may include tomato, mozzarella, prosciutto, salsiccia (sausage), artichokes, mushrooms and olives. The taste should be quite sparky.
Focaccia	Not the Ligurian thick focaccia, but a thin dough sprinkled with olive oil, salt and a herb, usually oregano or rosemary.
Frutti di Mare	Seafood pizza, usually with squid, mussels and scampi on a tomato base, but with no cheese.
Funghi	Mushroom and mozzarella pizza, often with no tomato.
Marinara	Despite the name, there's no seafood, just tomato, garlic and some oil. Called marinara because fishermen preferred this type of pizza as they contain no cheese (so they could eat it as an accompaniment to their catch). Italians are very particular about mixing cheese and seafood.
Napoletana	Tomato, oregano and olive oil.
Quattro Stagione	Meaning 'four seasons'. Each quarter of the pizza has a different topping. Strictly speaking, a good pizzaiolo won't mix unmatchable flavours on the same pizza. So if there is fresh seafood on one section, they won't put a cheese topping on another.

STAPLES

Pizza a taglio originated in Roma, probably in response to the chaos of a city that can't even wait the few minutes it takes to bake a freshly cooked pizza. Everybody eats them, sometimes as a mid-morning snack, maybe for lunch or perhaps even as a light dinner.

In the best pizza joints, the dough for pizza a taglio is machine-rolled. It's usually very thin and crispy, but can sometimes be more bready, like a focaccia. The most delectable toppings are the simple ones. Perhaps **pomodoro**, just tomato with a few basil leaves, or **patate con rosamarino,** finely shaved potato with a scattering of rosemary. Many toppings don't

STAPLES

include cheese, and modern interpretations tend to be creative without compromising the taste. **Radicchio** (chicory) with **gorgonzola** is a particularly good example.

Pizza cooked to order is a Neapolitan creation, perfected in the back streets but now being copied around the country. It, too, is defined by its simplicity: the most intense, complex-tasting San Marzano tomatoes, a few basil leaves and the local buffalo mozzarella all combine to make it a triumph. The most exquisite pizze are cooked in a **forno a legna** (wood-fired oven). These pizze are always thin, but the base isn't crispy and they will always be served hot, straight from the oven when you get them.

Both types of pizze are available all around the country. The real thing in Roma and Napoli has to be tasted to be believed.

Most places that make pizze to order will also offer **calzone**, sometimes translated as dialect for a 'boot'. Calzone use the same dough as a pizza, but folded in half so that they look somewhat like a flat Cornish pastie (although if you squint a bit they could even look like a boot). Calzone can be filled with similar things to those used to top a pizza.

Pizza a Taglio

Cereals, Pulses & Grains

Grains have always played a fundamental role in Italian cuisine. Even before there was wheat for flour there was **farro**, an ancient grain still in use today. This seedy heritage is stored in many of Italy's regional dishes such as **pizzoccheri** (buckwheat pasta) and the huge array of thick, resolutely flavoured soups such as the Friulani **orzo e fagioli**, barley with beans in a thick broth.

One of the most popular of all grains is **polenta**, the cornmeal staple of the north, although it only came about after Cristoforo Colombo brought it back from the Americas. To make polenta, finely ground corn is cooked with stock or milk for up to an hour (and at least 40 minutes) while being constantly stirred. The resulting paste can be scented with cheese or enriched with butter (or both). It's served hot and soft, perhaps with **ossobuco** (braised veal shanks), or left to set, then sliced and grilled or fried to reheat. Polenta served with milk was a classic belly-filler in poorer times, and is still popular with the kids, who could eat it until the **mucche** (cows) come home.

STAPLES

FABULOUSLY FASHIONABLE FARRO

Farro (Latin *Triticum dicoccum)* has to be the most fashionable grain in Italy today. This hearty grain is often translated as spelt, but also as emmer, a harder grain with higher magnesium and protein. The farro you'll find in Italy is virtually always emmer. Farro is an ancient grain, known to have been eaten by the Etruscans, and to have acted as a fuel for much of the imperial Roman legions. Yet the Roman elite shunned farro in favour of softer, easier to grind grains such as wheat, and it remained in relative obscurity (although the poor kept eating it) for much of the last 2000 years. The 1990s has seen a resurgence of farro in good restaurants across Italy. Expect to see it in soups such as Toscana's **zuppa di farro** or in upmarket restaurants, perhaps moistened with fish or crayfish stock.

Another grain popular throughout the north is **riso** (rice), responsible for that classic dish, **risotto**. Northern Italians must have spent a lot of time in the kitchen because this dish also has to be stirred the whole time it's cooked. Risotto that isn't stirred isn't risotto. The best are made from simple ingredients, such as chicken stock and mushrooms, or very good red wine, and finished with a dollop of butter or **mascarpone** (cheese) and usually a bit of freshly grated **parmigiano reggiano** (parmesan).

There are three common types of short-grain rice preferred by risotto makers: **arborio**, **carnaroli** and **vialone nano**. Arborio is the most popular and the cheapest of the three. Carnaroli, which was developed in Piemonte in the 1940s and has a hard core, is the hardest to overcook. It's also the most expensive. Vialone nano from the Veneto is also firm-centred, and is preferred by many cooks around the world as it can be par-cooked, cooled and finished later with little impact on the end result.

Risotto reaches its peak in Piemonte and the Veneto, with the Piemontese historically preferring theirs slightly drier and the Venetians preferring theirs creamier and a bit runnier. (See the recipe Herb Risotto in the Home Cooking & Traditions chapter.)

In Sicilia, they use rice on occasion, but you'll also find **cuscus** (cous-cous), just as in nearby Morocco and Tunisia. While this straw-coloured food looks like a grain, it's actually made from a mix of coarse and finely ground semolina flour, worked together with a little water and then formed into tiny granules. So while it is treated like a grain, it's actually more like a tiny piece of very hard pasta. Cuscus was once made by hand, a day-long process, but is now made industrially. In Sardegna you'll also find a similar product, **fregola**, which has slightly larger grains.

Dried beans are popular around the country, but nowhere as much as in Toscana, where they appear frequently in soups and also with fish and meats. The Tuscans have the nickname **mangia fagioli** (bean-eaters) for very good reason. Keep an eye out for the brown-and-white dappled **borlotti** beans and the extremely popular white **cannellini**.

Italians love **lenticchie** (lentils) and the best are from the tiny, secluded village of Castelluccio in western Umbria. Other regions, notably Molise and Abruzzo, also produce wholesome lentils. They are used in soups, or braised and served with meat such as **anatra** (duck) or **salsiccia** (sausage).

Ceci (chickpeas) are eaten roasted as a snack (sometimes sold from little street carts), but often used in soups or braises. A flour made from ground ceci is used in the Ligurian pancake-like **farinata** (see also Street Food in the Where to Eat & Drink chapter). In parts of the north you'll often see **orzo** (barley) listed on menus, especially in soups, and it's also used to make a coffee substitute – not for the **buongustaio** (connoisseur)!

Pasta

To most of the world, Italian food means pasta. As it does in most of Italy. As with all things in this wonderfully disjointed nation, each region does its own thing with what is essentially a simple mix of flour, water and, sometimes, egg. There are hundreds of shapes, from the straightforward **spaghetti** (long, thin strands of pasta) to the hand-made, golden yellow **pappardelle** (wide, flat pasta ribbons) to a curious dried pasta shaped like a penis (which may just be a gimmick, but is for sale in many speciality food shops).

Pasta existed in Liguria and Napoli long before Marco Polo went east. Although both regions still fight over who actually made pasta first, Italy made it popular in the world.

Most pasta can be divided into two groups: **pasta fresca** (fresh pasta) and **pastasciutta** (dry pasta). Differences occur in the way they are made and how they are used. The important thing with pasta is to cook it until the centre of each piece remains slightly hard and retains some bite. Cooking in this way is called **cuocere al dente**, and anything **al dente** has a feeling 'on the tooth' when you bite into it. An Italian will reject pasta that is not al dente.

The size and shape of each pasta is no accident. They absorb sauces differently, and each one is designed as part of a dish, so you won't see Italians putting a beef **ragù** (meat sauce) with a pasta designed for a light vegetable sauce. Each shape often has a literal meaning. Spaghetti actually means little strings; the flat ribbon pasta **tagliatelle** comes from the word **tagliare**, meaning 'to cut'; **orecchi-ette** are 'little ears'; and **strozzapreti** are 'priest-stranglers', a variety of short shapes, often with a twist in the dough.

Pasta is not usually rinsed after cooking, and is never cooked ahead in any self-respecting restaurant. So, you can always expect to wait at least the 10 or so minutes it takes to cook.

Bigoli con ragu

Egg Pasta

While a pasta is often made using wheat or semolina flour and water, in much of northern Italy the most common form is made with flour and eggs to produce pasta fresca. The favoured finely-ground flour is **tipo 00** (**doppio zero** or double 00), which is relatively high in protein. The local eggs there have vibrant yellow yolks, and the result is a golden pasta that is usually eaten fresh rather than dried.

The heartland of this pasta is in and around Emilia-Romagna, but these days you'll find hand-filled **tortellini** (small belly-button shaped filled pasta), thin little tagliatelle and delightful versions of fresh ravioli from the Veneto and Piemonte in the north, down to Napoli and beyond in the south.

Fresh egg pasta is usually eaten with slow-braised meats or rich sauces, although it can be eaten with melted butter and just a dusting of parmigiano. Pasta fresca makes better **pasta e fagioli**, the bean and pasta soup found throughout the north, and is essential in the luscious, lasagne-like **vincisgrassi**, made with liver and sometimes truffles, from Le Marche. Not all pasta fresca varieties contain eggs, although most do.

The more popular types of pasta fresca are as follows.

Bigoli
A thick version of spaghetti from the Veneto, often made by hand and sometimes using wholemeal flour. Usually served with an anchovy or meat sauce.

Cannelloni
Large pasta sheets rolled around a filling of minced meat, eggs and spinach, covered with bechamel and baked. A dry, tubular version also exists.

Fettuccine
A Roman version of tagliatelle.

Lasagne
Flat sheets used in the classic dish of the same name. The sheets are also available dried.

Pappardelle
Broad, flattish noodles from Toscana, usually served with a duck or rabbit ragù.

Ravioli
Originally from Liguria. Flat squares of pasta topped with a filling of minced meat or vegetables and another flat sheet pressed on top. **Raviolini** are the smaller stuffed pasta, and **ravioloni** the bigger.

Egg Pasta Dough

The best egg pasta is made with **tipo 00** (doppio zero) flour, though most plain, unbleached flour will do. You can use all egg yolks for a richer, more golden dough. The recipe makes enough pasta for one: increase the quantities as desired.

Ingredients

110g	plain flour or 00
1	egg, lightly beaten
1	generous pinch of salt

To make pasta the hard way, place the flour and salt together on the bench, make a well in the centre, and work in the egg by hand, kneading until it makes a smooth, firm dough. The easy way (which Italians don't approve of as much) is to throw the flour and salt into a food processor and add the egg, pulsing to mix as much as possible. You'll still need to tip the mixture out onto the bench and knead it together by hand. Let the dough sit and rest wrapped in a damp tea-towel or plastic wrap for at least an hour.

Ideally the pasta dough is rolled by hand using a long, wooden rolling pin (dust the rolling pin with extra flour to prevent sticking). Alternatively use a pasta-rolling machine and follow the manufacturer's instructions. Only roll one portion of dough through a machine at one time, unless your arms are long enough to stretch as far as the dough.

This basic rolled pasta can be cut into shapes such as tagliatelle, lasagne, for tortellini and many other shapes.

To flavour the pasta dough, you can add pureed cooked spinach, chopped herbs, squid ink, tomato paste or saffron dissolved in a little water. Cut down the amount of egg used by the same proportion as any wet ingredient that is added.

Tagliatelle
Classic Emilia-Romagnan pasta strips about 5mm wide, are long and flat. Similar versions are called **taglierini**, **tajarin** and **tagliolini**.

Tortellini
Originally from Bologna, these tiny mouthfuls of meat-stuffed pasta are fashioned in the shape of Venus' belly button. Larger versions such as **tortelli** are often stuffed with vegetarian fillings such as pumpkin while **tortelloni**, the really big ones, may contain a filling of goat's cheese.

Trenette
A Ligurian fresh pasta made to look like longish, thin tongues. Usually served with pesto and potato or green beans.

Dry Pasta

Pastasciutta is virtually always made from **semolino** (durum wheat) flour and water because semolino's higher protein content gives the pasta more 'bite'. Most dried pastas originated in the south, particularly those that are known internationally, such as spaghetti and **penne**. Pastasciutta is often served with vegetarian (or vegetable-based) sauces, generally a bit runnier and less rich than sauces served with pasta fresca.

Following are some varieties of pastasciutta.

Bucatini
A long pasta like spaghetti, but with a hole down the centre. Traditionally found from Lazio to Calabria. The name comes from **bucato**, meaning 'with a hole'.

Cavatelli
Round, flat pasta disks made by squashing small balls of dough with the heel of the palm, originally found in Puglia (and some say Molise). The sauce is usually tomato or vegetable-based, although it is sometimes served with a light meat ragù.

Gnocchetti
Despite sounding like it should be small gnocchi, this is a tiny dry pasta with a shell pattern on one side. Sometimes used in soups or with a tomato sauce.

Linguine
Long flat pasta cut similar to tagliatelle but made without eggs. The name comes from **lingua**, the word for 'tongue'.

Maccheroni
Generally used to mean the macaroni we know, although the term can be applied to pasta in general or tubular pasta in particular. In Molise they call **maccheroni alla chitarra** (flattish, hand-rolled spaghetti, see the Regional Variations chapter) maccheroni.

Orecchiette
The classic 'little ear'-shaped pasta of Puglia, usually served with **cime di rapa** (bitter, leafy broccoli-like turnip tops).

Penne
A traditionally Roman pasta that takes its name from **penna**, meaning 'pen' because the tip looks like the nib from a fountain pen. Basically they are smallish tubes cut at an angle. Often served **all'arrabbiata** (with spicy tomato-based sauce).

Pinci
Thick dried spaghetti from Toscana. Traditionally hand rolled and made with durum wheat flour. Tomato-based sauces are usual.

Rigatoni
Like tubular penne but with ridges on it to help it hold more sauce.

Spaghetti
'Little string' pasta originally from Roma. Best sauces include **carbonara** (egg, parmigiano and pancetta), **aglio e olio** (garlic and olive oil) and **con le vongole** (clams). Thick meat sauces such as **ragù alla bolognese** are a less successful and a more recent innovation.

Stringozzi
Named after the leather cord that the locals reputedly wanted to strangle tax collectors with, stringozzi is served in a similar manner to umbrici. A long pasta made with hand-milled flour but cut to form squarish strands rather than round ones.

Umbrici
Hand-made thick pasta typical of Umbria, made by rolling dough through the fingers. Classic accompaniment is butter and some shaved truffles. Also called **umbricelli**, or **ceriole**.

Other Pasta
Canederli
The big dumplings of Trentino and Alto Adige, made with stale bread, and often flavoured with **speck** (smoked matured ham) or liver. Sometimes served in broth.

Culingiones
A cross between potato ravioli and gnocchi, this Sardinian speciality is scented with a filling of wild mint and **pecorino** cheese. Sometimes called **culungiones**.

Gnocchi
Small potato dumplings that, at their best, are as light as a cloud. Typically served with tomato sauce or meat ragù, or sometimes baked.

Gnocchi alla romana
Totally unlike the other gnocchi. From Roma, these are round disks of cooked semolina paste, set, cut into flattish rounds and baked with cheese.

Pizzoccheri
Flat, wide but short buckwheat noodles of Valtellina in northern Lombardia. Usually served with chunks of potato, browned garlic, cabbage and melted **bitto** cheese.

Fruits & Vegetables

To see the passing of the seasons in Italy, all you need is a market. So tied to the seasons are the locals that the sight of row after row of **asparagi** (asparagus) obviously means it's May; a glut of **pesche** (peaches) probably means you're in August; and when the shelves fill with **Treviso radicchio** (chicory, a bitter salad leaf) it usually means you're well into autumn.

The markets are mesmerising places, but similarly seasonal are most **frutta e verdura**, the fruit and vegetable shops (see the Shopping chapter). The idea of buying what's in season and of preserving food that's abundant, is ingrained in the Italian psyche.

The variety of fresh produce available at any one time is reasonably limited. **Mele** (apples) seem to be a staple all year – but if you like them crispy only buy in autumn. From north to south the ingredients you see are often the same. Flattish **cipolle** (onions), ropes of **aglio** (garlic), mounds of **carciofi** (artichokes), deep red **pomodori** (tomatoes) sold on the vine and **melanzane** (eggplant) may be for sale in the fabulous shoulder-rubbing chaos of one of Messina's markets, but you'll see virtually the same produce in a frutta e verdura in Liguria. It's what each region does with the ingredients that differs. And what each area specialises in, they do to a joyous excess.

Some ingredients, though, are truly regional. You don't often see **cavolo nero** (black cabbage) outside of Toscana, yet within the region you can't avoid the stuff when in season. **Melanzane violette** (purple eggplants) are isolated to Sicilia and a part of Liguria, while the **fico d'India** (prickly pear) is only found in the far south and on the island of Sardegna.

Apart from the cultivated produce, many Italians have a taste for the wild (see Wild Food later in this chapter).

Rucola (rocket, also known as **ruchetta**) is one green which is cultivated and grown semi-wild. The cultivated version is traditionally larger and softer-leafed, with a mild, peppery taste and is cut from the young, new growth close to the ground. 'Wild' rucola is generally found on a stem, is smaller and has a mustardy bite. Both are now cultivated and are actually separate species, although rucola and ruchetta are used interchangeably as you travel from one town to the next.

One item worth trying is Treviso radicchio which originates, as the name suggests, in the town of the same name in the Veneto. It's a long-leafed version of the much-loved, bitter, red radicchio. The flavour is milder and more refined, and it is more expensive.

Finocchio (fennel) is seen throughout the country, often growing wild on the side of train tracks and the road. Finocchio is also the slang term for a gay man, so be sure you're in the right place and at the right time when you request one, or you may get the other.

Chicory tops, Trani market, Puglia

While the fresh fruit and vegetables you'll see in the markets are impressive, you can generally expect them to be heavily cooked when you eat them in restaurants. **Piselli** (peas) and **broccoli** are usually on the grey side while **carote** (carrots) tend to be so soft you can squash them on your tongue. Similarly, **insalate** (salads) in restaurants, are usually made from iceberg lettuce and sadly not those pert, soft, well-flavoured leaves which you saw at the market.

Wild Asparagus

WILD FOOD

Bang, bang, ba-BANG. You know it's autumn when the hills of Umbria resound with the blasts of gunshot. Spring is relatively silent, apart from the sound of fishing reels spinning, but autumn is the **cinghiale** (wild boar) season. So the grey, fierce-looking cinghiale (they resemble those found in Asterix comics) live tentatively in the forests, while fatigue-clad men chase after them with shotguns.

The quest for wild food is carried out by both men and women, from Valle d'Aosta to Sicilia. **Finocchio selvaggia** (wild fennel) is essential for some intriguing pasta of Sicilia. **Ortiche** (nettles) are used with onions to make **frittate** (thick, firm omelettes) and asparagi and **cipolle selvatiche** (wild onions, sometimes called **lampascioni**) from Molise and Puglia are even bottled for export.

Born out of centuries of self-reliance, hunting and gathering have taken on a special meaning and much of the locals' time and energy. It's also taking its toll on the environment. **Trota** (trout) are now introduced to the rivers from **ittico genico** (fish farms), while even the wild boar of Umbria are a relatively new addition, being a foreign breed introduced after the majority of the indigenous boars were hunted out in the 1960s.

If you don't want to collect your own ortiche or asparagi, then keep an eye out for the words **selvatica** or **selvaggina** at the markets, meaning the food is wild and not harvested. Not everything wild is necessarily of interest, such as the **carciofi selvatica** (wild artichokes) we saw in Sicilia. Carciofi are related to the humble thistle, and carciofi selvatica are decidedly thistle-like.

Meat, Poultry & Game

Where for generations there was relative poverty in Italy, a new-found prosperity means that meat is now the focus of many meals. **Antipasto** ('before pasta', an appetiser) tends to be dominated by **salumi** (see Salumi next), pasta is more likely to be stuffed with meat or served with meat ragù, and the focus of most meals, at least in restaurants or on special occasions, is now the meat course. While you may see tender **fiori di zucca** (zucchini or squash flowers), firm-headed carciofi and glossy red or green **peperoni** (capsicums) in the markets, the fabulous restaurant fare is more likely to be from an animal than a plant.

FINDING YOURSELF HORSE

Along with the usual suspects you'd find in most **macellerie** (butchers), you may also notice the signs for **carne equina**, meaning horse meat (also called **cavallo**). Now, meat from horses isn't just pet food – many Italians love the stuff, and for years it has been fed to children and the infirm, in the belief that it will improve their cardiopulmonary system. It's a sweetish meat, quite delicious if it's cooked right, but not as highly regarded today as it once was.

Horse meat is not totally uncool, however – you're as likely to see pretty young **signorine** as you are gruff old men buying the stuff. Carne equina is popular in virtually every region, and may be served just as beef is – perhaps braised, with polenta, grilled with lemon squeezed over the top, or even in little patties.

Despite the widespread popularity of the horse butcher, the meat rarely appears on restaurant menus, although you may see **asino** (ass or donkey) in its place.

Luckily, Italy excels in the quality of her meat. **Vitello** (veal) is everywhere, always pale, superbly tender, often milk-fed and delicious. In Toscana the **bistecca di manzo** (beef T-bone, called **bistecca alla fiorentina** in Firenze) rivals the world's best in quality and taste. The **maiale** or **carne suino** (pork), especially of Umbria and Sardegna, has to be tasted to be believed. And although most of the sheep you'll see on your travels are bred for milking, the **agnello** (lamb) is sensational, particularly **abbacchio**, the tender milk-fed lamb that reaches its zenith in Lazio.

The same high praise can also be given to poultry. The birds are raised more naturally here, fed on grains and allowed to age without as many hormones in the feed, so the flavour of their meat is more intense.

Besides **pollo** (chicken) you'll find **piccione** (pigeon), **faraona** (guinea fowl), **anitra/anatra** (duck), **tacchino** (turkey) and, if you're really lucky, **oca** (goose). Most of the smaller birds are sold in their entirety, minus a few feathers. This means that cock's combs and some residual feathers aren't uncommon (and neither are a few organs). Wild birds, including anatra and **fagiano** (pheasant), are often hung until 'high' to develop their flavour and increase the tenderness.

Italians tend to serve most of their meats, including the prime cuts, well-done. Many cheaper cuts are **stracotto** (cooked for a very long time, literally 'overcooked'), such as in a braise or ragù.

Butchers' display, Florence

Salumi

Salumi is a broad term that takes in all the **prosciutto** (preserved ham), **salsiccia** (roughly translating as sausages) and related pig products as well as other meat smallgoods, including **salami**.

The humble pig reaches its greatest heights in the salumi of Italy. But to list all the variations is fruitless. Often **salami** (preserved sausage) is described simply as **nostrano**, meaning 'ours' or 'local'. This same name means it will be heavier, almost Germanic in taste in Trentino in the north; gently fragrant in Emilia-Romagna; fiery with peperoncino in Puglia; and positively reeking with garlic and fennel in Sicilia. There are differences even within a region. Find a salami you like by asking for an **assaggio** (taste).

While you can buy salumi everywhere, many families still make their own. They do this out of desire to maintain a tradition, simply because they can and it's good to save money or – and this is the most likely – because they honestly think theirs is the best.

Usually the pig would meet its maker in early December, so that any cured meats will have most of the winter to age before the weather warms up. The pigs also tend to be at peak condition after eating well in the autumn. Specialist butchers are known to travel from village to village to help with the slaughter.

SALUMI AT A GLANCE

Bresaola	Air-cured loin of raw beef sliced so thin you can read your postcards through it (well, nearly).
Capocollo	Dry-cured pork sausage scented with red wine and herbs.
Coppa	Cylindrical pieces of raw, cured pork that is thinly sliced and served as antipasto.
Culatello	Pork from underneath the buttock, air-cured in a moist environment. It is very, very tasty, and very, very costly.
Guanciale	Cured raw pig's cheek. Fantastic used in cooking, particularly in pasta sauces.
Lonza	Meaning 'loin', in this case specifically of pork cured with garlic.
Mortadella	A very large sausage made from minced pork studded with lard and black pepper. Sold in slices.
Pancetta	Cured belly pork, similar to unsmoked bacon.

STAPLES

Prosciutto cotto	Cooked ham that is similar to English-style cooked (baked or boiled) hams. The northern Italian versions are best.
Prosciutto crudo	The typical Italian ham made from raw legs of (preferably female) pigs. The legs are salted and air-cured, usually in mountainous regions in fresh air. Buongustai tend to favour prosciutti from regions such as San Daniele (for pressed) and Langhirano (for unpressed). Each has its own character from the pigs and the curing environment.
Prosciutto	Prosciutto is quite remarkable. It must be sliced finer than paper, and its beautiful, sweet perfume starts to dissipate as soon as it is cut. While prosciutto is made all over Italy, many versions are heavily salted (**prosciutto crudo salato**), compared to those from around Parma and San Daniele, considered more sweet (**prosciutto dolce**). Many private houses have their own ham-stands, keep the prosciutto in their own **cantine** (cellars) and carve it at each meal. Good prosciutto is very soft and delicate and truly memorable, like a lover's kiss. Italian prosciutto is rivalled only by the jamõn iberico de bellota of Spain.

Salame	Singular of salami. General term for a sausage that is made from chopped meat and fat, and is often cured, aged and eaten raw.
Salsiccia	The general name for sausage.
Soppressa, soppressata	Meaty, generally coarse-textured salame found in central and southern regions. Often heavily flavoured with **peperoncino** (chilli). There can be many salame with this name.
Speck	Cured, smoked, uncooked prosciutto and belly pork. The best is from Alto Adige and Trentino.

Seafood

Italy's long, thin shape and the fact that three-quarters of it is mountainous mean that her inhabitants have always clung to the coast where they could. With the exception of Sardegna – where malaria was prevalent until the last half century or so – the heavily stocked Adriatic, Ionian, Ligurian and Tyrrhenian seas were to prove a rich source of food.

But as pollution, overfishing and the pressures of population growth have taken their toll on fish numbers, **frutti di mare** (seafood) have become more of a luxury item. The seemingly large catches arriving at harbours around the country every day (except Sunday) are just a fraction of what fishermen used to catch with less effort.

Fishing boats in Trani Harbour, Trani, Puglia

The best thing about the local seafood is its freshness. Rarely will an Italian be happy to buy fish more than a few hours old. Often the creatures are still alive: **cozze** (mussels) will close when you tap them, the **polpo** (octopus) may be slowly squirming around in its tray, and the **scampi** (shrimp) leaping out of the buckets. Even in Roman times freshness was important; there is evidence that the ancient market near the forum in Roma contained fish tanks so that Romans could buy live fish.

STAPLES

Fresh anchovies, Napoli, Campania

Sardine fillets, Rome, Lazio

Spend any amount of time and a bit of money in Italy and you will invariably end up eating seafood. The locals favour polpo, **seppia** (cuttlefish) and lots of tiny fish known in some areas as **neonati** or **bianchetti**, usually fried and eaten whole. In Liguria, Calabria and Sicilia, in particular, **pescespada** (swordfish) is highly prized.

One thing that seems remarkable to outsiders is that locals eat so much imported, preserved fish – **stoccafisso** (air-dried cod) and **baccalà** (salted cod) – when there's plenty of fresh fish. This is especially true in Liguria where **burrida** (stewed stoccafisso) is eaten by a population predominantly descended from seafarers. The explanation is that many Ligurians were often on long voyages, and preserved fish kept for long periods.

The best days to shop for seafood or eat it in restaurants are Tuesdays and Fridays, particularly if you're not on the coast. These days coincide with the big fish markets. And while at some stage it was essential for restaurants to note on a menu if an item has been **surgelato** (frozen), this practice has lapsed.

DATES OF THE SEA

You may be offered raw seafood on your travels, particularly in the regions of Abruzzo, Le Marche, Molise and Puglia. And while the scampi are deliciously sweet and the **datteri di mare** ('dates' of the sea, a brown bivalve mollusc) can be complex and lingering, take care. Cholera outbreaks have led to the serving of raw seafood being banned. The threat of fines hasn't deterred flavour-chasers and many restaurants, however, who defy the authorities. You can still find plenty of places to taste raw seafood. If you dare.

Fishing Nets, Trani, Puglia

Cheese

If General Charles de Gaulle reckoned he had trouble governing a country that had 365 cheeses, then it's no wonder Italy has had no luck finding a long-term leader lately, as their cheeses number closer to 450 these days. That Italy produces so many types of cheeses is a source of great wonder, but a fact little known outside her borders.

Italians love their **formaggio** (cheese), even when it's not from their region. Cheese is used in every course of the meal. A **pecorino** (ewe's milk cheese) may be served as an antipasto with broad beans, the first pasta course may have salted **ricotta** grated over, a main course can be **vitello parmigiano** (veal with a fine layer of superb parmigiano reggiano melted over), while the sweet could be the **cialzons** (like a ravioli) of Friuli, scented with smoked ricotta.

If you love cheese, you will love Italy. And if you can afford to devote a few kilojoules every day of your stay to the discovery of formaggio you will be duly rewarded. From the haunting, intensely likeable **gorgonzola**, a blue mould cheese made in Lombardia and Piemonte, to the nuttiness of really good **pecorino sardo**, the ewe's milk cheese from Sardegna, the range is only surpassed by the quality.

Basically Italy can be divided into cheese regions based on the animal whose milk is used: cow, goat, sheep and buffalo. Much of the north towards the alps is graced with cows, but you'll find some sensational **formaggio di capra** (goat's milk cheeses) in Piemonte and Valle d'Aosta. Cows also dominate the area, including the fertile

Parmigiano reggiano

plains in and around Emilia-Romagna. This is the heartland of the so-called 'King of Cheeses', parmigiano reggiano, although often you won't actually see the cows as they're kept under cover. The centre and south of the country are blessed mostly with sheep (although there are quite a few cows in the far south), as is Sardegna, while buffalo have a small hold in the area around Napoli and a scattering beyond that.

Half a wheel of cheese in shop window, Reggio Emilia

While parmigiano and gorgonzola have gained a name overseas, much of Italy's great cheese is simply known as pecorino. There exists a **DOC** (Denominazione di Origine Controllata) system for cheeses similar to that of wine (see DOC under Wine in the Drinks chapter) to protect the origin and integrity of cheese styles. About 22 cheeses have gained DOC status. Of these, seven are from sheep.

A CHEESE LEXICON	
Dolce	Sweet, signifying a young cheese with a sweetish, often nutty taste
Pastorizzato	Pasteurised, which not all cheeses are. The best usually aren't, but if you're concerned, ask the vendor
Piccante	Piquant, meaning the cheese is sharp, often aged and sometimes acidic
Stagionato	Aged
Vecchio	Old
Stravecchio	Really old

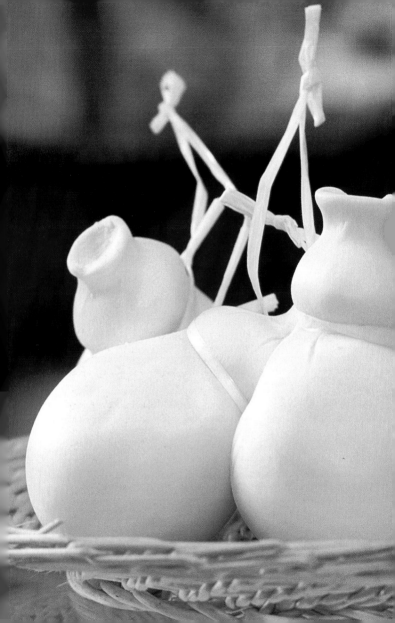

KING OF CHEESE

Parmigiano reggiano is a granular cheese produced around parts of the Po River in Italy's north, particularly in Emilia-Romagna. There's a lot of mystique about the cheese, and a fair amount of history. It has been in use for at least the last 700 years and apparently locals used to use a wheel as a deposit on a house. It's said that local banks actually own the vaults that store the cheeses nowadays, such is its value.

Parmigiano is a hard, cooked cheese, made with both the morning and evening milk. Small manufacturers are used to showing enthusiastic visitors around their factories, but you'll need to speak Italian. The day we visited one boutique producer on the outskirts of Modena, there were 20 well-behaved schoolchildren watching the show, mesmerised by the whirling curds and sniffing the scent of fresh milk. There's the unmistakable whiff of the cows, a sure sign of freshness. While the curd is heated, it isn't pasteurised, which means that the character of the milk is left intact.

Draining curd

Scamorza, Matera, Basilicata

The milk is skimmed, placed in huge, copper-lined basins, cultured, heated, and then whizzed with a machine that looks like a small outboard motor. The cheesemakers dip their hands into the basins and feel for the granular texture of the curd to make sure it's just right. They then lift the curd into cheesecloth. Each vat's curd is gathered with care into a single cloth, cut in half, drained over the whey in two cheesecloths and placed in moulds. The huge wheels are then placed in brine for the better part of a month.

Much of the leftover whey is heated to make ricotta which cheesemakers sell straight from the draining baskets. The rest of the whey is pumped out the back of the cheese factory and fed to pigs.

There are 6000 cheeses in the storeroom, yet they only make 16 wheels in the morning, and about the same at night. The wheels each weigh about 45kg when fresh (less as they age) and are stacked on shelves that tower over the cheesemaker. The parmigiano is aged for at least a year, usually two. Every two weeks they are turned and wiped clean. While this was once done by hand, a machine now works its way up and down each row automatically.

At some time towards the end of each parmigiano's maturation, professional testers take each cheese and hit them all over with a small hammer. An expert ear can pick up faint hollow sounds – a sign of cracks or faults in the cheese – and if it doesn't meet a certain standard, it's rejected.

At the Giglio warehouse in Reggio nell'Emilia, there is space to mature 120,000 wheels of parmigiano. From one end of the storeroom you can barely see the other – a feat made harder by the fact that the far wall has a huge, life-like picture of even more cheeses on shelves, so it looks like the warehouse runs forever.

Alberto Molini, who is in charge of these 120,000 wheels, has been listening to the sound of his mallet hitting cheeses for over 30 years. Yet even he can't be 100% sure of the quality of each cheese until it is cut. If he hears a 'ping' rather than a solid 'thud' he sometimes opens a cheese to see how it has ripened. Only then can he be sure.

Alberto spins the cheese and hits it constantly on all the edges and sides with the deft, almost musical skill you'd expect from a Carribean drummer. We listen carefully and can barely hear sound differences in one cheese. The rind of the suspect cheese is scored, and small, traditional knives (shaped like a fat apostrophe) are inserted. Three in the top, three in the bottom and as the last is inserted, the parmigiano suddenly pops open, splitting neatly down the middle with a satisfying sigh.

Alberto points out the problem: a small crack down the side of the cheese. But the cheese has matured fabulously, tasting mellow, sweet, salty, complex and nutty all at once. It had already aged to full term and so will be sold that day. Alberto shows us little white dots in the parmigiano, a sign, he assures us, of a cheese that has aged long, and aged well. The white spots are protein, not salt.

Alberto is a big man, but dwarfed by the cheeses and his factory. Unlike virtually all other Italians we meet, he doesn't want his picture taken, laughing that "a photo can't make me look thinner" – one of the prices of working with cheese!

Parmigiano reggiano (and the lesser grana padano) are marked on the rind with their name, the producer and the consortium that oversees their production as well as the date. The consortium checks every cheese before it is sold, and if it doesn't meet every standard set down by law (including a good hammering), the outside has crosses burnt into it.

Every wheel is worth a pile of money so there is a lot of fraud to counter. To be sure you're getting the real thing, never buy pre-grated cheese, and always buy a wedge where you can see the distinctive marks on the rind. Cheese marked with crosses may still be okay, but while you're in Italy you may as well have the real thing. The real thing, eaten with a drizzle of olive oil, shaved onto risotto, or washed down with a glass of good Italian red is an experience of almost regal proportions.

Some Better Known Cheeses

Asiago

A scalded-curd cow's milk cheese with a sweetish taste from the alpine regions of the Veneto. Until the turn of the century it was made with ewe's milk and some locals still call it **pegorin**, meaning sheep in dialect. There are at least three types but the best is Asiago d'Allevo.

Bra

A sweet and mild cow's cheese named after a town in Piemonte. Originally it was made by nomadic herdsmen, but matured and sold in Bra. Sold after maturing from 45 days up to 6 months.

Burrata

A delightful combination of cream wrapped in smooth, young cow's milk mozzarella. Originally designed as a way to conserve the cream, but now a must-try cheese while you're in Italy as it doesn't travel well.

Caciocavallo

A group of southern cheeses that look like bulbous bags that have been tied in pairs and then slung over a rod (called a **cavallo**, meaning 'horse') to cure. Usually it's an ewe's milk cheese or a combination, but in Sicilia it's made from cow's milk.

Caciotta (casciotta, cacio)

Usually a semi-firm, lightly cooked sheep's milk cheese (sometimes mixed with cow's) that is favoured in Toscana and Le Marche, although sometimes the term simply refers to any cheese. Eaten from fresh and sweet to quite firm without being dry. **Caciotta al tartufo** are sheep milk cheeses with the addition of specks of black truffle.

Capra, caprino

The general name for goat's milk cheeses, of particular importance in Piemonte and Valle d'Aosta.

Castelmagno

A softish, cow's milk cheese from the alpine village of the same name in Piemonte. The cheese has a white mould on the outside and specks of greeny-blue mould inside. Traditionally matured for 4–6 months on beaten earth floors in caves. Records show that it was used as a unit of exchange as far back as 1277. Standards have dropped in the last 50 years as herdsmen have left the Alps in search of a better life.

Fontina

A rich, heady, scalded-curd cow's milk cheese with a smooth texture that is used extensively in its homeland of Valle d'Aosta, particularly in the **fonduta** (a dish not dissimilar to a fondue). Cheeses are made within two

Latteria cheese production, gathering the curd from base

hours of milking, dry-salted and kept in brine-dampened cloths for two months. The best is considered to come from summer milk. An ancient cheese with a recorded history stretching back to the thirteenth century.

Gorgonzola
A particularly pungent blue cheese originally from northern Lombardia but now more often made in the nearby town of Novara in Piemonte. It's sold as **piccante** and **dolce**, depending on the age and its level of sweetness. Dolce is younger and piccante tends to be more powerful, yet creamier. Gorgonzola originated when an innkeeper in the Valsassina area stored stracchino cheese in his cellar for a bit too long, and some developed a blue mould. He served it regardless to the local cheesemakers who loved it and copied his method. Or so the legend goes...

Grana padano
The not-so-poor cousin of parmigiano and often substituted for it when sold grated. Grana is still better than any so-called parmesan made outside of Italy. It's made in regions of the north, particularly Lombardia, and has its own protection under law.

Mascarpone
Not really a cheese, but a cultured cream that is used extensively in desserts of the north. It's essential for the best **tiramisù** (see Some Common Dolci later in this chapter). A delightful cheese when mixed with gorgonzola.

Montasio
An ancient Friulian cow's cheese (at least since the 13th century) also made in parts of the Veneto, with a hard, smooth texture and soft yellow colour. It's used as a table cheese and is the most important ingredient in the Friulian dish of **frico**, an addictive fried cheese patty.

Mozzarella di bufala
This is the classic porcelain white, super-fresh cheese which is essential for the best pizze and a sheer joy to eat fresh (see Campania in the Regional Variations chapter).

Parmigiano reggiano
The hard cheese used all over Italy for grating onto pasta and in other savoury dishes or as a table cheese. One of the greatest of all the world's cheeses. See the boxed text King of Cheese earlier in this chapter.

Pecorino
The general name given to sheep's milk cheeses. A lot of pecorino comes from the south and the cheeses are consistently good. Most are part-cooked and have a semi-firm texture and nutty taste. Some **dolce** have a soft green

colour and a delightful, almost herbaceous tang. **Pecorino sardo** is a version of sheep's milk cheese from Sardegna, the masters of pecorino. Sardegna also makes most of the **pecorino romano** that is sold in Lazio.

Provolone
Originally from Basilicata, this incredibly popular cow's cheese is made with spun curd (similar to mozzarella), then worked into huge squashed pear-shaped cheeses held in shape with a cord. It's usually eaten dolce and mild, but is sometimes used **stagionato** (aged) and grated. These are the giant pale cheeses that most **formaggiaio** (cheese vendors) are likely to have on display.

Ricotta
While not actually classified as a cheese by the Italian government, this by-product of the cheese-making process is divine. As the name suggests, the whey left over after making cheese is re-cooked (**cotto** means 'cooked'), and the resultant white mass is drained in little baskets. The best are generally from sheep – pale, lightly perfumed and with a soft texture that dances on the tongue.

Robbiola
A range of rich, creamy cow's milk cheeses that tend to become harder and more piquant as they age. They take their name from the town of Robbio in Lombardia. Not to be confused with **robiola**, a soft goat's milk cheese from Valle d'Aosta.

Scamorza
Cow's curd spun in a similar way to mozzarella, formed into balls, tied around the middle and hung in pairs to mature. Often smoked. The good ones are incredible, the ordinary very ordinary.

Stracchino
Cow's cheese made from the naturally condensed milk of exhausted cows that have been making the seasonal migration from the hills to the mountains and vice versa (**stracco** means 'exhausted' in dialect). A wonderful, fleeting soft cheese with a creamy colour and a light, dreamy texture.

Taleggio
Washed-rind cow's cheese with a soft texture, an orangey skin and a mouth-filling, heady taste. Italians only eat them soft and almost runny. (the stuff usually sent overseas would be considered unripe in Italy.) These days most taleggi are made on the plains in Piemonte, and ripened in the Valsassina in Lombardia, using the natural, snow-chilled air currents which seep down through caves and into special ripening chambers.

BLESSED ARE THE CHEESEMAKERS

Luigi spends much of his day up to his armpits in warm milk, slaving over a culture or two. It's the only way to produce the firm, yet sweet **latteria**, the cow's milk cheese that the locals love.

Latteria cheesemakers are the traditional artisans of the curd in Friuli, and Luigi Vanone is considered one of the best. He's a young, lean, yet obviously strong man, no more than 30, and a living link to the cheesemakers of the past.

There used to be a cheesemaker in every village, now there are only about 100 left in the whole region. Latteria is an unpasteurised cheese, hand-made in copper-lined vats twice a day, every day. The vats were designed to be fired by wood, but these days a diesel flame keeps the milk warm. Ten local farmers bring in the milk from between 7.30 and 8.20am, as well as between 8.15 and 8.45pm each evening. If the milk isn't there then, it isn't used, so they make sure it's delivered on time. With unpasteurised cheese the rules regarding the milk are very strict.

We arrive at 10am to find the curds already being cultured. The room smells fresh and sweet. A little of last night's milk has been kept warm in a water bath for 10 hours to create a light yoghurt to add to the cheese. Rennet has been stirred into the morning's milk an hour or two before, and Luigi takes some of the mixture and tests it with a series of different chemicals.

"That's the new way," he grins. "But the real way is to feel the grain like this." Luigi reaches deep into the vat and pulls up some of the curd which has separated out from the whey and lies near the bottom. He presses it in his hand and feels the texture, how it presses together, how granular it is, how the remaining whey runs through his fingers.

"Nearly there," he says. If he used the chemical analysis alone, it would have him making the cheese already but, fortunately for us, Luigi's instinct knows better.

A few minutes after showing us the grain, the amiable atmosphere of the room becomes controlled tension as the first vat of curd is ready to drain. Luigi uses a flexible metal rod that is used to run around the base of each vat, loosening the curd which has started to settle. He is bent double, literally, the full length of his arms often under the liquid. Working with another person, Luigi lays cheesecloth out along the metal rod, and collects in it enough curd to make one cheese. In 20 minutes the first 19 cheeses are made. They're gathered in cheesecloth, drained, plopped into metal rings, stacked and pressed.

In the middle of the cheese-making a customer comes in to buy a slab of butter. It's Luigi who serves him, taking extraordinary care to wash his hands before and after the transaction. He doesn't look hassled,

but doesn't miss a beat serving a second customer who comes in wanting cheese a few minutes later.

Nearly 2000 litres (3200 pints) of milk are brought in today, and that will make 30 wheels of cheese, each weighing about 7kg. Luigi doesn't get paid in cash for making cheese for the farmers, but takes a percentage of the finished product. It's in his interests to maximise the amount made, as well as the quality.

His storeroom, smelling like warm hay, is stocked with the farmers' cheeses, all marked with the date made and the 'Latteria Sociale Ravosa' stamp. They will be turned and wiped by hand every two days until sold, anything up to a year later. The wheels used to be stored in the cellar of the same building, a place best suited to maturing cheese, but a new coolroom has saved Luigi lugging the wheels up and down stairs. His own cheeses, however, are still stored in the cellar.

As we leave Luigi's, we see cheeses stacked up in the back of a small van, ready for delivery. Most villagers know roughly what time to come by so as not to interrupt Luigi, and soon many more people arrive. They pop the cheese on the front seat of their Fiats or can be seen bustling up the street with whole wheels clutched under their arms.

Soups

While the humble **minestrone** (vegetable soup) is known well beyond the borders of Italy, the soups that are eaten across the country are far more varied, and minestrone is isolated mostly to a part of the north. Each region has its own soup, known variously as **zuppe** and **minestre**, but it's the Tuscans who've done the most with the dish. In fact, instead of the normal menu heading **primi** (meaning first course, see the Understanding the Menu chapter) they tend to list all first courses under the heading 'minestre'.

In the rest of Italy, a minestra is usually thinner than a zuppa, which is more likely to have pureed vegetables, bread or well-cooked pulses to thicken it. As a general rule, the word minestre is also used more in the north than in the south.

Another classification for soup is **brodo**, meaning broth, such as **tortellini in brodo** and **brodetto**. Many of the dishes that are classified as soups could just as easily be classified as stews or heartier dishes, their texture is so dense.

Some Common Soups

Brodetto
Originally from the Veneto (known locally as **broeto**), this is a fish broth made with small assorted Adriatic seafood in a stock scented with onions, capsicum and sometimes tomato. Now it can be found up and down the Adriatic coast.

Minestrone
Traditional soup from Lombardia made with legumes and vegetables (peas, tomatoes, beans), with pieces of bacon, parsley and garlic. Served cold in summer and with pesto in Liguria.

Orzo e fagioli
Thick bean and barley soup popular in Friuli.

Pasta e fagioli
Thick borlotti bean soup with pasta added at the end. Probably at its best in the Veneto.

Ribollita
A very dense vegetable soup from Toscana thickened with stale bread. The name means 'reboiled' and it must be left a day before reheating and eating. It usually includes cabbage.

Risi e bisi
Classic Venetian thick soup of rice cooked in a pea pod-scented broth and with fresh peas added.

Minestrone with pesto, Liguria

Risi e Bisi

This is a Venetian dish meaning 'rice and peas' in dialect. It's not exactly a runny soup, or a risotto, but kind of a cross between the two. Venetians would expect to eat theirs with a fork, but it's just as good runnier and eaten with a spoon.

Ingredients

400g	fresh young peas in pod
1.3	litres chicken stock
2	tablespoons finely chopped flat-leaf parsley
2	tablespoons butter
1	medium–sized onion, finely chopped
4	slices prosciutto, cut into strips
200g	risotto rice
50g	parmigiano reggiano cheese, grated

Peas in a pod, Sardegna

Shell the peas and rinse the pods well.

Heat the chicken stock with the pods and simmer for 15 minutes. Strain and discard the pods.

Heat the butter in a large, heavy-based saucepan and fry the onion gently for 5 minutes. Stir in the parsley and prosciutto and continue frying without colouring the onion for 5 minutes more.

Add the rice and peas and cook for another 2 minutes, then stir in the chicken stock, perhaps some salt and pepper. Bring to the boil, stir and turn down the heat. Simmer, stirring occasionally, for about 25 minutes or until the rice is cooked through. The texture should be like a thick soup or a runny risotto. If you need more liquid, add water or chicken stock.

Stir in the cheese and serve hot. A small grating of fresh nutmeg 5 minutes before serving adds a nice touch.

Serves 4 as a starter

Stracciatella
Chicken or light meat broth with egg and parmesan whisked through. Originally from Roma.

Tortellini in brodo
Little 'belly button' pasta filled with minced veal and/or pork and served in a light chicken broth.

Cardoncelli

STAPLES

Fungi

If you are travelling in Italy in autumn or early winter, the fungi alone – from the haunting, intense and intensely likeable **tartufi bianchi** (white truffle) to fresh **porcini** – can make your trip worthwhile. In autumn, cars parked in obscure parts of the countryside don't usually mean picnics or even clandestine or youthful liaisons (although they could), but are a sign that the weather is ideal for mushroom foraging.

Mushrooms can be found where there are lots of trees, moisture and cool weather, even in the south. Because so much of the countryside is mountainous, and relatively large tracts are still forested, mushrooms are particularly bountiful in the north, and in Toscana and Umbria.

Don't expect to be alone if you want to forage, however, as locals take to the forests in unimaginable numbers. It's a local passion. In Trentino the foragers are so determined that there are even mycologist police, who check the fungi that's been gathered and is for sale in shops. The good news is that if you don't want to forage, many wild species are sold in markets and at the **frutta e verdura** (fruit and vegetable shops).

FUNGI FACTS

There are several hundred types of fungi growing in the hills of Italy. Over 50 species are edible, including a few **tartufi** (truffles), the true porcini (*Boletus edulis*) and its related species, as well as wood blewits *(tricholoma nudum)* and other brightly coloured varieties.

Each forager is allowed to pick 3kg of mushrooms a day. Many claim to find over 100kg of mushrooms in a season, preserving their collection by drying or placing them **sotto olio** (under oil) for the year ahead.

The only summer mushroom of note is the golden-coloured **cantarello** (chanterelle).

Several Italians die every year from eating mushrooms they've found themselves. So, do your research, take an expert, and don't pick (or even touch) any species that could be mistaken for something else.

TRUFFLE HUNTERS

Giovanni watches a tiny red fly. It moves erratically, zig-zagging as flies do. But this particular fly keeps doubling back and forth, and seems to be hovering over a single point on the ground. Giovanni works out the precise spot, digs carefully about 15cm into the dirt, and pulls up a gnarled, jet-black piece of fungi with the most unusual smell

Giovanni, his dog and the fly are all looking for **tartufi**, in this case **tartufi neri** (black truffles). This pungent, edible fungi is one of the most highly sought after (and equally expensive) foods in the world and all **trifulaû** (truffle hunters) have their own secret methods and favourite areas to search.

Truffles grow underground in a symbiotic relationship with the roots of oak, willow, hazelnut and other trees. There are two main species that are valued by the buongustai: tartufo nero and the white truffle, **tartufo bianco**. Both are cold-season tartufi, available only from about October to March, but peaking in early winter. Depending on whom you talk to – and which region they live in – the best are widely considered to be the white variety, although both neri and bianchi have their own irresistible allure.

The smell of tartufi is apparently similar to a sex hormone in pigs, so locals used to use pigs in the hunt, as the French still do. Italians these days use either their own noses (not so efficient), look out for tiny red flies hovering above certain parts of the ground (a very difficult task) or train dogs to sniff out the tartufi. Giovanni generally uses a truffle dog rather than flies to find up to 100 kg (200 lb) of truffles in a good year.

With tartufi bianchi the dogs can be trained to recognise the smell of a truffle as it starts to ripen, a process that only takes about four hours and one that is ideally interrupted by the truffle-hunter digging it up. Once ripe, tartufi in the ground keep well for only about two weeks, so being able to find them in that critical four-hour ripening period means a truffle-hunter can stay one step ahead of the competition. The market for tartufi is much bigger than the number found each year, and hunters keep their favoured areas very much to themselves.

There is much conjecture and pride associated with tartufi. Whose is the best? Which region produces the most? It is said that a fair proportion of the tartufi neri sold in Périgord (France) were born in Italy. Even Alba's legendary **Mercato del Tartufo** (truffle market) in Piemonte is known to sell truffles from Umbria and Le Marche. Whatever the truth of origin, the best places for buying tartufi are definitely Alba for the bianchi, and Norcia (and environs) in Umbria for the neri. Both have festivals to celebrate the fungi (see the Celebrating with Food chapter).

When cooking with tartufi, the neri can be heated without problem, and people in abundant tartufi-producing areas even eat them roasted. Tartufi bianchi, on the other hand, mustn't be heated above 80°C or they lose their aroma. They are never cooked, but rather shaved over the top of a dish just before it is served. The best way to get the most flavour from a truffle is to store it with

The truffle hunter, Norcia, Umbria

STAPLES

eggs or rice, which will absorb the perfume. You'll end up with a divine frittata or risotto even after you've gobbled down the truffle.

Always buy truffles by their Latin names – *Tuber melanosporum* is black, *Tuber magnatum pico* is white – as the business is rife with fraud. Several people were jailed in the 1990s for a billion-lire scam involving fairly worthless Chinese 'truffles' scented with truffle oil. Out of season you may encounter the summer truffle (*Tuber aestivum*), which looks similar to tartufo nero, but is overpriced and somewhat overrated.

Preserved truffle for sale in jars, tins and the like have only a ghostly impression of fresh tartufi and are best left for those unfortunate enough to visit truffle areas out of season. Some truffled products, however, such as mushroom pastes, are a more affordable and often acceptable souvenir.

Olive Oil & Olives

Olio d'oliva (olive oil) is a gift from the gods. How else can you explain something so simple, so versatile and, dare we say it, healthy?

The dullish-looking olive tree has a kind of philosophical importance to the people of Italy. It is symbolic of the Mediterranean, the climate, the culture and its people. The olive branch is the universal emblem of peace, the trunk means good luck and prosperity, and the oil is the divine essence.

Not surprisingly, then, thousands of hectares of Italian countryside are given over to the stuff. For all the hype, however, there's not really that much to it. You basically take a bunch of olives, smash them up and press them. You take the liquid that comes out and centrifuge it (or let it stand) to separate the oil from the water.

The differences in quality come in the techniques. The best oils are made from hand-picked olives, which are often ground with stone mills and gently pressed between cotton mats. Dodgy operators, on the other hand, may let the olives fall from the tree naturally when ripe – it's a lot cheaper than paying for them to be picked. They will heat the crushed olive paste to extract more oil and finally run all sorts of hideous chemicals through the paste to get out every last drop of oil.

The best olive oil, and the only one worth spending your time and money on, is **olio d'oliva extravergine** (extra-virgin olive oil). The classification for this is principally a chemical analysis, where the oleic acid content must be less than 1%. Lower acid usually means more flavour and aroma. To be called extravergine, it is also required that the oil be mechanically (as opposed to chemically) extracted. And extravergine must meet a flavour profile tested by highly structured, professionally run, blind tastings.

The quality of olive oil depends on the region in which the olives are grown, their variety, the ripeness at which they're picked, how soon they're crushed and the crushing method. Filtration can clear a cloudy oil, but often inadvertently removes the mouth-feel of a truly wonderful oil. To many the most sought-after oil is that which runs free when the olive paste is spread on stacked mats, but before any pressure is applied. This free-run oil is usually more viscous, pungent and finer-tasting than the oil that comes later.

Green olives tend to produce more bitter, yet fruitier oils; riper olives tend to lead to sweeter, milder oils. As you travel the country you will see how the oil varies, and how the food is paired with the oil. In Liguria olive oil is sweetish and mellow with a lot of finesse; in Toscana it is more robust, greener and a bit sharp; while in Puglia the flavour tends to be more rounded, but still with a lusty, gutsy taste.

To some extent the best oils will depend on your sense of taste. Single-estate oils from Toscana can be incredible, and the taste reflects the care that has gone into their making. Exceptional oil is not the sole preserve of the Tuscans. Great oils can be found near Imperia in Liguria, around Spoleto in Umbria and near Andria in Puglia. Because of Italy's unique micro-climates, single-estate oils can be fabulous from everywhere in the country, such as Le Marche and Sicilia.

Store your olive oil in a dark, cool place and use it within a year of buying and within two months of opening. It won't get better with time, although some people believe green oils peak about two months after pressing. Oils are pressed in late autumn and early winter (November–December), and this is the best time to buy.

Oil olives contain a lot more oil than table olives, about 20–25% compared to 12–15%, and are usually of different varieties. Leccino, Frantoio, Moraiolo, Ogliarola, Corantina, Nocellara de Belice, Gentile, Canino, Biancolilla and Carolea are the most popular Italian cultivars for oil.

Table olives play a much lesser role in the food of Italy than the oil. Big, fleshy, green, sweet **cerignole** from Puglia and tiny little Ligurian olives compete with Sicilian for the hearts of Italians. Green table olives are often sold pitted, sometimes stuffed with a tiny piece of capsicum (pepper), while the black are usually sold whole (the good ones are often too soft to pit), and sometimes marinated or roasted.

Table olives are sometimes cooked into dishes from the south as well as in the more rustic food of Umbria and Sardegna. They even show up in rabbit stews. Cooks in Le Marche do fabulous fried stuffed olives, known as **olive ripiene all'ascolane.**

Olive grove

STAPLES

ACETO BALSAMICO

The condiments on the Italian table will be familiar to most kitchens. Salt is often seen on the table but pepper is not, although it appears in every kitchen. Wine vinegar and olive oil are usually served with the salad, and in the far north you may be offered **senape** (mustard) or **cren** (horseradish) with your ham. There isn't much need for extras, though, as most food arrives well seasoned and heady with flavour.

Twenty years ago the world outside of Modena had hardly heard about **aceto balsamico** (balsamic vinegar), and look at it now. This brown, somewhat mystical substance sits on fashionable menus and supermarket shelves around the globe, and we can't seem to get enough of it. But the real aceto balsamico is a rare and beautiful thing.

It was originally designed as a cordial to be sipped after dinner, a drink of **contemplazione** (contemplation), and every household around Modena (and in quite a few other districts) made their own concoction. It's an incredibly complex, lingering, yet exquisitely balanced condiment that hardly deserves to be called a vinegar at all. In fact you could describe the taste as sweet by comparison with 'real' vinegars.

Aceto balsamico is made by placing cooked must (unfermented juice) from Trebbiano grapes in a series of ever-decreasing sized barrels made of different timbers – cherry, mulberry, oak, chestnut and even juniper – over a number of years until the liquid is quite thick. The intensely hot summers really heat the attics where the vinegar is stored, up to 50°C, so the must condenses as it evaporates. Modena's sharp winters are also essential for the process, and balsamics made elsewhere are never quite the same. Once the must has been aged for at least 12 years it can be blended with other barrels (which have to be at least as old) to produce a classic balsamico.

While the balsamico for sale in Montreal or Bristol may carry Modena's name, it's well known that far more balsamic vinegar is sold around the world than is ever made in the region. In order to protect the original **aceto balsamico tradizionale di Modena**, a consortium has been set up to blind taste and select those balsamico that meet a certain standard. Only 10% of what is offered makes the grade and the rest is sold in various watered-down forms (mixed with boiled red wine vinegar, for instance) as aceto balsamico, without the reference to 'tradizionale'.

Aceto balsamico tradizionale di Modena is aged for at least 12 years, and aceto balsamico tradizionale di Modena extravecchio is aged for at least 25 years. Look for the distinctive, curvaceous 100 ml (31/2 fl oz) bottles and the paper seal of the consortium, and expect to pay more than you had imagined for a taste you won't believe.

The tourist office in Modena (Piazza Grande, 17. Phone 059 20 66 60) can organise visits to a balsamico producer with about one day's notice during the working week.

Herbs & Spices

What would the food of Italy be without fresh **erbe** (herbs)? The herbs that make up the Italian kitchen aren't numerous, but all are essential and make a difference whether they are used fresh or dried.

Aglio (garlic) and **cipolle** (onions) are considered herbs and their taste goes hand in hand with many Italian dishes. Garlic, however, is used in fewer dishes than you'd think.

More widespread is the use of **prezzemolo** (flat-leaf parsley), which is often added when onion is fried at the start of a dish, as well as at the end. Fresh **basilico**, basil, is used extensively from north to south, particularly with tomatoes and in the Ligurian pinenut and basil paste, **pesto**.

Rosmarino, robust-flavoured rosemary, is used fresh and dried to flavour poultry and pork in particular. Fresh **salvia** (sage) is very good with poultry and veal, and essential in **saltimbocca**, a Roman speciality of veal topped with sage and prosciutto. **Timo** (thyme), **maggiorana** (marjoram) and **menta** (mint) play minor roles. Two of the few herbs that are popular dried are **origano** (oregano) and **lauro** (bay leaves), although the fresh also plays a part in many dishes.

The **spezie** or **droghe** (spices) that most kitchens use are quite simple too. The most common, apart from **sale** (salt) and **pepe** (pepper) has to be **peperoncino** (chilli), particularly the further south you travel. Also common are **cannella** (cinnamon) and **noce moscata** (nutmeg), which are used in sweet as well as savoury dishes.

Basil, used all over Italy

Gelati, Granita & Sorbetti

Sicilians like to take the credit for having invented Italian ice cream (**gelato**; plural **gelati**), which might surprise the Arabs who brought the technology to Sicilia. One thing's for sure, no other nation today can boast such consistently good frozen desserts.

Gelati is the most accessible, lickably soft ice cream in existence and has to be tasted in Italy to be fully understood. **Artigianale** (artisan or home-made) gelati is available at most towns of any size and the best is flavoured with real fruit or real espresso coffee. Manufactured syrups are starting to make inroads. Look for 'artigianale' or **produzione propria** (production of the proprietor) and **nostra produzione** ('our production') signs as well as gelati that is served from stainless steel-containers rather than plastic – a sign that they are at least churned on the premises.

Gelati

Other frozen sweets include **granite** (singular, **granita**), sorbetti (sorbets) and sometimes **semifreddi** (semi-frozen). **Granite** are slushy ices that take their name from their granular texture. The most popular flavours are **limone** (lemon) and **caffè** (coffee), and they are served in many bars in the south during the warmer months. **Caffè granita con panna** is the classic espresso ice topped with a thick blanket of whipped cream and served with a **brioche** (a pastry), a spoon and a straw.

Sorbetti are made from fruit and sugar, usually without egg (or just with egg white) and without dairy products. In the streets of Napoli a sorbetto can be a refreshing, slushy iced drink made from fresh lemon, while in the north it can resemble the French sorbet, like an icy gelato.

Many semifreddi are served frozen, but they are often just chilled to fridge-cold. A semifreddo has a moussey texture and is served at least fridge-cold, unlike many cakes which are served at room temperature. When semifreddi are frozen, they do not (or at least should not) set hard and the texture should always remain closer to a mousse.

THE GELATI DISPLAY

No one makes ice cream like the Italians, and you should take every opportunity to try the range of flavours. You'll see the locals doing just that, as gelati is the snack food of the nation.

At many **gelaterie** (gelati shops), you'll need to pay at the cash register before you order. Ask for a **cono** (cone) or a **coppa** (cup) and suggest a size – **piccolo** (small), **medio** (medium) or **grande** (large) – or the number of flavours you want to try (**un gusto**, **due gusti** ... one flavour, two flavours ...). Here are some of the most popular versions.

Albicocca	Apricot
Arancia	Orange
Bacio	Hazelnut pieces and chocolate (a take-off of the Perugina chocolate)
Banana	Banana
Caffè	Coffee
Cassata	Candied fruit and chocolate bits in a creamy base (Sicilian inspired)
Cioccolato	Chocolate
Cocco	Coconut
Crema	Vanilla, usually with egg yolks
Fior di latte	Milk or milk with cream, usually with a subtle fragrance from the type of milk used
Fragole	Strawberry; **fragole di bosco** is wild strawberry, a summer flavour not to be missed
Frutta de bosco	Fruits of the forest; berries
Giandu/gianduia	Smooth hazelnut and chocolate
Limone	Lemon, often without dairy products
Liquorizia	Liquorice
Melone	Melon
Nocciola	Hazelnut
Panna	Cream, usually vanilla-scented
Panna cotta/ creme caramel	'Cooked cream', a creamy base with caramel through or on top
Pesca	Peach
Pistacchio	Pistachio
Stracciatella	With fine pieces of chocolate swirled through a vanilla gelato base
Tiramisù	Ideally made from mascarpone with coffee and **marsala** (fortified wine) and sometimes **savoiardi** (sponge fingers) biscuits
Zabaione/ zabaglione	Marsala and egg yolk
Zuppa inglese	Trifle flavoured, often with cake pieces

Sweets

Italian desserts and **dolci** (sweets) tend to fall into a few categories; frozen, pastry and fruit – fruit easily being the most popular after meals. Cakes, while a must at many special occasions, are not often seen in day-to-day life.

Dolci are usually bought from shops when they're served in an Italian household. The end of big family meals will often include fruit, while other preferences are for **biscotti** (biscuits) or **torte** (cakes) made at a local **pasticceria** (pastry shop). So the shops have continued to flourish and the standard of bought pastries, cakes and biscotti is remarkably high. At someone's house, the home-made dessert you are likely to be offered is the **crostata**, a simple, delicious pastry tart.

One thing Italians excel at, but in a different way from the Swiss and Belgians, is **cioccolato** (chocolate). In fact, it was to Piemonte that the Swiss came to learn about how to roast, blend and temper chocolate when it first became a fashionable sweet in Europe. Mostly it is **gianduia**, the

Polentina, cake from Como, Lombardia

STAPLES

hazelnut and chocolate combination, that the Italians now do the best. Very good chocolatiers exist everywhere from Torino (in particular) to Napoli. Bars, **alimentari** (food stores) and most **tabacchi** (tobacco shops that also sell sweets) sell mass-produced Italian chocolate that is well worth trying. The most famous brands are Perugina from Umbria and Ferrero from Piemonte and are found world-wide.

Some Common Dolci

Biscotti
These are crisp, often double-baked biscuits served with caffè or **Vin Santo** (a sweet dessert wine). Varieties include cantucci, brutti ma buoni, ricciarelli and ossi dei morti.

Cannoli
Long, fried, crisp pastry tubes filled with sweet ricotta, often flavoured with candied fruit, pistachios etc.

Pistachio cannoli

Cassata (alla siciliana)
A cake of Arabic origin with sponge, sweet ricotta, candied citron, vanilla and pistachios.

Crespelle
Crepes.

Crostata
Shortcrust pastry tart topped with jam, fruit or even ricotta.

Crostoli
Crisp-fried pastries sprinkled with icing sugar. Served at festivals in the Trentino–Alto Adige region and the names can include **chiacchiere** (gossip) and **bugie** (lies).

Panna cotta

Panettone

The classic Easter and Christmas cake from Milano, now available all year. It's a yeast-risen dough, fragrant with candied citron and other candied peel and fruit. Supposedly named after the baker named Tony who invented it for his lover (as in pane of Tony).

Panna cotta

Literally, 'cooked cream', this is the widespread, gelatine-thickened dessert that can be really delicious.

Strudel

Classic apple strudel found in the far north. Sometimes filled with ricotta instead of apple.

Tartufo

Translating as 'truffle' because it looks like the fungus. Usually a packaged cocoa-dusted or chocolate-coated ball of ice cream filled with nuts.

Torrone

Nougat of almonds or hazelnuts. Sensational varieties can be found in Piemonte and Le Marche.

Tiramisù

Sponge cake or savoiardi biscuits soaked in coffee and liqueur and layered with sweetened mascarpone. The whole lot is topped with bitter cocoa and a good one can change the way you look at life.

Zabaglione/zabaione

A whipped-egg dessert with marsala or good red wine. Similar to the French sabayon.

Zuccotto

Dome-shaped dessert of sponge cake with a filling of semifreddo, liqueur, custard and chocolate.

Zuppa inglese

While the name means 'English soup', it is actually the Italian version of trifle made with sponge cake layered with chocolate, custard and cream. They don't use any jelly.

drinks

Coffee and wine dominate the Italian drinks map, and not surprisingly, too, since the quality of both is impeccable, whether they be served in the local **osteria** (simple eating-house) or in a fancy **ristorante** (restaurant). But to focus only on these drinks would be to short-change the excellent aperitifs, liqueurs, sparkling waters and fruit-based drinks also available.

Wine

Italy is a wine lover's dream. Despite the big names such as **Barolo** and **Amarone**, the vast majority of Italian wines are little known outside of the country. This means that there's still some great drinking to be had at very reasonable prices. Such an oversight partly stems from the amount of cheap, sometimes shockingly sweet or ghastly wines that were exported around the world in decades past. It's not unusual to think of **Lambrusco** as something that left many of us with numbing headaches after too many parties, or to regard **Chianti** as that rough wine in raffia-coated bottles.

So it's a delight to realise that Lambrusco from Emilia-Romagna is actually a bone-dry, refreshingly fizzy red, and Chianti an agreeable wine full of resolute fruit flavours without a hint of lolly-water.

Italy produces about a fifth of the world's wine, but it has never made the big time internationally until recently, mostly because it didn't want to. Wine, like food, is a part of that year-long celebration called life, and not the preserve of the rich, the well-travelled or the wine snob. To some extent, that is all changing as entrepreneurial winemakers finely hone techniques, and even more entrepreneurial marketers tell the world that Italian wines are different to the stuff they know from France or California, are cheaper and often at least as good.

Understanding Italian wine is incredibly complex, but many good books in English do exist (see the Recommended Reading chapter), and if you want to find out for yourself, there is at least a century's worth of research ahead; one estimate puts the number of Italian wines at over a million, if each registered estate produced a single style.

As you travel around Italy, you will find that a meal without wine, even a cheap wine, isn't as good. You'll find that the wine and food of a region tend to complement each other beautifully. And you'll find no end of people willing to '**salute!**' life, love and liberty with a glass of fermented grape juice.

BOTTOMS UP

While Italians drink the most wine per head of any nation, they don't often get drunk. In fact, wine is virtually always drunk with a meal and a surprising number of Italians drink quite moderately, even when they're eating. But they do drink often, and you'll find wine is served with every lunch and dinner.

History

The grape was introduced to Italy probably by the Etruscans, about whom we know relatively little. But the earliest inhabitants we know of who drank fermented grape juice were the Greeks. Greece settled much of lower Italy under its Magna Graecia (Greater Greece) empire and much of the mass plantings of vines was to produce wine to take back to Athens. Italy's capacity to produce a lot of wine was evident even then, with the name *Enotria*, or Land of Wine, being given first to Calabria and then to the whole of the lower Italian peninsula.

The Romans didn't mind a drop of the old *vino* (wine) either, and set in place some vast areas of cultivation. Amphorae were the carriers of the day, and most of what was drunk probably wouldn't pass muster even at a student piss-up today. Chances are it was oxidised, rough and young.

If wine helped fuel a few too many toga parties (was this part of the imperial Roman downfall?), it certainly helped in the pagan celebrations of much of Italy over the next few hundred years. In fact, many harvest **sagre** (feasting festivals) would have been fairly drab affairs if not for the use of wine to liven up the proceedings. As Christianity gradually took a hold of the country, region after region continued to use wine in celebrations that included Christ as well as seasonal produce. The contribution of nuns and monks to the Italian liquor cabinet that we know and love today is, dare we say it, of biblical proportions.

The wines of Italy have had a rough ride over the last two centuries, being branded as second-rate by French and English journalists in the 19th century. Often the quality was poor, but this had more to do with poverty of the people than anything else. Wine, like the rest of Italy's cucina, isn't accorded any noble status. It was and remains an intrinsic, albeit enjoyable, part of life. Some critics say that Italians spend far too much time drinking the stuff, and not enough making it.

Dew covered vine leaf near Orvieto, Umbria

Typical trellis at vineyard near Bressanone

Times are changing, and the wine production of Italy is contracting in quantity, while increasing in quality. While there will always be rough, appalling, cheap wines, there are many saving graces. Generally they have a more austere, somewhat more food-orientated taste than their French counterparts to which they are often compared. For example, **amarognolo**, the bitter almond taste present (and desirable) in many Italian whites and some red wines, is not often found in wines from elsewhere.

DRINK DRIVING

Despite (or perhaps because of) the law against drink driving, it still happens with frightening frequency. There's no such thing as a random breath test, and Italians don't seem to take too much notice of how much they consume before they hop into the front of their Panda and tootle off home. Locals warn that on Sunday afternoons and public holidays it's not as safe on the roads as you'd like to think. (That's even if you don't think it's safe at all.) Even in the service centres on the **autostrade** (motorway), you'll see drivers pop into the bar for a quick glass of **grappa** (distilled fermented grape must) before driving their Alfa Romeo out at 160km an hour. One leading autostrade bar is at least taking the problem seriously and is displaying this sign: "Safety on The Road. We do not serve spirits (>21 degrees) at the bar between 10pm and 6am."

Grape Varieties

Estimates vary about the number of grape varieties in Italy, but the short, always correct answer to the question is 'heaps'. Italy boasts at least 1000 varieties (some suggest as many as 2000), of which about 400 are known to be in production. Many are clones of common types such as **Sangiovese**, while others are distinct varieties.

One thing is for sure, the grapes of a region are usually distinct to that region even if the same variety of grape exists elsewhere. This means that the wines of, say, a town such as Barbaresco are distinctly and consistently different from those of nearby Barolo, even though both use the same grape variety, **Nebbiolo** (from **nebbia**, meaning 'fog'). Each has its aficionados.

To add to the confusion, different grape varieties are given the same name. So Trebbiano Toscano, Trebbiano di Soave and Trebbiano di Lugana can all suffer from the poor performance of one, when it's the other that is to blame. Yet they are all different varieties, or at least clones, and the wines bear little resemblance to one another.

The major players in Italian wine production today are **Trebbiano** and Sangiovese and their related varieties (albeit some only by name). The Trebbianos occupy over 100,000 hectares of vineyards, and are the most widely planted type in Italy. Most of the grapes end up in reasonably light but spirited white wines or in blends. A small amount of Trebbiano also winds up in **passito** wines, often sweetish wines made by drying the grapes before crushing, such as the Tuscan **vin santo** (see the boxed text Passito in the Wine Styles section later in this chapter). A type of Trebbiano also goes into the **Marsala** you'll find in Sicilia.

DRINKS

EST! EST!! EST!!!

In the year 1000, a wine-loving cardinal, Fugger, was travelling to Roma. Because he didn't want to drink just any old wine, he sent a servant on ahead. Every time the servant found an inn that served wine of quality, he was to write **est** ('this is it') on the inn's door. When the servant found a wine in Montefiascone in Northern Lazio, he was so blown away that he wrote 'est! est!! est!!!' on the door. Apparently Fugger did eventually make it to Roma after stopping for three days at the inn. What state he arrived in, we don't know. We also don't know if he ever made it home again, though he eventually settled in Montefiascone. While some medieval myths get better with a bit of wine-blurred hindsight, we actually know where Fugger is buried: in Montefiascone's church, San Flaviano.

Sangiovese is the most prolifically planted variety in the region of Toscana through to the central south. Like Trebbiano, it's a collection of various grapes under the one banner, but in this case it is a red grape. Much of the time it is used in blends, but the large **Sangiovese grosso** grape flies solo to make the famed **Brunello di Montalcino** wine, while the **Sangiovese piccolo**, a smaller-berried vine, is used extensively in the well-known Chianti and **Chianti Classico** (see Toscana in the Wines by Region section in this chapter).

Other important grape varieties include the powerful red Nebbiolo, that is harder to tame to make great wine than the **Pinot Nero** (Pinot Noir) grape. **Barbera** is the more commonly used red grape variety of the north, particularly around Asti and Alba in Piemonte, and the **Moscato** grape is used from Piemonte to Sicilia, with differing results and in differing wines. The best known Moscato wine is Moscato d'Asti, one ordinary version of which used to be known as '**Spumante**'. Sicilia makes great dessert wine, particularly the Moscato di Pantelleria from the island of the same name.

The last two centuries have seen the steady influx of proven, noble, French varieties with a lot of success. Cabernet Sauvignon and Chardonnay are used extensively in Toscana, with great results. Merlot grapes do wonders for many blends and are now the third most popular red grape planted in Italy, while Pinot Nero is proving to be a viable wine of the north. Pinot Nero is also mixed into sparkling wine.

In the far south the most popular grape varieties are the old ones, such as **Aglianico**, planted in Basilicata about the 6th century BC, and other ancient varieties with names that evoke images of the bacchanalia, such as **Greco** and **Grechetto**.

See the Wines by Region section in this chapter for a guide to which grape varieties are in some of the more relevant wines.

Quality assurance

DOCG

In addition to the DOC system there is a further check to help ensure the standard of traditional Italian wines. **Denominazione di Origine Controllata e Garantita (DOCG)** is a more assured guarantee of quality, where wines are checked for high quality as well as typicality. Relatively few wines make the DOCG status. While the system commenced in 1963 at the same time as DOC, it wasn't until 1980 that Brunello di Montalcino was declared the first DOCG wine.

The DOCG classification has been the object of some derision because some obviously inferior wines made the leap from DOC. Proposed changes to the legislation state that the wine must prove itself by reputation before it makes the big move to DOCG, and that the wine must spend at least five years as a DOC.

For all the detractors, a wine with a DOCG is a far better bet for the uninitiated than any other classification currently available. DOCG wines are easily recognisable by the pink label wrapped either around the neck of the bottle or taped over the top.

SUPER TUSCANS

One of the major drawbacks of the DOC and DOCG systems was that it failed to recognise the great wines of individual producers who did things in an unorthodox way. Some Tuscans, for reasons of clever marketing as well as quality, were quick to realise that wines that had a rich, complex, internationally acceptable taste could be sold for far more money than the local wines would ever achieve. So great wines were developed to appeal to buyers in New York as much as those in Milano. Some smart, English-speaking wine scribes started calling the new wines Super Tuscans and the name has stuck.

The sad thing was that despite the international acclaim these wines received, Italy still recognised them as vino da tavola, the lowest possible classification. Despite recent attempts to reclassify them as IGT wines (see IGT & Vino da Tavola below), they are still known internationally as Super Tuscans. These days, brilliant wines from other regions such as Piemonte, Friuli and Alto Adige are also pushing traditional boundaries and producing fabulous wine.

DRINKS

IGT & Vino da Tavola

The DOC and DOCG systems can impede the development and improvement of wines. Until recently any wine that wasn't entitled to bear DOC or DOCG on the label was known as a **vino da tavola**, a table wine. Anyone trying to improve wine, say, by mixing the same Sangiovese grape that is used to make the esteemed Brunello di Montalcino with a bit of Cabernet Sauvignon for easier, earlier drinking, would lead to these wines being classified as the lowest of wines. In 1992 a new system was instituted to help recognise some of these wines (sometimes known as Super Tuscans) called **Indicazione Geographica Tipica** or **IGT**. Many compare IGT to the French *vin de pays*. While the IGT system attempts to classify wines, many great, modern-style wines are not listed for political or bureau-cratic reasons (and also because it's trying to classify the unclassifiable).

At the end of the day, you usually get what you pay for and certain blends from individual wineries should be judged on their own merit, just as they are in California, the Medoc and Coonawarra.

People tending vines near La Morra, (Barolo country), Piemonte

Wine Styles

Italy has all the major wine styles found elsewhere, plus a few more besides. There's **frizzante**, the fizzy wines, including **Metodo Tradizionale** (Méthode Champenoise). Often these can be referred to as **spumante**, the word **spuma** referring to the froth that arises as they are poured. The most famous is the Moscato d'Asti (no longer allowed to be called Spumante), and the Veneto's **Prosecco**. Prosecco Brut is a spumante, but it's as dry as any sparkling wine.

Red wines, the most common wines in Italy, are known as **vini rossi**, white wines as **vini bianchi** and rosé-style wines are called **vini rosati**. Along with these are **vino da contemplazione/meditazione** (wines of contemplation/meditation). One from an Eolian island off the coast of Sicilia is Passito di Pantelleria made from partially-dried grapes. The result is a surprisingly lush yet not overly sweet wine with a length and character that is not really suited to dessert, or to the meal proper. It's more suited to sitting around and meditating upon the joys of life.

PASSITO

One of the distinguishing features of Italian wine is the use of the **passito** (raisining) method. Grapes are removed from the vine as usual, but instead of crushing them immediately, they are laid out to dry, usually on wooden racks (a process called **appasimento**). The grapes tend to become raisin-like, drying out to varying degrees and usually going all mouldy in the process. Inside each grape the juice condenses and becomes sweeter.

These wines are often sweet, although not as sweet as many dessert varieties. Many Italians think of them as after-dinner wines.

However, some passito wines aren't sweet at all. One of the most famous is the Amarone della Valpolicella. Three grape varieties are used, and each one is affected differently during appasimento by the mold 'noble rot', *botrytis cinerea*. The tannins are concentrated along with the sugars. A special high-alcohol tolerant yeast is used to produce a wine unlike that from anywhere else and without a hint of excessive sweetness. Other passito wines of note are vin santo, some Moscato and Sagrantino di Montefalco.

Wine By Region

Every region makes wine, and traditionally each rural family made their own whenever they could. It's still possible to taste the simple wines that some families produce, and some of them are quite drinkable.

Some say that it was the Etruscans or Phoenicians who brought grapes to the centre and north of Italy, and the Greeks who established vineyards in the south, thus leading to two different styles. But more likely the current difference in wine perception and quality from the north and south is in the care and attitude of the winemakers.

Those of the south have not looked for outside approval and make wine in the way they always have because it was to drink, not to fiddle around with, and definitely not to be used as a sign of status. So the wines of the south have had difficulties with quality, some currently being addressed.

Every region produces wines of note, and some are blockbusters that appeal to the international palate. There are, however, any number of wines that are uniquely Italian, very drinkable and aren't on English-language lists of must-tries.

Valle d'Aosta

The smallest of Italy's regions is also the smallest producer. Vineyards cling to often terraced hills, and Valle d'Aosta lays claim to Europe's highest classified vineyard at Morgex. Wines generally aren't of much significance outside the region, as Valle d'Aosta produces less wine than its people consume. Local varieties of interest include Blanc de Valdigne and Vien de Nus. Labels can be written in Italian or French.

DRINKS

Vino Bianco

Chambave Moscato The Moscato grape grown around Chambave produces a wine that is quite dry and aromatic and should be consumed while young. Of greater note is the passito version which has golden hints and is a deeply perfumed dessert wine that ages well.

Vino Rosso

Donnaz/Donnas Made from a clone of the Nebbiolo grape, it is a light-style red with a raspberry aroma. Will age well over five years.

Piemonte

Piemonte is widely regarded, along with Toscana, as making the best reds in Italy, despite being outperformed in the quantity stakes by five other regions. The quality comes from tradition and respect for the grape.

Barolo tasting, Roberto Voerzio winery, La Morra, Piemonte

Notably, the greatest wines come from local varieties (somewhat unlike Toscana). The varieties have their own character, all the more reason to try them, though the flavours can take some getting used to.

This is the most organised region for wine tourism. Towns such as La Morra, Barolo, Barbaresco, Roppolo, Grinzane Cavour and others have public **enoteche** (wine stores) for tasting and buying the local wine.

DRINKS

Vino Bianco

Arneis di Roero A lesser known wine (not to be confused with the simple 'Roero', a red wine) made with an old grape variety, Arneis. Considered by some as a sexy, bold wine, and by others as simply trendy.

Gavi Sometimes called Cortese di Gavi after the grape Cortese. A prestigious, flinty and lightly acidic white with many loyal followers. Straw-yellow in colour and with citrus (lime) characteristics, it goes well with **primi piatti** ('first plate', first course) and fish.

Vino Rosso

Barbaresco A robust elegant red wine made with Nebbiolo grapes from around the villages of Barbaresco, Neive and Tresio. Lacks the power of a big Barolo, but is ready to drink at a younger age. Recent increases in quality and accolades have seen prices soar. Suits roasts and ripe cheeses.

Barbera One of Piemonte's most widely planted grape varieties. A versatile variety that can produce wines ranging from the light frizzante to intense and long-lived styles. Most well known DOCs are those from Asti and Alba.

Barolo Outstanding red wine made from Nebbiolo grapes of the Langhe district. Distinctive characteristics of truffles, garnet in colour with fantastic aging potential of up to 10 years. Tends to be tannic when young, but develops into a velvety savoury wine. Excellent in and with **brasato al Barolo** (meats braised in Barolo), game and risotto.

Dolcetto d'Alba The Dolcetto is a black grape variety grown extensively throughout southern Piemonte. The most outstanding DOC comes from the hills of Alba. Deep purple and rich but not sweet.

Monferrato When aged, good with pasta and boiled meat.

Nebbiolo d'Alba Great alternative in style and price to the intense Barolo and Barbaresco of the region. Good with red meat, game and truffle-based dishes.

Frizzante
Moscato d'Asti Once known as Spumante. Exported versions were (and sometimes still are) sickly sweet and none too classy, but the real thing is elegantly fragrant and lightly bubbled or frizzante. Made mostly from Moscato Bianco, Moscato di Canelli and Brachetto varieties in the provinces of Asti, Cuneo and Alessandria.

Rosato
Grignolino d'Asti Rarely found outside Piemonte. Made from the Grignolino grape, this wine is light in colour and sometimes slightly bitter. Is good as an **aperitivo** (pre-meal drink) or with rich food typical of the region.

Liguria
It's hard to believe that this small-yielding, steeply hilled region has over 100 grape varieties in production. The amazing thing is, Liguria doesn't actually produce that much wine (second lowest in Italy, only after Valle d'Aosta), but they have a long history of self-reliance. Most of the good wines are white, and are often made with Vermentino, such as the fashionable Cinque Terre.

Vino Bianco
Cinque Terre Made from the Bosco, Vermentino and Albarola grapes this light dry wine's quality does not match up to its fame.

Vino Rosso
Ormeasco Its rich and velvety bouquet is the Ligurian answer to the Piemontese Dolcetto. From a subzone of the Arroscio Valley in the newer DOC area of the Riveria Ligure di Ponente.

Rossese di Dolceacqua The Rossese grapes, from Dolceacqua and the hills behind San Remo and Ventimiglia, make a wine that is both warm and rustic. This wine can vary from light, Beaujolais style to a richer, fruit-driven wine.

Vino da Dessert
Sciacchetrá A rare passito version of the famous Cinque Terre. Golden in colour and at least 17% alcohol. Well worth keeping an eye out for.

Lombardia
The industrial, financial and fashion heartland of Italy loves its wine, but the local production is relatively modest. (They're probably too busy

DRINKS

designing, fighting bribery allegations and making money to work on the grapes.) But good wines are to be found, particularly in the Valtellina near the Swiss border, though much of the best is exported north without ever going through Milano. Another production area is the **Oltrepò Pavese** on 'the other side' (south) of the Po River, as well as around Brescia and Bergamot. The most favoured drops are the sparkling wines of Franciacorta and some passito Nebbiolo from Valtellina.

Vino Bianco

Methode Champenoise di Franciacorta A champagne-style wine made from Chardonnay and Pinot Nero.

Vino Rosso

Barbera di Oltrepò Pavese Bonarda Ruby red in colour. Good with salami, first courses and grilled meats.

Franciacorta Rosso Cabernet Franc, Barbera, Nebbiolo and Merlot. Best drunk within the first four years and goes well with game and roast.

Valtellina Sfursat Wine from Valtellina made from Nebbiolo. Garnet in colour and with an intense, spicy fragrance. Good aging potential. Excellent with game, meat and ripe cheese.

Trentino–Alto Adige

Everywhere you look when you drive north into Alto Adige are vines next to the roads – vines on terraced hills, vines on rolling hills, vines by lakes. With such a cool climate, the north is perfect for aromatic whites and the south, particularly in Trentino, for fine flavoured reds. The region produces an enormous quantity of DOC wine (over 50% of production) and fully a third of all wine produced leaves the country. (Most of it hardly travels any distance, finding its way to Austria just over the border.) Much of the newer style wine is made with French varieties, such as Merlot, Chardonnay and Pinot Grigio (Pinot Gris). The Riesling Renano (Rhine Riesling) is also good.

Vino Bianco

Traminer Aromatico (Gewurztraminer). The classic aromatic white wine from the area that claims to be the origin of the grape.

Hillside vineyard near Bressanone, Alto Adige

DRINKS

Vino Rosso
Alto Adige Cabernet Ruby red in colour with characteristic herbaceousness and intense fragrance. Good with roasts, grilled meats and ripe cheeses.

Terolego Rotaliano A deep red, tannic wine with great aging potential.

Vino da Dessert
Moscato The region produces both a **giallo** (yellow) and a **rosa** (pink) version. Good with strudel.

Friuli–Venezia Giulia
Friuli–Venezia Giulia is best known by many outsiders for the quality of their wine. In fact, vines positively flourish in Friuli, and locals make an industry out of growing all kinds of root stock and selling them around the world. Local grape varieties include the red Refosco as well as Picolit, making a rare, sweet wine. It was in Friuli, too, that individual grape varieties were first made into truly smooth and flavourful grappa which had previously just been something highly alcoholic you made with scraps.

Collio

The region of hills towards the border with the former Yugoslavia has some of the most blessed micro-climates in the land, producing many different wines from a variety of grapes.

Collio Orientali de Friuli

The best part of the Collio makes the finest whites in Friuli, again with a range of grapes. The reds are interesting too. Look for the fascinating **Schioppettino**, meaning 'tongue splitter' because the acid balance means you can only taste it up either side of your tongue.

Grave del Friuli From one of the largest wine-growing zones in the province, with over half the DOCs of Friuli being produced here. Merlot and some good whites excel.

Veneto

The Veneto is a big player on the Italian wine scene, producing 20% of all the DOC wine (by volume) in the country. Both reds and whites tend to favour local grape varieties, leading to wines of unusual, yet very typical local character. The area around Verona is particularly blessed, boasting both Soave and Valpolicella, two of the foremost wine regions in the country. Prosecco, a sparkling wine, is a particularly great way to start a meal.

Vino Bianco

Colli Euganei Moscato Golden-yellow in colour, with an intense fragrance characteristic of Moscato. Good with all desserts and fruit salad.

Soave Sprightly, fresh and lively white wines that taste of the soil in which they are grown. Great with rice dishes.

Vino Rosso

Amarone della Valpolicella Like driving a Ferrari in sheepskin gloves, the mix of strength and smoothness is fascinating. The wine has a slight bitter almond taste which marries beautifully with food. Made in the passito method. A similarly-made wine, Recioto della Valpolicella, is used after dinner and has the strength with sweetness and a thicker texture.

Bardolino Fragrant red wine, ruby red in colour, and best drunk young. Goes well with a light primi piatti and soft cheeses.

Valpolicella A highly regarded, easy-drinking wine from the same zone as Amarone, but made without the passito method.

DRINKS

Frizzante
Prosecco di Conegliano Lightly fizzy wine from the Prosecco grape. Choose from **brut** (dry), **dolce** (sweet) or **amabile** (in-between).

Emilia-Romagna

While Emilia-Romagna produces some absolutely amazing food, such as **parmigiano** (parmesan cheese), **prosciutto** (cured ham), and **aceto balsamico** (balsamic vinegar), the wines aren't nearly as well received by outsiders. Lambrusco is the light-hearted, lightly bubbled red that wine snobs like to deride, and the DOCG wine Albana hasn't received the acclaim that other 'guaranteed' wines have. Both are delightful food wines, and marry with the rich, buttery food of the region perfectly. When you can't enjoy the sheer, unadulterated pleasure of a little bit of (thankfully dry) red fizz then surely the fun has gone from life.

Vino Bianco
Albana di Romagna (dry/passito). Straw colour tends to golden yellow with aging. A dry or medium sweet white wine. The dry style is a good accompaniment to soups and fish-based dishes, the medium sweet with fruit and desserts.

Vino Rosso
Lambrusco Reggiano Lightly frizzante (sparkling) red wine. Ruby red in colour, with hints of violets on the palate. Goes well with salami, **gnocco fritto** (a single fried potato dumpling) and Modena's famous dish **zampone** (stuffed pig's trotter).

Sangiovese di Romagna Ruby red in colour with an intense fragrance. A hint of sharpness makes it excellent with roasts and red meat.

Toscana

It is the Tuscans who've led the charge, no, the stampede, among some northern winemakers for overseas recognition. Having weaned us onto Italian wine in the 1970s with cheap, raffia-wrapped bottled Chianti, they're now using some of the most innovative and modern techniques in the country to produce outstanding wines.

Chianti is still the drop of the masses. It is very drinkable, and can be very good. But the most excit-

DRINKS

ing things are happening in those little fortified hill-top villages, whose wine-making traditions are being revised to increase quality, notably Montalcino, Montepulciano and San Gimignano. Toscana also started the trend of untraditional, yet exceptional, wines called Super Tuscans (see the boxed Super Tuscans earlier in this chapter).

Barrels in wine cellar at Altesino, near Montalcino, Toscana

Vino Bianco

Vernaccia di San Gimignano Ancient grape variety grown since the 13th century around the village of San Gimignano. Italy's first DOC wine and the second white wine to gain DOCG status. An aromatic and steely wine, full of fresh fruit flavours.

Vino Rosso

Brunello di Montalcino One of Italy's most prized and expensive wines. Made from the versatile Sangiovese grape in Montalcino, south of Siena. Garnet red in colour with an intense palate and ethereal fragrance. This rich, complex wine requires by DOCG law a minimum of three to five years' aging. Great accompaniment for roasts, game and wild boar.

Chianti A light, easy-drinking style, ruby red in colour and produced in large quantities in seven zones in Central Italy. After World War II the quality declined, though renewed interest and new technology are bringing it back to its heights. Typically bottled in **fiaschi** (flasks covered with straw). Chianti Colli Senesi is the largest Chianti-producing zone with a youthful style. Chianti Rufina produces good quality wine while Chianti Colli Pisane is known for its light, soft style.

Chianti Classico From a zone that is the historical heartland of Chianti (roughly between Siena and Florence), this is where the majority of really good quality Chianti comes from. This zone has a DOCG to guarantee the quality.

Rosso di Montalcino Although this wine is made from the Sangiovese grapes that are rejected when the famous Brunello is made, it is by no means second-rate. The rich fruit flavour of this wine is impressive in its own right. Under a relatively new DOC ruling, the wine can be appreciated after only one year of aging.

Rosso di Montepulciano The lighter and younger cousin to the Vino Nobile di Montepulciano. A great alternative to the Nobile, in both ready-to-drink style and price.

Vino Nobile di Montepulciano The beautiful hill town of Montepulciano in Toscana produces what was referred to by Francesco Redi in the 17th century as the 'king of wines'. Today's progressive wine-making continues to uphold the quality of this distinguished wine. Produced from predominantly Sangiovese grapes, or Prugnolo Gentile, as they are known locally.

Vino da Dessert

Vin Santo The name literally means 'holy wine', indicating that the wine may have been used in Mass. Traditionally a sipping wine, it is made from semi-dried Trebbiano Toscano, Malvasia and Grechetto grapes. The grapes are pressed and sealed in **caratelli** (small barrels) for three years. The wine varies from sweet to semi-sweet and dry. It's usually golden amber in colour and beautifully aromatic, and at its best is one of Italy's best dessert wines.

Umbria

The harsh terrain of much of Umbria isn't the best place to produce wine, but the region does have a few highlights. Wines from small producers around Lago di Trasimeno have interest, if not always loads of class, and much of the wine suits the pork-heavy food of the region. Interestingly, one of the country's best Champagne-style wines comes from an Umbrian producer, Lungarotti. The best local white, Orvieto, is as gorgeous as the town that bears its name.

Vino Bianco

Orvieto Classico This famous, must-try wine is produced by blending five grape varieties: Trebbiano Procanico, Grechetto, Verdello, Drupeggio and Malvasia. Is produced as both a dry and semi-sweet wine.

DRINKS

Vino Rosso

Sagrantino di Montefalco A passito wine that was, until relatively recently, known only locally. It is fast becoming known by outsiders for its mix of strength with velvety texture. The dry is very good, sometimes astounding, but the sweet version also has its own fans.

Le Marche

There's not much land to grow grapes in Le Marche, what with the Appennini mountains on one side and the sea on the other. But what is produced, particularly the white, is highly regarded. Thanks to the Verdicchio grape and some clever marketing with an amphora-shaped bottle and a label describing the wine's history, Le Marche is a contender in white wine sales internationally. The wine has grown in stature and remains true to the region and perfect for a **brodetto** (fish stew) of Adriatic seafood.

Vino Bianco

Verdicchio dei Castelli di Jesi The delicate Verdicchio grapes produce wines that range from crisp and clean with yellow-green hues to a rich gold and textured with a little age. Goes beautifully with the local seafood. Try it with fish soups and shellfish.

Verdicchio di Matelica The lesser-known of the two outstanding Verdicchios. Some claim that the original Verdicchio came from here.

Vino Rosso

Rosso Cónero A deep ruby-red, quality wine with a full, round flavour. Very limited amounts are produced in the hills around Ancona.

Rosso Piceno Produced from 60% Sangiovese and 40% Montepulciano, this smooth, composed wine benefits greatly with three years of aging.

Lazio

The region that contains the country's political capital seems content to produce wine for drinking in Roma's trattorie. Most of Lazio's wines are white and unremarkable, but quite acceptable, particularly for the price. The wine can often seem sharp, possibly to suit the full-on taste of Roman food, and locals can often be seen watering it down. Depending on how good the bottle (or carafe) you order is, you may want to do this too.

Grigolino vines near Asti, Piemonte

DRINKS

Delivery of Frascati wine to a restaurant in Roma, Lazio

Vino Bianco

Colli Albani Made in the hills of Alban this dry white wine has a delicate fragrance and an almost apple-like flavour. Good as an aperitivo or served with fish.

Frascati Produced from Malavasia and Trebbiano grapes (with small amounts of Greco, Bellone and Bombino) in the famous hill town (yes, another one) of Frascati. A lot of Frascati is exported internationally but the best you'll drink will be in Italy, and within the wine's first year of bottling. The wine is delicate and aromatic and goes well with eggs, vegetables and light primi piatti.

Vino Rosso

Torre Ercolana Limited wine from Anagni, south-east of Rome. Made from a blend of Cenanese, Cabernet and Merlot. An impressive and opulent wine.

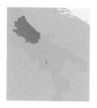

Abruzzo/Molise

The great wine of Abruzzo has, confusingly enough, the same name as a great wine of Toscana – Montepulciano is both a grape and a town. Here, it is the grape that produces a wine bold enough to cope with the pork-based products of the region. Molise has only a couple of classified wines, but uses many non-DOC varieties in its table wines.

Vino Bianco

Trebbiano d'Abruzzo A fresh, crisp wine that loses its simple appeal when served too cold.

Vino Rosso

Biferno Rosso One of Molise's best-known wines. Produced from the Montepulciano d'Abruzzo grapes, it is a lighter style wine, ruby red in colour and has an intense fragrance. Can be aged for up to four years. Goes well with salami, lamb and pork.

Montepulciano d'Abruzzo Produced from the local Montepulciano d'Abruzzo grapes. This fruit-driven wine intensifies and rounds out with age. Ruby red in colour. Good with grilled meat, game and roasts.

Vino Rosato

Ceresuolo d'Abruzzo Rosé version of the Montepulciano d'Abruzzo. Goes well with the pastas and soups of Abruzzo.

Campania

For a region once noted for its wines (writers during the Renaissance apparently loved the stuff), Campania is now known for producing a lot of ready-to-drink styles without much pizzazz. The most common local vines are from ancient stock, such as Greco and Aglianico, both pre-dating the eruption of Monte Vesuvio. Nearly all the wine is outside any classification system, probably just how the locals like it.

Vino Bianco

Greco di Tufo Crisp white with decent fruit flavours. 'Greco' refers to many of the varieties brought in by the Greeks.

Vesuvio (Lacryma Christi) Some say it's more famous for the name (Christ's Tears) than the taste. This was probably the same variety that was buried under Monte Vesuvio's famous eruption.

Vino Rosso

Taurasi Made from the ancient Aglianico grape, this is a deep, rich red with the potential for long aging. Some call it the Barolo of the south.

Puglia

The biggest producer in Italy, Puglia has suffered under the international tendency not to blend wines. For years, much of the region's production was exported for use in other wines or vermouth. The result now is a region with a huge output, but with less notion of quality than you'd hope. Things are changing, and there are a few gems to be found.

DRINKS

Vino Bianco

Locorotondo From the town of the same name, it's a very pale wine with a similarly light and subtle taste. It goes brilliantly with fish.

Vino Rosso

Castel del Monte The most well known DOC in Puglia, with rosé and white styles as well, but it is the red that turns heads. The riserva (aged for three years) is the best buy.

Salice Salentino A smooth, deep-flavoured red with a touch of bitterness as you'd expect from a grape made from Negro Amaro ('black bitter').

'Coperto' pergola style trellising, Puglia

Basilicata

Despite being an ancient wine-growing region (Greeks introduced the Aglianico variety in about the 6th century BC), Basilicata only produces one DOC wine. The funny thing is, it's the same grape variety that the Greeks liked. When you're on a good thing, stick to it.

Vino Rosso

Aglianico del Vulture Some describe this as the great unknown red of the south. The trick is to not drink it too young or it seems austere and unfriendly. And don't drink too much while you're in Matera or you'll get totally lost in the old city.

Calabria

Calabria used to be called 'Enotria' by the Greeks, the 'Land of Wine', because they recognised the potential of the vine here. It is the varieties that the Greeks introduced that still set the scene, particularly Greco, which goes into most of the local whites. But the only real wine of note that is found outside its area of production is Cirò, which many regard as the oldest wine in the world.

Cirò

From slopes along the Ionian coast, an ancient wine that is said to be getting better all the time. Elegant and with a lifted bouquet, it comes as red and, more recently, white and rosé.

Sicilia

While the average wines in Sicilia nowadays are a light-style red and a refreshing white (Corvo is the most commonly recommended wine), it is Marsala that the isle is famous for. Invented over 200 years ago by an Englishman, John Woodhouse, who had some experience from Jerez in Spain, Marsala is making a comeback. DOC rules have banned the addition of eggs, cream and syrups and the results include dry styles that have wine critics swooning.

Vino Rosso

Marsala The most famous wine of the isle comes in dry and sweet styles. The dry is amber in colour with an almond/woody aroma and palate. Excellent as an aperitivo or with desserts and cheeses.

Vino da Dessert

Moscato di Pantelleria A wine of fabled intensity and rarity from one of the Eolian islands. Many call this a benchmark Moscato, with its floral bouquet and lingering taste, but no cloying sweetness.

Sardegna

It was the Spanish who brought one of the region's best known grapes to Sardegna. Grenache, known locally as Cannonau, is found in several regions, and is particularly good from around Oliena, where, incidentally (and thankfully), the most interesting food is also to be found.

Vino Bianco

Vermentino di Gallura Made from the Vermentino grape in a traditionally bold style. Its strong flavours marry well with **burrida**, the oily fish stew of the region.

Vino Rosso

Cannonau di Alghero Both a dry and passito style of this wine are available. The dry version is an excellent table wine with decent complexity. The passito is only all right.

DRINKS

Other Alcoholic Drinks

While wine is the major drink of Italy, the bar shelves groan under the weight of many more tipples, most made from ancient herbal recipes, sometimes by monks or nuns. Because of the secret nature of the ingredients, most of them are known by their brand name, and many are found all over the country.

Aperitivi

Italians, those who drink before dinner, like something with a bitter taste, something that stimulates the palate. Many aperitivi are herbaceous and have a very addictive slightly bitter nuance. Often it is a hint of quinine that does the trick. Quite a few of the aperitivi can also be served as digestivi.

Aperol

This orange pre-dinner drink has a lower alcohol content than most. Made with rhubarb and ginseng, among other ingredients, it's finding favour with those who want a bitter palate-lifter without the alcohol of Campari.

Bellini

The classic drink of fresh white peach juice combined with the sparkling Prosecco of the Veneto.

Campari

Probably the most common of the aperitivi, it's a red-coloured, spirit-based drink with a bitter, palate-cleansing taste. Once you've got a taste for it, it's hard to drink others. Bitter Campari means the straight drink, while Campari Soda is a pre-mixed bottle of Campari with soda water.

Crodino

Fizzy non-alcoholic bitters.

Fernet-Branca

Like a form of bitters, using blossoms and 'rare' aromatic herbs, also available in a mint style.

Negroni

A cocktail of Campari, vermouth and gin.

Pastis

The anise-flavoured drink of the southern French is drunk around the French border of Liguria and Valle d'Aosta.

Punt e Mes

A brown, thickish Milanese drink with a vermouth base and alpine herbs. Usually served straight, or with a slice of orange, it is a delectable mix of bitterness and sweetness.

DRINKS

Caffe corretto, (espresso with the addition of grappa)

Ramazzotti
A Milanese drink with a more lifted, mintier aroma than Punt e Mes, and less bitter taste, but similarly dark in colour. Drink straight or with an orange slice.

San Bitter
Similar to an alcohol-free Campari (also a similar red in colour).

Vermouth
Wine-based drinks scented with herbs, the most famous being Cinzano.

GRAPPA

Grappa

To sum up the majority of Italian **digestivi** (digestives) in one word, you only need to say **grappa**. Grappa is the single most popular digestivo in the country, favoured from the alps to the isles. In its roughest form it is made from the distilled **vinacce** (crushed grape skins and stalks) from any type of grape, is extremely high in alcohol and tastes like it's made from barbed wire. At its best, grappa is made from the vinacce of high quality grapes of one variety, has a distinctive taste and is as smooth as velvet. It's always clear, and is the favoured after-dinner drink of most Italian men.

Peach grappa

Another strong alcohol digestivo is **acqua vita**, made by distilling any fruit or vegetable. It could be **mirtilli** (like a wild blueberry), **pesche** (peach) or grape varieties such as Chardonnay. The difference is the use of whole fruit rather than the pressings, so the result is a smoother drink. It's also popularly added to coffee to make a caffè corretto (see the boxed text Coffee Decoder later in this chapter).

Other digestivi include **Centerba**, a powerful drink from Abruzzo made with aromatic and digestive herbs. It's a very pale green, gorgeous colour though it often comes in a raffia bottle and clocks in at 70% alcohol. Another more common digestivo is **Cynar**, made from distilled artichokes. It's a dark brown colour, has a herbaceous hint and can also be used as an aperitivo.

Liquori
There are many **liquori** (liqueurs) in Italy, often flavoured with berries or fruit, but they aren't often drunk. These are the most common.

Amaretto
Almost syrupy almond liqueur with a hint of bitterness underneath the sweetness. Used extensively in desserts.

Limoncello
A duckling-coloured lemon drink that comes from the Amalfi coast and is now becoming more popular. The best is made from fresh lemons, pure alcohol, sugar and water. Sweet, fragrant, powerful and very easy to drink.

Sambuca
Aniseed flavour, popular with younger drinkers. Often served **con la mosca**, 'with the fly' (coffee bean), which Italians don't usually eat.

Menu board outside restaurant in Bolzano

Birre (Beer)
In a land flooded with wine, it's not surprising that Italians don't drink a lot of beer. But it is popular and younger Italians have taken to beer and have no hesitation in guzzling it down with pizza.

Italian brewing is mainly concentrated in the north and many brewers have Austrian roots which may explain their German-sounding names. The most common Italian beers are nearly all crisp and light Pilsener-style lagers which are perfect to quench your thirst on hot summer days. While Italian beers aren't going to challenge the great beers of Belgium and Germany there are a few worth trying. The most popular breweries are Dreher, Moretti and Peroni and while these are all good, if you want to try something different, down a Forst Sixtus, a Splügen or a Gran Riserva.

You can also find Guinness, Theakstons Bitter Ale and Heineken.

DRINKS

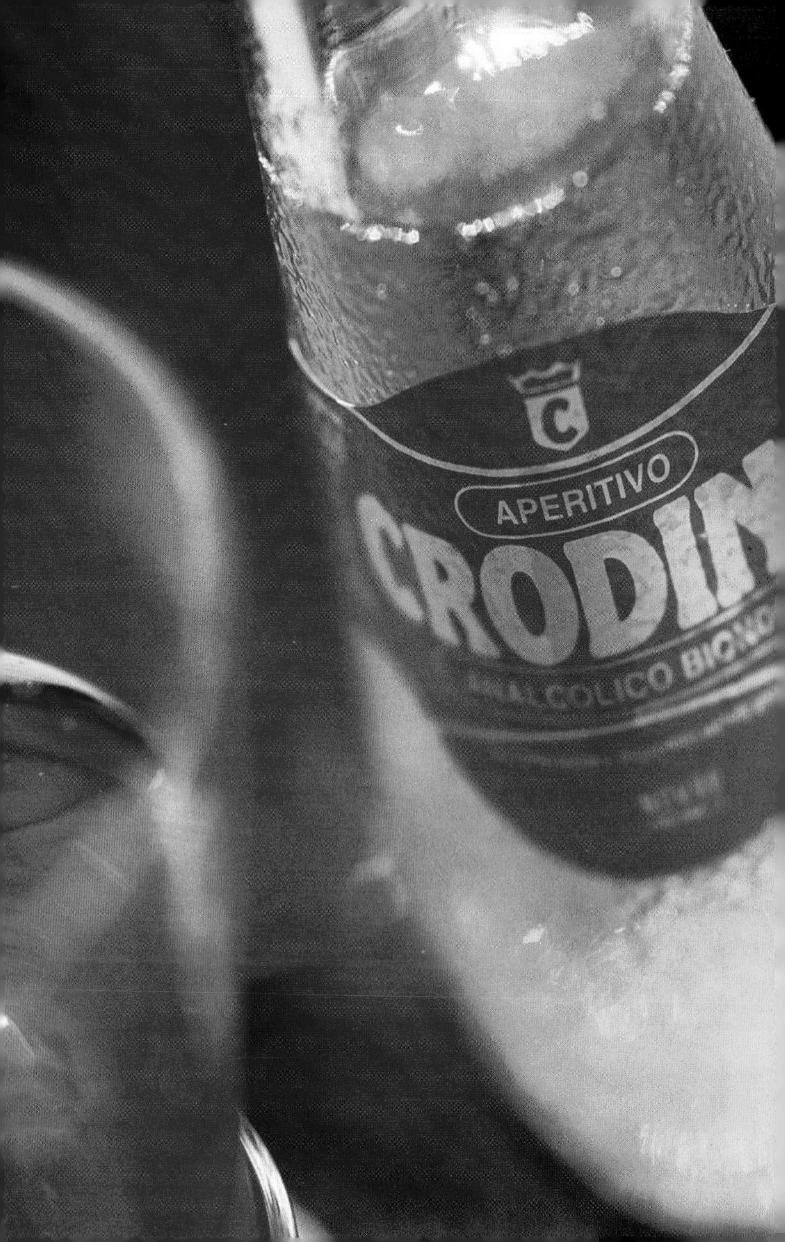
APERITIVO
CRODIN

Non-Alcoholic Drinks
Coffee & Tea

Okay, get this: coffee in Italy isn't like anywhere else in the world. It's better. So don't come thinking of **caffè** (coffee) as the stuff that comes in a bottomless cup in North America, or that bitter, ungainly stuff you often find in Australia. And it isn't at all like the French *café*, despite its being made in similar machines.

The first thing to get your head around is the temperature. Coffee is served at the perfect temperature for flavour, **tiepido** (tepid). This means that the **crema**, the rich, caramel-coloured foam on top of an espresso, preserves the aroma without being bitter. It also means that the milk is heated with steam to create a

Coffee granita with cream

schiuma, the thick, rich, dense and quite wet foam that captures the essence of the crema. If you don't like your coffee at this temperature, then ask for it **molto caldo** (very hot), deal with the deep sigh from the barman, and don't expect it to taste as good as it could.

Italians ADORE their caffè. They duck into bars for a quick fix and are gone in the time it takes to say *"Buongiorno. Come vai ...?"* Usually it is a simple caffè (a short black or espresso in English) but could include a little grappa in the cooler months (see caffè corretto in the Coffee Decoder in this chapter). They invariably sugar their coffee. In some areas the barmen may do this for you if you don't ask them not to, although thankfully this habit is quite rare.

Italians don't offer instant coffee. Even at home the classic Moka stove-top espresso machine is used. To offer instant coffee would be considered decidedly poor form. Interestingly, espresso coffee contains less caffeine than instant or percolated coffee.

Great coffee doesn't need any additives, and so the horrific habits that Italian immigrants once practised in the New World (such as using salt, lemon peel and even mustard to lift the taste of the substandard coffee that was available there) are unheard of. So, too, the modern notion that coffee needs vanilla or hazelnut aromas and the like to make it seductive. When you've had the real thing, there's no going back.

By comparison with caffè, **tè** (tea) in Italy is a disappointment. In bars the water comes from the espresso machine and is not freshly boiled. The tea you buy in Italy is also a bit limp in taste (even the British brands seem different), and doesn't quite do the drink justice. You can find **tè freddo** (iced tea) in bars and this is often as good as you'll find in other countries.

Crodino, booze-free aperitif

COFFEE DECODER

The best place for a cheap coffee is in a bar (see the Where to Eat & Drink chapter), and great coffee is served at bars just about everywhere. Most Italians only drink cappuccino for breakfast and will look at you sideways if you order one after midday. But if that's what you want, then it's worth bearing the brunt.

Caffè
While the word means coffee, if used alone, it always implies the classical small espresso, which must always have a dense, light brown **crema** (foam) on top. Drunk by adult Italians of all ages and from all walks of life.

Caffè corretto
A caffè with a drop of strong alcohol added to 'correct' it. The alcohol is virtually always grappa and even if you don't normally take sugar in your coffee, this could well be the time to try a bit, as it rounds out the flavour. Caffè corretto is sometimes drunk at breakfast, especially during the cooler months.

Caffè decaffeinato
Decaffeinated coffee, available virtually everywhere in both of the above styles.

Caffè freddo
A shot of coffee in cold milk, a popular summer drink in southern parts.

Caffè latte
Similar to a French *café au lait* but not as milky or as large. Occasionally served in a glass, it's a milkier version of the cappuccino, with less foam.

Caffè lungo (doppio, americano)
A long coffee. While the name means 'double' it is usually the same amount of coffee grinds with extra water poured through. This tends to make the coffee more bitter and higher in caffeine than a straight caffè. Usually only ordered by tourists.

Caffè macchiato
An espresso 'stained' with just a dot of milk. You can order it **caldo**, with a dot of hot, foamed milk, or **freddo**, with a spot of cold milk.

Cappuccino (cappuccio)
The favoured breakfast of most Italians. A shot of espresso is topped with thick, richly foamed milk called **schiuma** (and sometimes dusted with bitter cocoa). It's named after the Capuchin monks, whose robes

are apparently the same colour as the milky brown coffee. Cappuccino also means little hood, but many people refer to it simply as a **cappuccio** (plural **cappucci**), especially in the north. This drink is outstanding virtually everywhere in Italy and has nothing to do with the appalling interpretations that masquerade as cappuccino around the world.

Latte macchiato
Warmed milk 'stained' with a shot of coffee, usually served in a long glass.

Macchiatone
A bigger version of a caffè macchiato caldo, but without as much milk or foam as a cappuccino. Not widely known. A great stepping stone to becoming a serious straight caffè drinker.

Ristretto (caffè ristretto)
A 'restricted' coffee. This is the real essence of the coffee bean as it is just the first dribble of coffee that comes from the machine when making an espresso, with a very concentrated (but not bitter) flavour. Curiously, it has less caffeine than an espresso.

Espresso coffee (caffè) being made

WATER, WATER, EVERYWHERE

It's still and the piazza is quiet. The morning rush to work has passed and there's hardly a soul left walking the streets. But as the clock strikes noon, there's the creak of doorways opening, and the burble of chatter starts to come nearer and nearer the square.

Noon is water time in the villages tucked inland in Abruzzo. Elderly women with bent backs, long skirts and thick black stockings start to gather around the communal tap in the centre of town. They clutch empty buckets and plastic water bottles, some even have crates full of them. This is spring water, piped down from the hills, and the locals know how good it is. They favour the water quality at noon, or at least that's the story. From the way they laugh, grip each other's arms and gesture wildly as they talk, it could be suggested that they all congregate at noon for the social life rather than acqua.

Not all water that comes out of these fountains is great, but most is, and it's favoured over normal tap water. Some public taps have the sign **acqua non-potabile** (water not for drinking) but if you see a congregation of locals filling every spare container they can with the stuff, it means it's not just reliable, but probably far better than bottled water. The sign comes from the fact that it may not have been scientifically tested, and the authorities are playing it safe.

The time and nature of the water collection varies with every town, but they virtually all have a stream of water spouting forth. Use it for everything from a quick wetting of the whistle to the filling of household containers. Even if you don't trust the water, the conversation and life around the watering hole is one of the most enjoyable facets of Italian culture of which every visitor can partake. If nothing else, it'll give you a thirst for life.

Water & Mineral Water

While tap water is drinkable (and in fact quite enjoyable) over much of Italy, locals still choose to drink bottled **acqua minerale** (mineral water). The reason? Because they can. Bottled mineral water is not only cheap and accessible, but it also reaches its most perfect form in Italy.

For the connoisseur, nothing comes close to the finely beaded water that Italy produces. The best tend to be naturally effervescent, with little beads of fizz that literally dance on the tongue and don't hurt the throat as you gulp it down. Even when there is added gas, the bubbles tend to be smaller and less aggressive than most other waters in the world. Even the still water leaves the palate joyously refreshed.

Historically, Italians would have chosen to drink spring water because the stuff coming from taps could be so hard (so full of minerals and salt) that it wasn't appetising. And there used to be problems with the safety.

But these days the bottled water tradition continues, as much because the waters are so crisp, clean and cleansing to the palate. You may even notice that the best bottled water can often be found in areas that still have poor-tasting tap water.

If you ask for water, even in a bar or at someone's home, it will be from a bottle, and more often than not it will be **frizzante** (sparkling) if you don't specify otherwise. Many waiters have learnt to recognise foreigner's preference for non-sparkling water and tend to check with you first. When asking for flat/still water you can ask for it **senza gas** or **naturale**. If you simply can't face bottled water then ask for **acqua del rubinetto** (tap water).

Fruit Drinks

Even a place blessed with countless grape varieties and a passion for alcohol in all its forms can find room for a bit of something fruity. And Italians have taken to simple fruit juices with the same ferocious quest for flavour that they turn to everything they consume.

Arancia, Sardegna

DRINKS

FRUIT TO GO

Every bar will have a range of tiny bottles of **succo (di frutta)** in the fridge under the bar. These dense, preserved fruit juices are quite intense, surprisingly true to the fresh fruit that they come from and reasonably pricey. They are generally made from concentrate and sometimes have sugar added. Most brands sell them in cute little bottles (about 180ml capacity), which can be mixed with soda water or drunk straight. Flavours include **arancia** (orange), **pere** (pear), **pesca** (peach), **mirtilli** (like a kind of blueberry), **albicocca** (apricot), **limone** (lemon), **lampone** (raspberry) and **pompelmo** (grapefruit).

For about the same amount of money you can buy a **spremuta**, a freshly squeezed juice pressed from the fruit while you wait. Just about any bar in the country can make this beautifully simple drink for you (including those on the autostrade). Look for **spremuta d'arancia, di pompelmo, misto** (mixed) and the wonderfully complex and beguilingly-coloured **aranciata rossa** ('red', blood orange, also known as **tarocco**). For something shockingly good try the **spremuta di limone**, often mixed with soda water and always served (as are most spremute) with sugar on the side.

Soft Drinks

Italians aren't traditionally big on the soft drink thing and they don't drink them as sweet as you'll find in many other countries. They often come in tiny bottles, although the can is becoming more popular, and the flavours tend to be limited.

Aranciata is the classic orange drink, with a bitter-orange flavour and less sugar than orange drinks elsewhere. **Aranciata amaro** is a more bitter version of aranciata, while **limonata** is the lemon version. Most have real fruit juice. The home-grown version of cola is **chinotto**, a dark, lightly herbaceous drink with a slightly bitter taste. It's a bit more adult than most cola drinks, and not to everyone's tastes, but is addictive.

One soft drink that doubles as an aperitivo is **crodino**, an orange-coloured drop with light fizz and a good mix of sweetness and bitterness for the experienced palate. Even more bitter is **sanbitter**, a brand of red soft drink that can be used as a non-alcoholic aperitivo offering (in some respects) in place of Campari.

Tè freddo (iced tea) is also drunk instead of soft drinks in the warmer months. This tè is virtually always of the bottled variety, often scented with lemon or peach.

home cooking
& traditions

Cooking, eating and sharing are the foundations of family life in Italy. So much more than mere sustenance, eating is a passion they are happy to spend time and energy enjoying. The features that attract us to Italian cucina were innovations of the home. Even today, you only need to visit the kitchen of a mother or grandmother to find the most rewarding culinary experiences.

Cooking is traditionally very close to the heart of Italians. In many areas a woman's suitability to marry depended on her cooking ability. It may have been the knowledge of how to make cheese, her success in foraging for mushrooms, or her ability to make pasta which first caught her partner's eye. Calabrian women were considered ready to wed only after they had mastered at least 12 pasta shapes. An Abruzzi woman always had to take her **chitarra** (wire pasta cutter) with her when she moved to her marital home. That old adage about 'the way to a man's heart is through his stomach' seemed to find credence in old Italy (although many think that's still aiming a bit too high).

Italian men, while not often traditionally or intimately involved in the day-to-day cooking, are very particular about the dishes that come out of the family kitchen. Most of them regard their wives as the best cooks in the world (after their mothers). They might test the pasta as it cooks or carve the ham. They will be there at the killing of the pig and will make all the salami for the year. And they will be eating with the kind of gusto reserved for times when you're master of your own castle.

Typically the female children are involved in the preparation of the meal. Girls are taught to make pasta at quite a young age (a skill many more modern Italian women are keen to forget as they see it as being tied to domesticity). Groups of women are known to sit around the kitchen table shelling **piselli** (peas) or **fave** (broad beans) for dinner.

The Italian kitchen tends to form the hub of the house. Life still revolves around what is happening in the kitchen, and the kitchen table is a place to learn about religion and politics, as well as cooking.

These days, urban and rural kitchens don't differ much. There's a stove (virtually always gas), a sink and very little bench space. It's only in the last 50 years or so that most homes had an oven. Before that, many would use communal, wood-fired ovens where they would roast or bake their dinner when the bread-baking had finished for the day. These days a home without an oven is virtually unheard of. Most sinks, too, only had running water within the last century.

On the table you may find a **crostata** (fruit tart) covered with a tea towel, waiting to be devoured. Despite the cliché, you may also find a tray with home-made pasta either drying or just sitting idle, waiting to be cooked.

Italians love to cook outdoors and you may often see them lighting a fire when out for a picnic. The smell of wood smoke is important for so many dishes. From the simple **bruschetta** (grilled bread) of Umbria and Toscana, to the **farinata** (chickpea pancake) of Liguria, the allure of food scented with wood smoke is highly sought after. The communal wine bars of Friuli may offer **polenta** (corn meal) cooked over an open fire (often cooked over fires indoors in winter) and at traditional polenta festivals you

Herb Risotto

Homely, comforting and reasonably simple to make, the most important utensil for a risotto is the stirring arm. A good risotto must be stirred the whole time so that starch can be released from the rice, adding a luscious creaminess that coats each still-firm grain. Don't compromise or it won't taste as good. If you don't want to stir the whole time or buy Italian **parmigiano** (parmesan cheese), you'd be better off cooking something else.

Ingredients

2	tablespoons butter
2	medium-sized onions, finely chopped
1	teaspoon salt
3	cloves garlic, crushed
400g	Vialone nano, Carnaroli or other risotto rice
250ml (1 cup)	decent quality white wine
1¹/₂l (6 cups)	chicken stock, simmering
4	tablespoons chopped fresh mixed herbs (parsley, thyme, basil, marjoram)
80g	parmigiano reggiano, freshly grated
	pepper to taste

Heat the butter in a large, heavy-based saucepan over a medium heat. Add the onion and salt and cook for a couple of minutes until soft. Stir in the garlic and cook for a minute longer.

Stir in the rice and fry gently until the grains are all warm inside (you can tell this by picking up one grain and squeezing it between thumb and finger to feel the heat). Turn up the heat and add the wine, stirring constantly until it has been incorporated. Turn the heat down.

Have the stock simmering gently on a back burner and when the wine has all been absorbed add the stock, one ladleful at a time, stirring constantly until each spoonful is absorbed.

After 20 minutes cooking time, start to test the rice occasionally to ensure it doesn't overcook. The rice is cooked when it has a creamy consistency, but each grain should retain its integrity. When it reaches this stage (and you may still have a little stock left over), add the herbs, two-thirds of the parmigiano, and salt and pepper to taste. Serve with the remainder of the cheese and some more black pepper on top.

Serves 6 as a primo ('first' course)

can still see well-built men stirring the meal in vast cast iron pots over open fires. Because of the cost and logistics of cooking over a fire, Italians these days bring the flames and smoke into their restaurants. There are eating houses all over the country specialising in wood-fired pizza, steaks or suckling pigs. But given half a chance, Italians will still light a fire and cook anything they can over the coals.

Unlike French cuisine, most of the art of the Italian cucina, the recipes and techniques, weren't written down. They were skills learned at a tender age, by girls watching their mothers and grandmothers. Generation after generation of women were expected to spend a fair amount of their day around the stove.

When recipes were written down, they included such obscure measurements as 'an abundance of basil', 'a chunk of butter' or to make a rabbit ragù, to chop rabbit into pieces 'bigger than if you were frying them'. Recipes always did, and still do to a large extent, expect the reader to have prior knowledge of cooking techniques. One of the great early texts on Italian food, *La Scienza in Cucina e l'Arte de Mangiar Bene* (*The Science of Cooking and the Art of Eating Well*) by Pellegrino Artusi, published in 1891, went a long way to correct this problem with better measurements. But it's still full of such curious, yet evocative guidance, such as to roll pasta as thin as a coin. It's now been translated into English (see the Recommended Reading chapter) and gives a great insight into the times, albeit it from a moneyed, Tuscan perspective.

The home kitchen isn't just for meals, but also for preserving any glut of produce. **Porcini** mushrooms are preserved here, a skill which has retained its importance as mushrooms from outside Italy (and of a lower quality) have been taking up space on shop shelves. Tomatoes are carted home by the box-load to become **sugo**, the all-important tomato sauce. Stone fruit such as **pesche** (peaches) and **albicocche** (apricots) are conserved in sugar syrup, perhaps spiced with **canelle** (cinnamon).

Much of this excess still comes from the family property wherever possible. A home with a garden that doesn't have some kind of fruit tree is highly unusual. Any space, even an apartment or flat, that doesn't have some potted herbs is rare.

This self-reliance came from the poverty of the people over the last century or two. While often there were shops selling many things, including bread, salame or pasta, many Italians couldn't afford to buy them, except once a year as a treat. The good thing is that despite the renewed prosperity, many of the practices are still alive. In Le Marche families still make cheeses to store in caves (see the Regional Variations chapter), and in Modena many families make their own balsamic vinegar.

HOME COOKING

Rows of potted geraniums on a balcony, Roma

LUNCH AT VINCENZA'S

"Of course Vincenza doesn't mind," says the local policeman as he translates for us. "She wants to cook you lunch."

Vincenza doesn't speak English or Italian but a Calabrese dialect. And she has the most infectious smile that you can imagine, albeit a well-lined, 70-something smile.

Vincenza's house is basically just two rooms, one on top of the other, high up on the hills overlooking the Tyrennhian Sea. Most of the villagers now live in the coastal town of the same name, making a living from the brief but lucrative summer holiday season. The elderly tend to live in the old town, a perilous 20-minute drive up a steep, winding road.

Vincenza moves with surprising agility up and down the rough cobbled streets of her town. She shops every day for lunch, today buying some fresh parmigiano, a little fruit and some veal. Everything is bought within 100m of her door.

Street in San Remo, Liguria

The kitchen is the one room downstairs, the bedroom upstairs. There are few windows, and when Vincenza was young, two families shared the space. A cousin's family of eight had the lower room, her family of six lived upstairs. Many of the family left to find fortune in Milano and Liguria, some ended up in Argentina, and the rest are in Australia. Vincenza lives here alone.

The tiny fire struggles to warm the space downstairs. Every day she carries glowing coals upstairs in a wide flat tray, to warm her bedroom. Sometimes she cooks over the fire, as they did when she was young. These days, though, she has a simple gas stove, and the rest of the room contains a rough, well-worn kitchen table and a sink.

Next to the stove are all the condiments. A little jar of **peperoncini** (chillies), a tall bottle of unbranded olive oil and some salt. That's it. We try to help with the preparations, but Vincenza won't hear of it. The table is set, a special cloth and fine serviettes appearing from a trunk in the corner. She does all this with thick arthritic-looking knuckles and a smile. The trunk is full of cooking pots and linen, from when the house was a bustling centre of activity. At least 10 saucepans and heavy-based casserole dishes are moved to find the things Vincenza needs.

Even at short notice, the meal is more than one course. A local peperoncino-flecked **salsicce** (sausage) is sliced as antipasto. Smoky, grilled, intense black olives that Vincenza has cured are drizzled with olive oil and are perfect washed down with a simple red wine.

The wine is made by a nephew, she tells us, and there's beer if we don't like it. The wine, while unrefined, is just right for the occasion. The perfectly cooked **al dente** ('on the tooth') spaghetti is tossed with tomatoes, chilli and olive oil. Even the veal has a taste and tenderness we don't recognise. We dress the salad ourselves, with some red wine vinegar and olive oil. It's just tomato and lettuce, but even these have a resolute character.

It's hard to communicate verbally over lunch with this woman with whom we've fallen in love. But the messages get through despite language barriers. Photo albums appear, a form of charades is played to allow us to communicate, we laugh unashamedly loudly at her humour and we are overcome with her spontaneity and warmth. And she feeds us just that little bit more than we were planning on eating, as always seems to be the case in Italy.

A neighbour's son drops by unannounced to fix Vincenza's television. He touches her arm affectionately, she responds with a hand upon his. You can tell she would dearly love to have some family living with her. He isn't here because his parents have forced him to come; he adores Vincenza and shows her respect. Even though we've already eaten, she asks her visitor three times if he is hungry.

HOME COOKING

Bolognese-style Meat Ragù

The hallmark of a good ragù is that it is cooked for hours and hours.

Ingredients

3	tablespoons butter
1	medium-sized onion, finely chopped
3	sticks celery, finely diced or minced
100g	carrots, peeled and finely diced or minced
300g	veal, minced (ground, preferably neck)
250g	pork, minced (ground, preferably neck)
250ml	(1 cup) full-cream milk
250ml	(1 cup) white wine (if it's not good enough to drink then it's definitely not good enough to eat)
440g	tinned Italian tomatoes, chopped (including juice)
1	tablespoon chopped flat-leaf parsley
1/4	tsp nutmeg
1	teaspoon salt
	pepper
	water

Heat the butter in a deep, heavy-based saucepan and fry the onion over a medium–high heat until translucent.

Add the celery and carrot and continue to fry for 2 minutes. Turn up the heat and add both minces, some cracked pepper and salt, breaking up the meat as it fries. Cook these ingredients together until all the liquid has evaporated.

Stir in the milk and reduce the heat to a simmer, stirring occasionally until the milk has evaporated. Add the nutmeg and stir.

Add the wine, stirring occasionally until it has evaporated, then add the tomatoes and 250ml (1 cup) water.

Turn the heat right down and barely simmer for 2–3 hours, stirring occasionally and adding 125ml (1/2 cup) water as needed. By the end, the full-flavoured oil should separate from the ragù, and the liquid should have boiled away.

Add the parsley, taste and adjust the salt and pepper and serve with home-made **tagliatelle** or **gnocchi**. Remember not to rinse your pasta after cooking it.

Toss a little ragù through the pasta rather than dolloping a spoonful on top. The ragù can be enriched at the end with extra butter or cream, and perhaps with sautéed finely diced chicken livers or mushrooms. Use only freshly-grated Italian parmigiano on top.

Serves 6

Utensils

The utensils of the Italian kitchen will be familiar to most; rolling pins, slotted spoons, paring and cooks' knives are all part of the culinary hardware. But there are a few implements that are rarely seen outside of Italy.

One has to be the polenta maker. It consists of a brass basin that sits on the stove, and a motor on top that slowly turns a paddle. Polenta, like risotto, must be stirred the whole time it's cooking, but the difference is in the action. While risotto needs a wooden spoon to stop the rice sticking to the bottom of the pan and to constantly move the grains, polenta is stirred without scraping the bottom of the pan. The modern polenta maker is an adaptation of the old style, where a cast-iron pot was held over a fire and an elaborate cog system allowed the meat to be cooked on a spit, while an arm at the end of the spit slowly stirred the polenta pot.

A polenta maker

Oil pourers

While it's mostly the affluent who own polenta makers, many will have a pasta maker. These are simple rolling machines with attachments for tagliatelle, **ravioli** and the like. They operate like a commercial dough-breaker, albeit on a tiny scale (about 100g of pasta dough at a time is ideal). Each pasta machine has a clamp so you can attach it to your kitchen table or bench, a handle to slot into each roller as you use it, and a brush to clean it with. You roll the dough through the machine, fold it over, roll it through again, and gradually reduce the gap between the rollers until you end up with a long sheet of pasta about 10cm wide and quite thin. At this point you can use the attachments. Pasta machines are never, ever, washed, as once they have water on them, they will start to stick. Instead they are brushed clean of flour, ready for the next use.

More specialised is the **spá'tzle** (dumpling) maker, used in Alto Adige and, to some extent, Trentino. Spá'tzle is an egg and flour paste that is so runny it can drip through the holes of a colander (one way to make them if you do not have the special tool). With the devised tool, you run a handle over what looks like a large-holed grater with very few holes. Each sweep of your hand pushes a dribble of paste through the holes and straight into boiling water underneath.

One knife that is sometimes seen in Italy is the **mezzaluna**. The name literally means 'half moon' and the knife has a smoothly curved shape with a handle on either end. Holding the handles vertically, you rock the blade from side to side and it chops everything in its path. It's particularly good for chopping herbs such as parsley.

celebrating
with food

When you live life as passionately as the Italians do, every day is a celebration. They require only the flimsiest excuses to rejoice. Even if you're only here for a few days, you'll encounter someone who has something to celebrate, be it a birthday, a religious occasion, a good harvest, or a victory for the Italian football team.

People on the Italian peninsula have always celebrated a harvest, some god or other, a wedding, a birth or the alignment of the sky/stars/moon or whatever. And when Christianity arrived, they simply put their new God as the figurehead. Most of these festivals were pretty wild affairs, such as the Saturnalia festival in Roman times, where a week of drunken revelry in honour of the god of disorder was marked by a pig sacrifice at the start, and a human sacrifice at the end.

Green & white asparagus bunches

Celebrations these days are more sedate affairs by comparison. But they can still be amazing, such as the snake festival of Le Marche. The tiny hamlet of Cocullo celebrates the feast day of San Domenico by draping poisonous (though de-fanged) snakes all over the saint's statue and themselves. Then each of the five leading snake-handlers and statue carriers get to eat a **ciambellona**, a cake in a ring-shape, which represents a snake biting its tail.

The biggest times for festivals these days centre around **Natale** (Christmas), **Pasqua** (Easter) and **Carnevale** (Carnival, the period leading up to Ash Wednesday, the first day of Lent). Religion plays a major part, along with a certain amount of superstition. For example, a piece of Christmas **panettone** (sweet cake) eaten on 3 February (San Biagio's day) is said to ward off sore throats for the rest of the year.

Many festivals are no longer held, and each year sees the number and nature of events change. Some are unpopular, some are too much work, while others are just too boring. But new festivals are being added all the time, perhaps by the local business community in order to increase tourism, by producers of certain products to create more interest in them, or by united citizens who just want to celebrate their good fortune in a certain way.

The classic way to celebrate any feast day is to precede it with a day of eating **magro** (lean) because the feast day is usually one of overindulgence in **grasso** (rich and not so lean – okay, fatty!). And while just about every festival has some kind of food involved, many of them are *only* about food. The general rule is that a **sagra** (feasting festival) will offer food (although

ASPARAGUS FESTIVAL

It's 10 am, but Santena's centre piazza is alive. Men in medieval dress are calling you to play their ancient games of skill, ringing hand-bells to attract players. For 1000 lira you can have three tries at smashing walnuts with a mallet as they come hurtling out of a wooden chute. Another game involves using a fishing rod fitted with a loop on the end of a piece of string. You slip it around the neck of a bottle, a skill that is far harder than it looks. Men race each other to be the first to lift their bottle and win some local **vino** (wine). On one side of the piazza, over 40 local Harley-Davidson riders are showing off their bikes and their girls. They do this most weekends, visiting all the festivals near Torino in Piemonte.

Santena is famous for its **asparagi** (asparagus), and the late-spring festival of asparagi is much like many of Italy's smaller festivals. The town square, normally quiet, bustles with life today. By nightfall, the stalls and games and asparagus stands will be gone and a band will rock the local youth. But the daytime belongs to the whole community, and when the church bells ring the community converges on the piazza.

Locals lay out bound bunches of asparagus on a huge table in the middle of the square, the focal point of the piazza. When lunchtime comes, crowds line up for a taste of asparagus, **salumi** (preserved meats) and pasta (with asparagus sauce, of course). Even the statue in the centre of town is of spears of asparagus pointing towards heaven. On each of four sides a maiden represents one of the seasons.

Locals tell us that Santena's sagra is only about 20 years old, and created to bind the community and build on the pride they have in their produce. It's like a fete or a fair – there's no big fanfare, no blow-up jumping castle for the kids, no video games or fire eaters. But there is a sense of culture and community, a sense of belonging and, above all, there's that Italian sense of spirit and fun.

A brass band strikes up, tuba and trombone notes lilting in the air, while the band members parade around in flat caps. The local heart research foundation sells balloons. Local artisans (and they are true artisans) are showing their wares – brass-workers, wood-carvers, wool-spinners and leather-workers compete for your attention, while another man finely hones hand-made tobacco pipes. Other stands sell **salsicce** (sausages), some laced with the local white truffle, local cheese or wine, advertising special prices for the sagra.

At lunchtime, everybody is eating asparagus, cooked in huge pots in the open air. There are no speeches, no philosophical calls to arms or local dignitaries promoting themselves. Instead, Santena is a community celebrating what it means to be a true community, with goodwill, nobility and dignity. And if that includes a Harley-Davidson club, then so be it.

A YEAR'S WORTH OF FESTIVALS

Check with local tourist offices to be sure of dates as they may change.

January
• On the 30th and 31st, Aosta, the largest town in Valle d'Aosta, holds Il Sapere del Sapore, where theatre, music and craft form an excuse for locals to gather and taste the wonderful cheeses, particularly **fontina**.

February
• The intriguing town of Umbria celebrates the end of the winter black truffle season with special restaurant menus and street stalls in the third week of February.

• In the days and weeks leading up to Ash Wednesday, Carnevale feasting and frivolity gain momentum to compensate for the abstinence during Lent. The last Friday of Carnevale means a huge **gnocchi** (potato dumpling) feast in the town of Verona in the Veneto. Papa Gnocco, dressed as a giant gnocco, is the patron of the event.

March
• Probably the biggest **polenta** (corn meal) festival in the country takes place in Monastero Bormido (Piemonte) in the first week of March. Great cauldrons of the stuff are cooked and served with sausages.

April
• On the 25th of the month, Venezia celebrates San Marco (whose name graces the city's only Piazza) with **risi e bisi**, a soupy rice dish with peas (see recipe in the Staples & Specialities chapter).

May
• Virtù, a festival of the seven virtues, is held on the first weekend in May at Teramo in Abruzzo. It's celebrated with a soup that has seven kinds of grain, but the most important thing is that it is made by seven virgins.

• Santena, near Torino in Piemonte, hosts a very low-key, but quite delightful gathering to celebrate their famed asparagus on the third Sunday. The festival is relatively new, like the town statue which shows a maiden in several stages of undress (representing the four seasons) underneath a bunch of asparagus.

CELEBRATING

• The normally sleepy town of Cocullo in Abruzzo goes snake-crazy on the first Thursday in May, with de-fanged snakes paraded around town. Those who carry a statue get to partake in ciambellone, circular cakes.

June
• Near Trapani in Sicilia, on the 24th of June, tuna is trapped and harpooned in a bloody ritual that dates back over 2000 years.

• Every second year Amalfi celebrates its famous lemons on the second Sunday in June. Any excessive frivolity can be blamed on the **limoncello** (lemon liqueur).

July
• Livorno, on the coast in Toscana, holds a sagra of the seafood stew, **cacciucco**, on the third Sunday.

August
• Pognana Lario, near Como in Lombardia, holds a sagra to celebrate gnocchi in about mid-August.

• Urbino in Le Marche holds a series of events to celebrate the festivals once held by Duca Federico. The big feast includes dishes that would have been served during the Renaissance.

September
• On the second or third Sunday, Mezzegra (near Como) holds a sagra del Missoltino to celebrate the fish of the region. Fish are air-dried, fried then marinated overnight before being served.

October
• For much of October, Alba in Piemonte holds a truffle festival, with street stalls at the weekend and specialties in restaurants. It also coincides with a donkey race.

November
• On one weekend of the month, the little hillside town of Cavoi in Sardegna holds a celebration of local bread, their brilliant potato, **pecorino** cheese and wine. Even better, it's free.

December
• Treviso radicchio, the long-leafed, red chicory is celebrated in the Veneto on the second weekend in December at the old Treviso market.

you'll normally be expected to pay), and at a **festa** (festival or celebration) you may have to bring your own.

Besides the usual eat, drink and be merry theme, many of these festivals have another agenda, and political parties are known to be involved. There's nothing wrong with that, in fact it's not so hard to imagine ideological communists and socialists holding festivals as celebrations of working people as much as to garner support. That is, after all, their philosophy.

Other festivals are blatant grabs for the tourist dollar. The sagra, for instance, is an excuse to sell cheap sunglasses, plastic toys and the like. But for the most part they are community-run, community-orientated and are put on to benefit the community. And while you wouldn't travel to a town for most of the festivals these days, they are fantastic to visit if you happen to be in the area.

regional
variations

When you think of Italian cucina, the likes of spaghetti bolognese, pizza, lasagne and Chianti might spring to mind. Now, you can forget the idea of 'Italian food'; there is hardly such thing. You are about to embark on a journey through the myriad of distinctive regional cuisines which make up the gastronomy of this wonderful country. There is no end to the discoveries you can make.

REGIONS

SWITZERLAND • LIECHTENSTEIN · AUSTRIA · HUNGARY

SLOVENIA

CROATIA

BOSNIA-HERCEGOVINA

FRANCE

MONACO

LIGURIAN SEA

ITALY

ADRIATIC SEA

Corsica (FRANCE)

✪ ROMA

Sardegna

TYRRHENIAN SEA

IONIAN SEA

Valle d'Aosta
Piemonte
Liguria
Lombardia
Trentino-Alto Adige
Friuli-Venezia Giulia
Veneto
Emilia-Romagna
Toscana
Umbria
Le Marche
Lazio
Abruzzo
Molise
Campania
Puglia
Basilicata
Calabria
Sicilia
Sardegna

Sicilia

MALTA

MEDITERRANEAN SEA

The food of Italy is a vast collection of regional dishes. The people of Abruzzo know that the people of nearby Puglia cook pasta. It's just that the pasta's different, cooked in a different style of sauce, and the Abruzzi may know nothing about how the Pugliese cook and serve their own. What's more, until recently they may not have particularly cared about the differences, believing (as they do with typical Italian modesty) that their pasta/cheese/wine is the best anyway.

Many dishes cross regional boundaries to a little or great extent. This regional guide is meant as a map to help you find your way through the maze of Italy's disparate cucina. To be used in conjunction with the dictionary, it's not meant as an exhaustive list, but rather as a **stuzzichino**, an appetiser to prepare you for Italy's incredible food, born through the geography, history and, most of all, from the locals' dedication to true flavours.

These are the textures, the smells, the tastes that await you in Italy.

Piazza Navona, Roma

Valle d'Aosta

The tiny region of Valle d'Aosta (Valley of Aosta) – tucked between France, Piemonte and Switzerland – is known to few outside Italy, although it has its own charms. Set against a backdrop of snow-capped Alps, the ruins of the Roman empire can still be seen today in this former Roman stronghold. Aosta has been the major town for about the last two millennia.

The proximity with France means that the region eventually fell under the rule of the House of Savoy and remains, to this day, fully bilingual. Valle d'Aosta's cucina is strongly influenced by the French, but Italian tradition has more obvious effect here than in the fiercely German Alto Adige.

Because of the harsh climate under the Alps, each season is celebrated with the arrival of special foods: fungi and **salumi** (preserved meats) in winter, eggs and aromatic herbs in spring, wild berries in summer and goose in autumn.

Potato is the main starch, although polenta plays its part. Once upon a time, meat from the goat antelope, chamois, was the staple, although it has been virtually hunted out. These days the meat is more likely to be **capretto** (kid) or **vitello** (veal). The locals, known as Valdostans, also use a fair amount of **maiale** (pork), and also **oca** (goose) may be turned into **salsicce** (sausage) or a variety of **prosciutti** (preserved meat).

Lardo, the fragrant, herb-scented lard, is a local speciality (particularly of Arnad) and is used in the best **boudin** (blood sausage). The boudin looks like its French namesake, and is made with beetroot, lardo and potato.

DON'T MISS

- **Boudin** – A dark red sausage that is usually made with beetroot and potato
- **Capra** – The local French-style goat's cheese that tastes fantastic
- **Fonduta** – Creamy, melted fontina cheese
- **Food Celebrations** – Arnad celebrates a **sagra** (feasting festival) of lardo in late August; La Thuile holds a festival of salami, tripe and polenta in February; and Oyace holds a sagra to rejoice in the cucina of fontina in mid-August. The tourist office in Aosta has a list of all events

City of Aosta, Valle d'Aosta

The major local cheese is **fontina**, a very smooth, creamy cheese with a divine, almost cashew nut hint. It's essential for **fonduta** (similar to a Swiss fondue). Fonduta is available canned everywhere, and is a viable alternative if you don't have the equipment or ingredients to make the dish yourself. Fontina can also be found melted over or into polenta for **polenta concia** or in the classic **costoletta alla valdostana**, a veal cutlet filled with fontina, crumbed and fried.

The **capra** (goat's cheese) of Valle d'Aosta is sublime. Look for it in the cheese shops of Courmayeur and Aosta.

One of the interesting traditions that is still followed is in the bread baked about a week before Christmas. Families all visit the local wood-fired bakery to make **copa**, a hard rye loaf. When we say hard, we mean hard. It's kept between posts in the attic for months and months before being cut (like wood, almost), dipped in wine or milk to soften, and eaten, perhaps with soup.

A cold climate usually means the locals like a strong drink, and the local coffee is just that, as well as being a social event. **Caffè valdostano** is made with coffee, **grappa** (distilled grape must) and sugar, and served in communal drinking pots, with separate spouts but one basin. Try not to suffer backwash if you're sharing one.

Piemonte

There's a certain French feel in landlocked Piemonte (Piedmont). You want proof? Well, Piemontese wines such as the great **Barolo** are designed to age better than most in Italy; the dishes tend to be more complex; they eat frog's legs; and distinguished towns such as Torino (Turin) carry a noble air. It's no wonder, when you look at how much the western reaches border France, albeit separated physically by the Alps.

Historically the region has had a diverse influence. Originally there were Celtic and Ligurian settlements, coming under the control of the Romans on their march north. Goths and Lombards came through, as did the Franks, but it was the House of Savoy from 1045 that exercised the most influence. Later, the Austrians and Russians held power, but the region actually spoke French for much of the last millennium.

After the unification of Italy, Torino became the capital for three years and the area has remained a powerhouse of economic and, to some extent, agricultural wealth ever since.

The winters are crisp, the summers far milder than regions further south, and the cucina has developed its own sense of place. The most famous food from Piemonte is the **tartufo bianco** (white truffle). These fungi grow under the ground in a symbiotic relationship with certain trees. They're particularly prevalent around the province of Alba, and have the most intoxicating perfume. Many **buongustai** (connoisseurs) from around the world believe tartufi bianchi are the closest thing to the perfect flavour. At prices of sometimes 2,000,000 lira a kilogram and upwards, they'd want to be. Alba holds the Fiera del Tartufo festival every year in October and their truffle market is held every Saturday morning during the season (October, November and December) at Palazzo Madelena, and along Via Emanuele. (See Truffles in the Staples & Specialties chapter.)

In and around Alba is a pretty good place for a food lover to be. **Cinzano**, essential in a martini and probably the most famous Italian aperitif in the 1980s, originated only 10km from here. Ferrero started their campaign of world chocolate domination from Alba, the *real* **Asti** sparkling wine (not sickly, but floral) is made just up the road, as are Barolo and its younger cousin, the luscious **Barbaresco**. Many wineries will take visitors if you ring ahead (see the Drinks chapter).

The stylish, gracious city of Torino may be the region's political centre, but it's also the coffee capital, boasting Lavazza as the biggest coffee roaster. Torino has some of the best caffès you'll find in Italy, meaning they're some of the best anywhere, and the coffee they serve is superb. The town is also the birthplace of modern chocolate. It was here that Europeans first learned to make chocolate into bars and improved on the drink that the

Napoli street market, Napoli, Campania

Aztecs had invented. The local chocolate is now often mixed with hazelnuts, which grow well in Piemonte, and **gianduia** (rich ground hazelnuts and chocolate) is a local culinary and economic success story.

Other flavours of the region include **bagna caôda** (or **bagna cauda**), a paste of anchovies, garlic, olive oil and sometimes cream, served with raw or blanched vegetables. Piemonte also does a great version of **bollito misto** ('boiled mixed'), offering up to seven types of boiled meat, served with three sauces: one of herb, fruit, and a honey & white mustard sauce (tasting far better than it sounds).

DON'T MISS

- **Caffè** – Make it your mission to find the best **caffè** (coffee) in the best **caffè** (bar) in Torino
- **Cioccolato** – Sure, you can buy the big brands at home, but wait until you try the ones from the small artisan-makers of Torino or Alba
- **Tartufi bianchi** – Indecently good white truffles of Alba
- **Vino** – From the light Dolcetto (no, it's not sweet) to the sadly maligned Moscato d'Asti (spumante) to two of the great wines of the world, Barolo and Barbaresco
- **Zabaglione** – A delicious dessert

Piemonte produces two-thirds of Italy's rice, and the paddy fields stretch on forever, especially around Vercelli and Novara. The Piemontese prefer their risotto a little drier than the Venetians, and the most typical is probably made with one of the great, complex red wines. Any risotto, though, is probably going to be memorable. The marshy rice paddies of the area are home to a proliferation of frogs, which don't last long around any passing buongustai.

The local sweets are influenced by the geography. Nuts are very good, particularly hazelnuts and almonds, often finding their way into **torrone**, a form of nougat. **Amaretti**, strong flavoured almond biscuits which come in many shapes and guises, are a virtual staple. Fine sponge cakes are seen in pastry shops, and are sometimes served with **zabaglione**, similar to a French sabayon. This whipped egg dessert, scented with wine or **marsala**, is luscious.

Liguria

It depends on what you want from Italy, but if you're looking for cliff-hanging villages, James Bond-style driving and all the glam of the Riviera, Liguria is for you. From the seemingly too-beautiful Cinque Terre, to the schmaltz of beachside resorts near Alassio, the whole region seems to flirt with the coast. That's because Liguria is almost exclusively a coastal region, shaped like a jagged boomerang over the Mare Ligure (Ligurian Sea).

Relatively little cheese is made here, since the hills behind the coast offer little room for cows or sheep to graze. Along the heavily cropped coast, flowers and olives compete with grape vines for space. Most of the greenhouses you see are for the huge flower industry, not food, and what happens inland is, and has always been, dependent on what is happening on the sea.

The Mare Ligure is colder than other Italian seas, and is less rich with seafood, although it still produces fine fish. The Ligurians were great sea-farers, and so the most typical dish of a place such as Albenga, **burrida** (fish stew), isn't actually based on fresh **triglie** (red mullet) or **orata** (bream) but rather on **stoccafisso** (stock fish, air-dried cod), the kind of fish that would keep on long voyages.

Well before the wealthy Genoan empire, it was the Neanderthals who were thought to have first inhabited the coastline. Then the Gauls and later the Greeks left their mark with wine and olives. The array of usual conquerors came and went, including those from Rome, France and Spain, and to some extent their embellishments to the cucina are still evident.

REGIONAL VARIATIONS

Bicycle next to locked gates of private beach, Spotorno, Liguria

DON'T MISS

- **Pesto** – A paste of fresh basil leaves, Sardinian sheep's milk cheese, pine nuts, garlic and Liguria's distinctive olive oil
- **Farinata** – The chickpea flour flat-bread (more like a pancake) that is at its best when cooked on a wood fire
- **Ligurian olives** – Small, dark, and delicious without a hint of bitterness
- **The Saturday market in San Remo** – The whole town goes crazy looking for a parking space as the market near Piazza degli Eroi Sanremesi leaps to life

Chickpea flour is used to make **farinata**, a flat pancake. **Pissadella** (an onion and anchovy flat bread, like a style of pizza) is the local version of the French *pissaladiere*, and garlic is used in glorious abundance compared with the rest of northern Italy.

Liguria's most famous contribution to the world is **pesto**, the basil, garlic, **pecorino** (ewe's-milk cheese) and pine nut paste, an adaptation of an imperial Roman dish. It is used to perfection on local pasta such as **trenette** (long flat pasta) or **trofie** (spiral-shaped pasta). Pesto also makes an important appearance in the **minestrone alla genovese**, the classic minestrone soup served with a dollop of the paste on top.

The vegetables of Liguria are among the finest in the country. You'll find asparagi and **carciofi violetti** (purple, spiny artichokes) from Albenga, citrus fruits from along the coast, and **melanzane violette** (purple eggplants), also found in Sicilia.

Liguria's local bread is **focaccia**, the flattish, yeast-risen dough brushed with oil and sprinkled with salt before baking. Sometimes olives or herbs are added to the top. The result is a loaf about 2cm high with a delightful texture. Liguria also invented the dried ravioli for long voyages, and the cake, **torte genovese**, known to most of us (thanks to the French) as genoise sponge. It was the Ligurians who invented the candied **castagne** (chestnuts) in Genova.

Olives abound around Imperia, and many find their way into the local oil. Ligurian oil is finer on the palate, in many ways more elegant than the strong, robust oils of further south. It is the perfect accompaniment to the food of the region. Ligurian table olives, known locally simply as **nostrano** (local) are small, elongated and black, as well as being delicious.

Liguria has fantastic markets, Genova and San Remo amongst them.

Lombardia

Oh Lombardia (Lombardy), it's like you're all dressed up with no place to go. This is the region led by the sprawling metropolis Milano (Milan), which leads the nation in fashion, design and making money. And yet it is Roma to the south that is political boss of the country.

The Milanese never let you forget that it is they who hold the economic strength in the country. Lombardia is the power base for the Lega Nord (The Northern League) who are pushing for secession of the north. But if Roma would be economically poorer without Milano, then Milano would be culturally poorer without Roma.

Historically Lombardia has fared a lot better than the south. While the last 2000 years have seen Lombards, Franks, Venetians, Austrians and others dominate the region, it has always had a very fertile and often wealthy past. The region was divided into city states between powerful families such as the Visconti, Pallavincini and Scaligeri during the Renaissance. This left many beautifully built, wealthy towns whose food culture, despite their proximity, developed quite distinctly from one another.

The north of the region borders on Switzerland, and fertile valleys, especially the Valtellina, have their own specialities. Further south lie the great lakes of Como, Iseo and Garda. Small fish from the lakes are eaten fried, and festivals of the fish tend to occur in summer (see the Celebrating with Food chapter).

Arborelle, fried fish, Lago Di Lecco, Lombardia

Further south, in and beyond Milano, the land becomes flatter but equally fertile around the Po River. **Riso** (rice) is grown, particularly towards the west, and there are plenty of cows for milk, cream, butter, cheese and meat. The cheeses are some of the most interesting in the country, such as **taleggio**, **gorgonzola** (both now also made in Piemonte), **bitto**, **grana padano** and **stracchino** (see Cheeses in the Staples & Specialities chapter). Try them with **mostarda**, the mustard fruits of Cremona.

DON'T MISS

- **Ossobuco** – Braised veal shanks where the bone marrow is better than the actual meat (which is saying a lot)
- **Pizzoccheri** – Buckwheat pasta with cabbage, potatoes and melted bitto cheese
- **Risotto alla milanese** – The creamy rice dish gilded with saffron, delectable with molten bone marrow
- **Shopping at Peck** – Milano's amazing food store and cafe not far from the Duomo
- **Visiting a cheesemaker** – For aged taleggio cheese, try Mauri, in the postcard-perfect Valsassina

Lombardia's dishes favour butter over olive oil, and risotto is a staple, as is polenta. Northerners are known, by those in the south, as the disparaging **polentone** (polenta-eaters) because corn meal, not pasta, is eaten at so many meals. Corn meal even makes an appearance in the almost biscuity-textured, crunchy **torta sbrisolona**, a cake made with almonds, grape must or wine, and plenty of butter.

The classic rice dish is probably **risotto alla milanese**, scented with saffron and bone marrow, adding that unctuous, desirable finish. Bone marrow is the best part of **ossobuco**. Ossobuco actually means 'bone hole', and refers specifically to sliced veal shanks braised with onions and vegetables and finished with **gremolata** (chopped parsley with garlic and lemon).

Pumpkins are a staple of the north and wouldn't be seen in some parts further south. They are used with mostarda in Cremona's **tortelli di zucca**, fresh pasta filled with pumpkin and amaretti biscuits.

One of the dishes that Lombardia has given the world is **minestrone**, the classic vegetable and legume soup with pasta cooked into it at the end. Milanese minestrone is virtually guaranteed to be better than any version you know.

Milano is the home of **panettone**, the light, yeast-risen candied fruit cake. But the most impressive part of Milano is Peck, the foodstore and cafe that offers some of the best shopping under one roof in Italy.

A really good dish from the far northern area of the Valtellina is **pizzoccheri**, flat, fresh buckwheat pasta with potatoes, cabbage, garlic and mild bitto cheese. **Grano saraceno** (buckwheat) is actually grown in Valtellina and used in **polenta taragna**, a polenta made using dark buckwheat with corn meal, lots of butter, and bitto or other cheese.

Trentino-Alto Adige

This landlocked region forms a bridge between the Latin and Teutonic worlds. The decidedly Germanic Alto Adige (butting up against Austria) looks to the north for cultural, linguistic and culinary influence, while Trentino is definitely more 'Italian' in feel. These areas are linked in many ways, including their status as a joint region, but in more ways they are quite distinct.

While Trentino had nearly 800 years of self-government under the rule of Trento, Alto Adige was part of Austria until its handover to Italy after WWI. Alto Adige still calls itself **Südtirol**, South Tyrol. The two regions were only united in 1948. Signs in Alto Adige are bilingual, men wear *lederhosen* and drink tall glasses of beer, while little girls with blonde plaits chomp on pretzels. The foods that make the region distinctive are those that hint at an Austrian influence.

Bread is often dense, scented with caraway or rye. Prosciutto is usually **cotto** (cooked), and **cotto e cren** (cooked ham with horseradish) is often served as the antipasto (if you can call it that). Alto Adige has no pasta of its own, a space that **canederli** (the large bread dumplings of the region) and **spá'tzle** (little flour and egg dumplings) fill admirably. Canederli can be flavoured with **speck** (smoked, cured pork), livers or herbs. They can be cooked in soup or served on the side of meats. Spá'tzle is a good first course with melted gorgonzola, or as part of a main course under the meat.

Speck is a must-try, although it is no longer made to the high standards that Alto Adige was once famous for. It looks like a form of streaky bacon, but is more herbaceous and cured for weeks before being smoked. The result is a firmer texture and more intense flavour. There's a local festival in May dedicated just to speck.

DON'T MISS

- **Gelato** – To be enjoyed as you stroll through the streets of Trento
- **Salsicce con crauti** – Sausages with sauerkraut
- **Speck** – Cured, cold-smoked pork belly is at its best here
- **The Strado del Vino** – A beautiful drive among beautiful vines

Crauti (sauerkraut) is very popular, particularly with sausages and other meats. **Gulasch**, a thinner version of the Hungarian goulash, is also served.

The **strudel** is very good, although its pastry is thicker and slightly less refined than you'd find in Vienna.

STRADA DEL VINO/WINE TRAIL

This sign-posted wine road leads off to the south of Bolzano (Bozen) in Alto Adige. The road winds delightfully through pretty villages, past the relatively unspoilt lake, Lago di Caldaro (Kalternsee) and seemingly manicured, orderly vineyards. It goes for about 40km (25 miles), finishing at Cortina all'Adige and you can re-enter the **autostrada** (motorway) near Mezzo-Lombardo. On the way you pass through Termeno (Tramin), home of the Traminer grape variety, and there are plenty of opportunities to drink the wine in nice gardens in the villages that you pass. In the town of Caldaro there's a small but interesting wine museum (Via dell'Oro, 1).

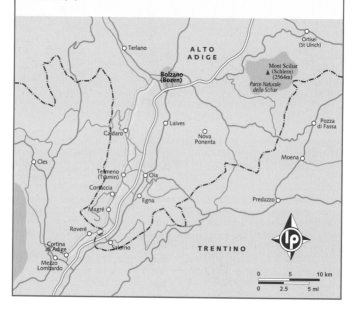

The region abounds with vines and fruit trees, particularly apples. The flanks of the ever-present Dolomiti Mountains are often flush with mushrooms, especially in the autumn. In fact, the Trentini are the most zealous of all foragers, and hold fungi festivals to celebrate their good fortune. The forests also provide the perfect **sotto bosco** (the 'under forest'). You will find wild berries, such as **fragole di bosco** (wild strawberries) and **mirtilli** (like French *myrtilles*, vaguely similar to blueberries).

Grapes are grown everywhere possible, even on steep slopes. The **Strada del Vino** (see the boxed text and map Strada del Vino) is worth a tour, and there are more than a few good wines along the way that you can try. Locals are particularly proud of the reds from Alto Adige, although outsiders and southern Italians tend to prefer the whites. Trentino produces a good mix of both (see the Drinks chapter).

White table grapes

Trentino's biggest town, and a major drawcard on its own, is Trento. If any town knows how to eat **gelato** (ice cream), this is it. From the very young to the more mature, strolling with gelati when the weather warms is a particularly Trentini thing to do. Interestingly, they often eat it (very elegantly) with a spoon, even from a cone.

Olives are grown in Trentino. The microclimate around Riva del Garda creates a light-flavoured oil without the gung-ho flavours of southern oils. If you're in Trentino–Alto Adige you can expect lard (lower in saturated fat than butter), butter and heavier food than further south.

Friuli-Venezia Giulia

You only need to talk to an elderly local from Friuli-Venezia Giulia to hear the history of the region. They talk of dispossession, of being overrun and of borders being drawn – the fate of the locals for too long.

Friuli-Venezia Giulia sits on a vital trading port, where three very different cultural groupings meet. The Germanic, Latin and Slavic cultures all come together here, creating tensions that have occasionally lead to all-out war over the last 2000 years.

The imperial Romans established Aquileia here, a city dubbed 'Second Roma' partly because of its importance to trade. Later, Attila the Hun swept through the area, as did the Lombards, then parts of the region came under Venetian rule. But it was the Austro-Hungarian empire, WWI and the subsequent (seemingly arbitrary) division of lands with the former Yugoslavia after WWII that still lingers in the minds of locals.

This often seething melting pot of cultures means that the food has lots of inherent character. You'll see **cotto e cren** (cooked ham and horseradish) and a version of the Hungarian classic **gulasch** (goulash), made here with larger chunks of meat and a runnier sauce than the original. Spices such as cinnamon and cloves are also used with more abandon.

These days Friuli-Venezia Giulia is positively flourishing, buoyed by specialist industries, such as chair making and Zanussi professional cooking equipment, coupled with a strong work ethic and a good sense of style. The region has a perfect climate for very good vines and wines.

The port town of Trieste, which became part of Italy in 1947, is the coffee capital of Italy, with thousands of tonnes of beans arriving daily. The inimitable Illy Caffè is based here, as are many smaller producers. While Trieste's **caffès** (cafes) are more sullen than those in many other cities, it's still worth promenading the caffè-laden avenue Via XX Settembre just to lounge around in them. The local cappuccino isn't as big as elsewhere, and is often topped with whipped cream. If you can, eat at a **buffet**, the local equivalent of the more traditionally Italian **osterie** (local restaurants).

Udine, in central Friuli, has more than its fair share of beautiful caffès, and the habit here is to sit with a newspaper, a book, a lover or a friend and mull over your coffee.

While Friuli-Venezia Giulia has reaches in the Alps, and there are beautiful beaches and lagoons on the coast, most of the particularly regional food is found in the fertile rolling hills.

Pasta seems to be an afterthought; in its place are polenta, gnocchi (often made with bread) and **cialzons**. Like a cross between ravioli and gnocchi, cialzons are made sweet (maybe with candied citron, chocolate and smoked ricotta) and savoury (perhaps with marjoram, spinach and cheese). It's considered traditional to have over 40 ingredients in each type. **Mesta e fasoi** is polenta cooked with beans and butter. Even the local bean soup, **orzo e fagioli** (barley and bean soup), uses **orzo** (barley) instead of the more usual pasta of other regions.

The local **latteria** (dairy farm) cheese is very good. Dishes often include other cheeses, such as **malga** from the mountain areas, or smoked ricotta. **Montasio** cheese is the distinctive taste in the superb **frico** (fried savoury cheese cakes).

DON'T MISS

- **Caffè crawling** – Swan around in one Udinese caffè after another and pretend to be the new Ernest Hemingway
- **Frico** – The savoury, fried montasio cheese 'cake'
- **Orzo e fagioli** – An enormously ugly but delicious barley and bean soup
- **Prosciutti San Daniele** – Many call this the best raw ham in Italy. It's worth spending a small fortune discovering its melt-apart texture, raunchy fragrance and sweet taste
- **Visiting a frasca** – Drink local wine under a pergola within an arm's reach of the vines they came from

Eating in Friuli-Venezia Giulia is as much about the experience as the food, particularly in a **frasca** (or **locanda**, a home-style wine bar). Traditionally wine producers could set one up – all they had to do was hang a branch outside the property. There was no sign, but everybody knew a frasca was in full swing. A frasca serves the wine of the estate and often some food to go with it.

One of the region's most famous foods is the sweet prosciutto of San Daniele. Local tradition is to use minimal salt and cure the legs of black pigs for 12–18 months. San Daniele's old town is given over in praise of ham, and if you want a whole leg, it's worth visiting. Most prosciutto-makers are on the outskirts of town and many sell direct to the public. The town also holds a prosciutto festival at the end of August each year, where locals parade down the street dressed as hams.

Veneto

To most visitors, the Veneto means Venezia (Venice). But the grande old dame with the canals is only one beautiful city in a region of beautiful cities. The remainder of the Veneto abounds with elegant old towns such as Padova and Verona, as well as fantastic food. From the **radicchio** (chicory) of Treviso to the **Amarone** wine of Valpolicella to the rice from Ferron, one of the oldest mills in Europe, to the fashionable dessert staple tiramisù, the Veneto has it all.

Veneto stretches from Venezia's canals to the Dolomiti (the Dolomites) in the north and Lago di Garda in the west. The far north is so Germanic it looks like parts of Austria, and the food has a Germanic feel (see Trentino-Alto Adige in this chapter).

Venezia's crumbling facades should hide many fantastic restaurants –

Panorama of gondolas, Veneto

after all, the seafaring culture of the empire was formidable and the envy of the world – but it's hard to find real food in a town with such a transient population. You'd be hard pressed to find a good meal in Venezia, particularly near the station. In many ways there is a sense of sadness to Venezia, a city that is rapidly losing its population.

You'll also discover far more about North American culture than anything Venetian while you're here. Even Michelin-starred restaurants in this city are shamelessly overpriced and arrogant, and the food isn't as good as you can find at similarly ranked restaurants elsewhere in Italy.

There's a bar that lays claim to having invented the **bellini**, a cocktail of peach pulp and **prosecco** wine, named after artist Giovanni Bellini, though you may find the contemporary drink expensive.

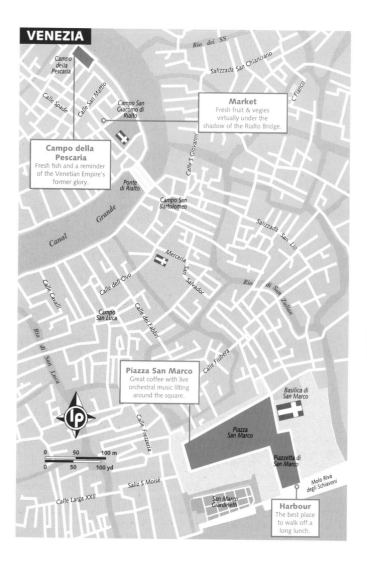

VENEZIA

Rio dei SS

Salizzada San Chianciano

C Franco

Campo della Pescaria

Calle Spade

Calle San Mattio

Campo San Giacomo di Rialto

Market
Fresh fruit & vegies virtually under the shadow of the Rialto Bridge.

Calle S Giovanni

Campo della Pescaria
Fresh fish and a reminder of the Venetian Empire's former glory.

Ponte di Rialto

Campo San Bartolomeo

Salizzada San Lio

Canal Grande

Merceria San Salvador

Rio di San Zulian

Calle Cavalli

Calle dell'Ovo

Campo San Luca

Calle dei Fabbri

Rio di San Luca

Calle Fiubera

Piazza San Marco
Great coffee with live orchestral music lilting around the square.

Calle Frezzeria

Basilica di San Marco

Piazza San Marco

Piazzetta di San Marco

Molo Riva degli Schiavoni

0   50   100 m
0   50   100 yd

Saliz S Moisè

Calle Larga XXII

San Marco Giardinetti

Harbour
The best place to walk off a long lunch.

But there is an upside. Venezia's fish markets retain some of their former glory, and the historic caffès in the Piazza San Marco, such as Florian, are a sheer joy to behold, despite the number of tourists. Usually a cover charge of 6500 lira for a live orchestra applies, and the price of a coffee will quadruple the moment you decide to sit down. Add the two together and that quick caffè is suddenly costing as much as a main course in a **trattoria** (eating-house) in another town, but it's worth every penny. It is Venezia, after all.

DON'T MISS

- **Padova's market** – One of the best in the nation
- **Treviso radicchio** – Refined, elegant flavours of a simple leafy vegetable
- **Old timing** – Sipping Amarone in Antica Bottega del Vino in Verona. There's been a restaurant on this site for most of the last 500 years
- **Posing** – Listening to the live orchestra outside Caffè Florian in Venezia's Piazza San Marco and feeling like you're smarter and better-looking than before you arrived
- **Risi e bisi** – The Venetian soupy rice dish flavoured with fresh peas
- **Tiramisù** – The home of this dessert is Treviso, so try it there and compare

The rest of the region more than makes up for Venezia. Elegant cities such as Verona and Padova glow with charm and wealth. Padova is well known for its market, set on two sides of a central palazzo (see the Shopping chapter for a floor plan), and good food seems to be found at just about every turn.

Seafood plays a big part in the cucina of the Veneto, but just as good are the rice dishes, such as **risi e bisi** (rice and peas, see recipe in the Staples & Specialities chapter). **Bigoli**, the local, thick, home-made spaghetti, is very satisfying, often served with a simple anchovy sauce. Polenta is very common, probably playing second only to risotto as a first course. You may be served polenta with **baccalà** (salt cod), **faraona** (guinea fowl), or **cavallo** (horse meat).

Emilia-Romagna

Is this every food lover's nirvana? You want **parmigiano reggiano** (parmesan cheese)? Tick. You want the real, lingering nuances of the true **aceto balsamico** (balsamic vinegar)? Tick. How about **lasagne** (baked pasta layers), **tortellini** (filled pasta morsels), **mortadella** (pork sausage), **prosciutto di Parma** (air-dried, salt-cured ham)? Tick, tick, tick, tick.

Emilia-Romagna has all that and more. This land of Ferraris and noble towns is often overlooked by visitors to Italy, who seem not to even know the region exists between Toscana and the north of Veneto and Lombardia. In some respects that's not surprising: outside the historical centres of the towns, the flat lands appear merely industrial, despite the prolific agriculture that occurs on every bit of land bigger than a postage stamp.

Some call this the gastronomic heart of Italy. And so it is. Or at least it is world renowned for its gastronomy, and should be known for the way it can affect the heart, physically and emotionally. Italians from the south like to think of Emilia-Romagna as the cholesterol capital. Here cow's milk, cream, butter, lard and pork reign supreme.

Olive oil is a relatively recent phenomenon, so too the water-based pasta of the south. In Emilia-Romagna the local pasta is truly golden with egg yolks, and more often than not is made by hand. The best is rolled with a pin, not through even the simplest of rolling machines.

The region was ruled by the Gauls, the Romans and every invader that came from the north, including the Goths and Normans, along with the Spanish from the west. The two papal states of Emilia and Romagna were joined on unification of Italy, but it is the noble families of the Renaissance that shaped the area's ambiance. It should come as no surprise that the region's most famous living son and exponent of its food is opera singer Luciano Pavarotti.

While the food of Emilia-Romagna can be rich, it's really the pasta that, above all, makes this a region for food-lovers. You can find parmigiano and prosciutto di Parma in other regions, but you can only try the fresh pasta at its source. Keep an eye out for **malmaritati**, translated as 'badly married', a dish of **fagioli** (beans) cooked with fresh egg pasta that has been cut into rough shapes.

The region also excels in tortellini, which can come simply boiled, tossed with butter and with a little parmigiano grated over, or in **brodo**, a light chicken broth. **Tortelli** and **tortelloni** are larger versions in the same shape.

Bologna's most misinterpreted dish has to be **tagliatelle al ragù**. When it left Italy's shores it somehow became 'spaghetti bolognaise', dished up weekly to countless English, Australians and Americans. The real bolognese dish is made by tossing a little rich, slow-cooked **ragù** (meat sauce, often

REGIONAL VARIATIONS

Pedroni family logo on a barrel of balsamic vinegar, Modena, Emilia-Romagna

made with veal and pork) through fresh egg noodles. The ragù is usually cooked with milk to cut the acid of the tomatoes and wine, and really good versions are finished with a touch of cream and finely diced, sautéed liver (see recipe in Home Cooking chapter).

Salumi (preserved meats) are done really well in Emilia-Romagna. Mortadella is the huge, delicious sausage made with finely pureed pork and dotted with bits of fat. You'll see it in every **salumeria** (smallgoods shop, delicatessen) of the region. Despite the similar look, don't think that the original mortadella tastes like the inferior 'baloney' sold some places outside Italy.

One of Emilia-Romagna's greatest foods is **culatello**, a joyously fragrant, beautifully soft, cured piece of pork taken from under the rump of the best pigs. Once the culatello has been cut out, the leg can no longer be used to make prosciutto, so the price for the finished product reflects not only its value, but the value lost from the whole leg. Culatello needs a more humid area to cure than prosciutto, and up to 18 months to ripen fully despite its small size. The name comes from the word **culo**, translating colloquially as 'arse'.

DON'T MISS

- **Aceto balsamico tradizionale di Modena** – Real, honest balsamic vinegar, good enough to make you swoon
- **Culatello and prosciutto Langhirano** – Some of the best prosciutto comes from Langhirano and the even more prized culatello is found in Parma
- **Food shopping in Bologna** – Apart from the market on Via Ugo Bassi, the salumerie and **formaggeri** (cheese shops) all make this some of the finest food shopping in Italy
- **Gelati in Reggio-nell'Emilia** – Great flavours, but the real treat is the elegant way some gelaterie form the ice cream into a rose shape on your cone
- **Parmigiano reggiano** – Known as the 'King of cheeses'. Try the real thing here because while it's copied around the world, nothing even comes close. The best never leaves the region
- **Tortellini in brodo** – Handmade pasta in the shape of a belly button served in a light broth is at its most delicate here

Other bits of pig also reach their pinnacle here. **Zampone**, stuffed pig's trotter, is a speciality from Modena. Emilia-Romagna is widely acknowledged as the home of **cotechini**, huge pork sausages scented with nutmeg, boiled in their skins for about an hour before being sliced to serve.

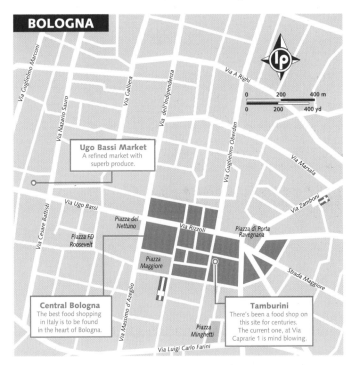

BOLOGNA

Ugo Bassi Market
A refined market with superb produce.

Central Bologna
The best food shopping in Italy is to be found in the heart of Bologna.

Tamburini
There's been a food shop on this site for centuries. The current one, at Via Caprarie 1 is mind blowing.

Via Guglielmo Marconi
Via Nazario Sauro
Via Galliera
Via dell'Indipendenza
Via A Righi
Via Guglielmo Oberdan
Via Marsala
Via Zamboni
Via Cesare Battisti
Via Ugo Bassi
Piazza del Nettuno
Via Rizzoli
Piazza di Porta Ravegnana
Piazza FD Roosevelt
Piazza Maggiore
Strada Maggiore
Via Massimo d'Azeglio
Piazza Minghetti
Via Luigi Carlo Farini

One widely known food that comes from Emilia-Romagna is **aceto balsamico** (balsamic vinegar). The amount sold internationally is estimated to be at least twice the amount legally produced in the area just outside of Modena. To protect the integrity of the product a consortium was set up to protect the real thing from being undermined, so look for the characteristic **aceto balsamico tradizionale di Modena** bottles and you'll be blown away by the taste (see Condiments in the Staples & Specialities chapter).

Toscana

What is it about Toscana (Tuscany) that non-Italians love so much? Is it the noble history? The fact that it is an historically important centre for art, literature and learning? Or is it the **bistecca alla fiorentina** (Florentine beef steak)? It could be any of these, but the bistecca seems to have the edge.

Toscana has been the region of the last decade (or two). Everyone outside Italy wants to live there, and just about every other person seems to have written a book about the place.

The region *is* beautiful. Underneath the heavily touristed heart, chaotic traffic and smelly streets, Firenze (Florence) is truly a world-class city in every sense. The country hills, with their rows of cedars, are as distinct as they are alluring, and the small, well-preserved towns retain their demure feel despite the influx of visitors. But Toscana has kept much local character and pride through centuries of animosity between cities. Pisa, Firenze and Siena are all serious historical rivals, and remain so even today. If Italy is a fragmented country, Toscana is the fragmented region.

Toscana was an Etruscan stronghold before the Romans came through, but it's the last 600 years that have given it the character it enjoys today. The Renaissance began here and artistic works are still a major drawcard.

The food is more complex than the cucina of further south, despite what many English-speaking recipe writers would have you think. While more northern European in its approach, thankfully it resounds with the flavour of brilliant ingredients, and maintains its Italian-ness that way.

Tuscans love meat. Visit the Firenze markets and you'll see more parts from more beasts than you previously thought existed. The pinnacle of all this carnivorous activity has to be the bistecca alla fiorentina, specially sourced from local white cattle, **la Chianina**. It's cut into T-bone steaks about 5cm thick and grilled over coals. Bistecca will come rare at a restaurant (forget well done as it will be burnt on the outside) and you pay by **l'etto** (hectogram), meaning each 100g in weight. In even the humblest of restaurants, your bistecca will probably cost over 50,000 lira and is enough to feed two people. While Chianina beef is becoming more scarce, you can still find it at many restaurants, as well as at markets.

Tuscans are jokingly called **mangia fagioli** or 'bean eaters', such is their passion for the humble legume. White **cannellini** beans and the dappled **borlotti** beans are favourites and often seen in soup, or served with sausages or braised meat.

Much of the food is also based on the **pane toscano**, the fine-textured salt-free bread. It's used to thicken soups, which the Tuscans are famous for, such as **ribollita**, a 'reboiled' bean and vegetable soup, flavoured with black cabbage and left to sit for a day before being served. The same pane

The Ponte Vecchio & River Arno, Florence, Toscana

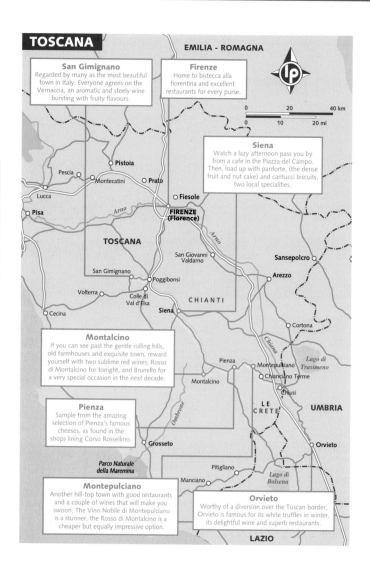

TOSCANA

EMILIA - ROMAGNA

San Gimignano
Regarded by many as the most beautiful town in Italy. Everyone agrees on the Vernaccia, an aromatic and steely wine bursting with fruity flavours.

Firenze
Home to bistecca alla fiorentina and excellent restaurants for every purse.

0   20   40 km
0   10   20 mi

Siena
Watch a lazy afternoon pass you by from a cafe in the Piazza del Campo. Then, load up with panforte, (the dense fruit and nut cake) and cantucci biscuits, two local specialities.

Pistoia

Pescia

Montecatini   Prato

Lucca

Arno

Fiesole

Pisa

FIRENZE (Florence)

TOSCANA

San Giovanni Valdarno

Sansepolcro

Arezzo

Arno

San Gimignano

Poggibonsi

Volterra

Colle di Val d'Elsa

CHIANTI

Cecina

Siena

Cortona

Chiana

Montalcino
If you can see past the gentle rolling hills, old farmhouses and exquisite town, reward yourself with two sublime red wines; Rosso di Montalcino for tonight, and Brunello for a very special occasion in the next decade.

Pienza

Montepulciano

Lago di Trasimeno

Chianciano Terme

Montalcino

Chiusi

Pienza
Sample from the amazing selection of Pienza's famous cheeses, as found in the shops lining Corso Rossellino.

LE CRETE

UMBRIA

Ombrone

Grosseto

Orvieto

Parco Naturale della Maremma

Pitigliano

Lago di Bolsena

Montepulciano
Another hill-top town with good restaurants and a couple of wines that will make you swoon. The Vino Nobile di Montepulciano is a stunner, the Rosso di Montalcino is a cheaper but equally impressive option.

Manciano

Orvieto
Worthy of a diversion over the Tuscan border, Orvieto is famous for its white truffles in winter, its delightful wine and superb restaurants.

LAZIO

is also used in **pappa**, a tomato and bread mush that has an extraordinary depth of flavour, and **panzanella**, a bread and tomato salad, which sometimes appears as runny as a thick soup.

One local pasta is **pinci**, similar to the Umbrian **umbricelli** (see Umbria later in this chapter), served with ragù or **sugo** (sauce). **Pappardelle**, fresh, flat egg noodles cut wider than **tagliatelle** and thinner than lasagne sheets, are also common. The noodles are mostly flat, but sometimes come with a crinkled edge, and may be served **alla lepre**, moistened with a little hare or rabbit ragù.

REGIONAL VARIATIONS

DON'T MISS

- **Bistecca alla fiorentina** –
  Not just a steak, but possibly the best steak you'll ever eat

- **Cacciucco** –
  Livornese seafood stew scented with red capsicums, tomato and lashings of garlic

- **Cantucci e Vin Santo** –
  Crisp biscotti dipped in the ambrosial Vin Santo wine as dessert

- **Driving the Toscana Trail** –
  The drive would satisfy most people, with towns as pretty as Montepulciano and Pienza, but real flavour-chasers will go berserk over what they can eat

- **Panforte in Siena** –
  This 'strong bread' reaches unparalleled excellence in its home city

- **Zuppa** –
  The bread-thickened soups such as ribollita and pappa

REGIONAL VARIATIONS

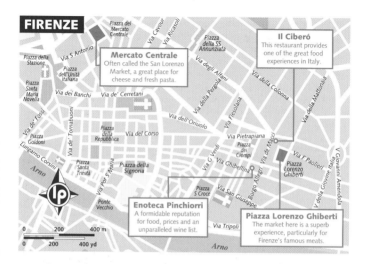

FIRENZE

Piazza del Mercato Centrale

Via Cavour

Via Ricasoli

Piazza della SS Annunziata

Il Ciberó
This restaurant provides one of the great food experiences in Italy.

Piazza della Stazione

Via S Antonio

Piazza dell'Unità Italiana

Mercato Centrale
Often called the San Lorenzo Market, a great place for cheese and fresh pasta.

Via degli Alfani

Via della Colonna

Via della Mattonaia

Piazza Santa Maria Novella

Via dei Banchi

Via de' Cerretani

Via dell'Oriuolo

Via della Pergola

Via Fiesolana

Via de' Fossi

Via de Tornabuoni

Piazza della Repubblica

Via del Corso

Via Pietrapiana

Piazza dei Ciompi

Via F Paolieri

V Giovanni Amendola

Piazza Goldoni

Lungarno Corsini

Arno

Piazza Santa Trinità

Via Por S Maria

Piazza della Signoria

Via G Verdi

Via Ghibellina

Via de' Macci

Piazza Lorenzo Ghiberti

Via della Giovine Italia

Ponte Vecchio

Piazza S Croce

Borgo Allegri

Via San Giuseppe

Enoteca Pinchiorri
A formidable reputation for food, prices and an unparalleled wine list.

Via Tripoli

Piazza Lorenzo Ghiberti
The market here is a superb experience, particularly for Firenze's famous meats.

Arno

0   200   400 m
0   200   400 yd

LP

While meat can dominate, the seafood of Toscana is also great, and you'll see it displayed in restaurant windows throughout the region. Livorno leads the region with seafood and they've created a seafood stew, **cacciucco**, which needs to have five types of fish, one for each 'c' in the name. The name comes from the Turkish *kukut*, meaning 'small fry'.

Toscana's wine is well known outside Italy's borders (see the Drinks chapter), perhaps more from their marketing nous and ready acceptance of French techniques than mere quality. While the Tuscans have led and often still lead Italy in terms of wine quality, up until the 1970s the export of poorly made Chianti probably did more international harm than good to the Italian wine image.

Cheese is central, particularly **caciotta**, the local name for cheese in general and pecorino in particular. Cheese was considered so important that women used to offer cheese-making as a dowry skill. The cheese of Pienza, a town near the Umbrian border, is one of the greatest pecorini in Italy.

Local sweets in Toscana are few but memorable. **Panforte**, the Sienese flat, hard cake with nuts and candied fruit is sensational. Instead of fancy sweets you'll see a range of dry textured, often double-baked **biscotti** (biscuits) such as **cantucci**, which are usually studded with almonds. They're good, especially when dipped into **vin santo**, the local sweet wine. Another popular biscotti are **ricciarelli**, made with marzipan.

Umbria

Umbria has been touted as the new Tuscany. Expats from the UK and US are buying and renovating run-down farm houses, which are far more affordable here. Tourists are finding that the hill-top towns have a charm and appeal that their more museum-like Tuscan counterparts can only dream about. The food, too, is a suitably strong drawcard.

Landlocked Umbria is sandwiched between the more wealthy and sophisticated Toscana on the one hand and Le Marche on the other. Lago di Trasimeno, the largest lake in central and southern Italy, moderates the extremes of temperature, but the weather can still be incredibly harsh in the Appennini and snow isn't uncommon, even in late autumn.

Umbrians are descended from the Umbrii, who roamed the area before the Etruscans. Then came the Romans and after that a relatively long period of instability, marked by self-governing city-states and many medieval fortresses. Then it was the Papal States. Umbria found lasting fame after St Benedetto, the patron saint of Europe, was born in Norcia, and St Francis was born in Assisi.

The Umbria of today is full of well-preserved villages with beautiful stone buildings and cobbled streets. Gorgeous countryside takes up a lot of the space in-between, although some inappropriate development is starting to encroach.

There are olives and vines, both of which the Umbrians have wrought with finesse. Many would suggest that the best olive oil in the world isn't actually from Toscana or Liguria, but rather from near Spoleto. The **Orvieto Classico** white wine and their version of **metodo tradizionale** (the *méthode champenoise* sparkling wine) are particularly good.

The heart of Umbrian food is the hearth. Wood fires are used for everything from **porchetta** (spit-roasted pig) to tiny birds to **bruschetta** (grilled bread appetisers) and mushrooms. In Umbria it is the pig that reigns supreme, followed closely by lamb, sheep's milk cheeses, truffles and anything wild that hasn't been hunted out. Umbrians love to hunt and **cinghiale** (wild boar) are fair game in autumn. Unfortunately, many species of wildlife, particularly small birds, deer and the cinghiale, have been hunted almost to extinction.

The local **porcini** mushrooms are some of the best in the land, and the elusive **tartufo nero** (black truffle) is found in winter, particularly around Norcia (see Truffles in the Staples & Specialities chapter). For those who can't make it to Piemonte, the **tartufo bianco** (white truffle) is sometimes found near Orvieto, a town worth visiting for its wine alone.

Norcia, snuggled in the mountains to Umbria's east, is a food-lover's dream. Even if you're not there when the pungent **tartufi** (truffles) are in season, there are more than enough attractions. The local pecorino cheese is good, particularly the ricotta rolled in wheat germ. **Pecorino di tartufo** is a semi-hard cheese studded with pieces of truffle. If you leave it in your warm car while you take an artery-cleansing climb through nearby Monti Sibillini, you could find the intoxicating, evocative aroma to be a suffocating one on your return.

The pork butchers of Norcia are famed around the country, giving the name **norcineria** (signifying quality) to good butchers in Roma and beyond. Their prosciutto is saltier, coarser, but more fragrant and complex than those of Parma and San Daniele. Cinghiale make a decent prosciutto, but the **salsicce** (cured sausages) from them are even better. About 30 minutes from Norcia is Castelluccio, set on a high plain, and home to the best lentils in Italy.

Interior of Norcineria, Norcia, Umbria

Umbria has its own pasta, most notably umbricelli (sometimes called **ceriole** or **ombricelli**), and **stringozzi**. Both are made by hand with the same water-based dough. Umbricelli are round and string-like, but not as fine as spaghetti, while stringozzi are more squarish, but equally long. Both strangozzi and umbricelli are often served with a meat ragù (perhaps including pork), tartufi nero, or a tomato sugo.

DON'T MISS

- **Tartufi neri** – The black winter truffles of Umbria are some of the best anywhere

- **Lenticchie** – The tiny, pale green lentils of Castelluccio are the best in Italy

- **Porchetta** – Suckling pig stuffed with its liver, wild fennel and rosemary, then spit-roasted over a wood fire, lending the meat a dreamy aroma

- **Salsiccia di cinghiale** – Wild boar sausages (usually about the size of a thumb) are sweet and rich and very good

- **Strangozzi and umbricelli** – The handmade pasta is as satisfying to the soul as it is to the stomach

- **Visiting Norcia** – For the tartufi, the prosciutto, the mountains, and especially the refreshingly different people

Most of the bread in Umbria is the type made without salt, sometimes called pane toscano, here simply known as **pane**. Bread made with salt is called **pane con sale**.

Umbria isn't particularly famed for desserts, but the figs and plums are good in summer. Of more interest is the chocolate of Perugia. Chocoholics from around the world will know the brand name Perugina and associate it with 'baci' or hazelnut 'kisses'.

Marche

Mention Le Marche (The Marches) to most visitors to Italy and the reaction is usually a great blank. It's virtually isolated from Umbria on the west by the Appennini, and tempered by the Adriatic on the east. Le Marche can seem a forgotten region, which is curious, considering some parts are only three hours' drive from Roma.

Le Marche takes its name from its autonomous provinces, each called a **marca**. Originally the Piceni, one of the area's oldest tribes, held sway, then Roma took control, and later the Longobards. But it is the Vatican and the noble families of the 15th and 16th centuries that have left their mark. It's a region of distinguished, sophisticated towns such as Urbino, tempered with a bit of wilderness. The locals know it too, and there's a whiff of exuberant, wild spirit beneath their amiable exterior.

Le Marche's regional cucina is a result of the narrow strip of flat land near the coast and long valleys running from the Appennini in the west. The seaside resorts look sombre and deserted in winter, over-full in season, and sadly over-developed the whole time. But inland, Le Marche's heart is still warm, the welcome real, and the food pretty darned sensational. Truffles and pig products resemble those of nearby Norcia (see Umbria in this chapter), while the clean air and medieval villages are slowly gaining the recognition they deserve.

DON'T MISS

- **Olive ripiene all'ascolana** – Olives stuffed with chicken and/or veal with cheese and herbs. Particularly good in Ascoli Piceno

- **Ciauscolo** – A decadently soft pork salame from Visso that is actually spreadable

- **Formaggio di fossa** – Ewe's milk cheese (often from near Urbino), aged in caves or ditches. It can be hard to find, but must be sampled

- **Mistrá** – Along with anisetta, this is the local anise-scented digestivo (post-meal drink) usually served 'con la mosca' ('with the fly') – with two or three whole coffee beans

- **Vincisgrassi** – A rich, baked dish with layers of egg pasta, chicken livers, ragù, cream and truffle. Like every lasagne you've never had

Catching up, Ascoli, Piceno, Le Marche

Olives do quite well here, producing sublime oil and some great table olives. Ascoli Piceno, an unassuming town with lovely wide streets, is known for its **olive ripiene**, stuffed green olives, filled with a mixture of veal, pork and/or chicken, then crumbed and fried. They are luxuriously addictive. So too porcini, the wild mushrooms that abound in autumn.

Wild mushrooms for sale, Florence, Juliet Coombe

Lumache (snails) are popular in the north, the **coniglio** (rabbit) can be superb, and the **lonza** (cured pork loin) of Macerata is legendary. For those who aren't weight-watching, seek out Macerata's **vincisgrassi**, a lasagne of ragù, truffles, chicken liver and cream with a taste to make your heart stop (or at least you think it might).

Le Marche's cheese is very good, and includes a sweetish **casciotta d'Urbino**, made with three parts sheep's milk and one part cow's. But for something to really knock your socks off, try the **formaggio di fossa**, ewe's milk cheese that is kept in caves or trenches for 100 days (**fossa** means 'trench'). Straw is packed around the cheese, and unlike most cave-ripened cheeses, they aren't turned, wiped or even checked – the cave is closed the whole time. The result is an earthy, almost truffle-perfumed cheese that comes in odd shapes. Families still take their cheese to be cured as they have done for centuries, in much the same way as families around Modena still make balsamic vinegar. They look at you sideways when you ask if everybody makes their own cheese like this – as if everybody wouldn't!

Le Marche's seafood is similar to that of Abruzzi (see Abruzzo & Molise in this chapter). The markets at seaside towns such as San Benedetto del Tronto can be very good. The local version of brodetto (fish stew) is considered one of the best in the country, and the *really* good versions only have fish and no seafood. One of the most celebrated versions is the **brodetto all'anconetana**, containing 13 types of fish. Price constraints mean that finding a fish-only brodetto these days is half the battle. The other half is paying for it.

Lazio

Talk about Lazio (Latium) and you'll have to talk about Roma (Rome). The national capital is tied up with so much history, and has had such an effect on the region and the nation that it's hard not to think of Roma as Lazio itself. But this would give the wrong impression, particularly when it comes to food. While Roma has a cucina founded on the poverty of those in the street (as opposed to wealthy families), the region's cuisine has developed quite distinctly.

Roma's dishes tend to speak of an impoverished people who loved meat so much that they would eat almost any part of a beast. So, while the whole of Italy loves offal, it is in Roma that the love reaches its apogee. The rest of Lazio, however, is more or less the transitional step you'd expect to find between the honest simplicity of Campania and the richer, more complex food of Toscana.

DON'T MISS

- **Carciofi** – Artichokes: try the stuffed **carciofi alla romana**, or **alla giudea** (Jewish style, deep-fried whole)

- **Gelati** – The best gelati in Roma is some of the best in the world

- **I Mercati** – Roma's markets abound with not only local produce but with food from all over the country. The best are Testaccio, Campo dei Fiori and the more earthy and exotic one in Piazza Vittorio Emanuele II, not too far from Stazione Termini. No matter where you are there's usually a market close by

- **Pajata (Pagliata)** – These surprisingly delicious veal entrails (with the milk still inside) are often eaten roasted or tossed through penne or rigatoni

- **Saltimbocca alla romana** – Tender, milk-fed veal is lightly fried, topped with fresh sage and prosciutto and quickly grilled. The name means to 'jump in the mouth' and the flavours tend to do cartwheels on the tongue

- **Volpetti** – Right near Testaccio market is one of the finest food shops in Italy

Sheep have most influenced the food of the region, so keep an eye out for **abbacchio** (milk-fed lamb) and the famed **pecorino romano** cheese – imitations called Romano cheese which are made in other countries don't even come close.

Roma is Roma is Roma. The ancient empire, with all its cultural, artistic and academic wealth, fell into the doldrums with the arrival of the so-called barbarians (basically everyone who was opposed to Roma). But the agricultural practices continued as they always had in the rest of Lazio. Sheep were farmed, the artichoke – a form of thistle – flourished, wheat and farro continued to be sown.

There has always been an underclass in Roma. At times, even in the heyday of the Empire, up to a third of the inhabitants of the eternal city were given a bread ration to prevent them from starving to death. Impoverished Romans used to sit by while the moneyed aristrocrats lived off the proverbial fattened calves. Sitting in **osterie** (neighbourhood inns) near the abattoirs, the impoverished watched as all the beasts' innards (the **quinto quarto**, the fifth quarter) were chucked out, and worked out how to cook them. How else can you explain dishes like **pajata**, veal intestines still filled with the congealed milk that the animal had drunk just before its demise? Most of what is now considered Roman cucina developed from these osterie, especially those near the abattoirs in Testaccio and Trastevere. There are still restaurants opposite where the abattoirs once were, producing dishes from the parts of animals that the wealthy didn't want.

Roman food is not all offal, but a lot of it is. When you see the word **coratella** in a dish, it implies that you'll be eating lights (lungs), kidneys and the heart. Often these dishes are cooked with **carciofi**, the wonderful artichoke that in Roma is rounder, fleshier and better-tasting than virtually anywhere in the country. It cuts the richness of the offal and leaves the palate refreshed if not cleansed. At other times tomato is used with offal, and the expression 'in umido', while normally meaning cooked in a broth, in Lazio tends to mean cooked in a broth scented with tomato.

Poverty also led to the judicious use of other ingredients. Pork is commonly used, but sparingly. **Spaghetti alla carbonara** is the classic pasta dish, with a gorgeous, barely-there sauce of egg, pecorino and **guanciale** (cured pig's cheek). Guanciale is also used in **pasta all'amatriciana**, with a sauce of tomato, garlic and **peperoncini** (chillies). Small amounts of prosciutto and sage are used to spark up the veal dish **saltimbocca**, while even the humble chicken broth is given a lift by the judicious use of parmigiano and whisked egg to make the soup **stracciatella**. Many Roman restaurants serve **gnocchi all romana**, semolina-based discs baked with ragù or tomato sugo, on Thursdays.

Sadly, Roman food isn't what it once was. The transient population of politicians, students, historians and tourists means many restaurants offer the kind of food you wouldn't go back for because you won't be going back. Great places do exist, but the number of affordable, quality eateries has dropped in the last few years. You can also be burnt with service charges at Roman bars, particularly around the tourist haunts. Before you sit down for coffee know that the price could skyrocket the minute you take your seat.

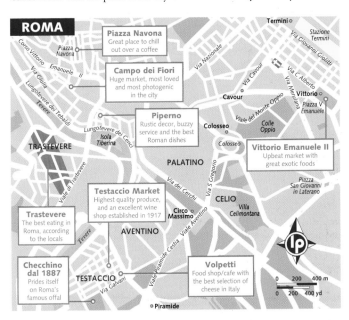

ROMA

Piazza Navona
Great place to chill out over a coffee

Campo dei Fiori
Huge market, most loved and most photogenic in the city

Piperno
Rustic decor, buzzy service and the best Roman dishes

Testaccio Market
Highest quality produce, and an excellent wine shop established in 1917

Trastevere
The best eating in Roma, according to the locals

Checchino dal 1887
Prides itself on Roma's famous offal

Vittorio Emanuele II
Upbeat market with great exotic foods

Volpetti
Food shop/cafe with the best selection of cheese in Italy

Lazio gave the world **lattuga romana** (cos or romaine lettuce), but don't expect to see it in caesar salad because, despite the Mediterranean accent, caesar salad was created in Mexico.

Roma was built on the Via Salaria, the salt road, where traders set up camp on the banks of the Rio Tevere. By the amounts used, often quite excessive, you get the impression that they still love their salt. If you aren't used to eating salt, be prepared for a lip-sticking, water-drinking few days when you first arrive.

Abruzzo & Molise

To many Italians and visitors alike, Abruzzo and Molise are one and the same. While Molise, immediately to the south of Abruzzo on the Adriatic coast, became an independent region within Italy in 1963, its similarities with Abruzzo are far greater than its differences.

In many ways the regions (known collectively as Abruzzi) form a bridge between the more conservative north and the gung-ho south: driving in Abruzzi is only semi-chaotic; locals eat a variety of both egg and water-based pasta; and they have the life-loving attitude of the southerners as well as the organisational skills that distinguish the north.

What's not hills, sea or mountain is invariably heavily cropped; olives and vines compete for space along the roadside, particularly in the north. Both Abruzzo and Molise touch the coast and have peaks in the Appennini. Traditionally, many clusters of houses in the valleys of Abruzzi were virtually inaccessible to outsiders.

The locals herded sheep, often for month-long voyages to find food or to sell the animals at market, creating huge **tratturi**, sheep routes that can be as wide as an eight-lane road. Because of the isolation, Christianity took longer to reach here than virtually anywhere else in what is now Italy. As a result the locals tend to be even more superstitious than the rest of the country, and their harvest festivals are some of the most pagan in origin.

Abruzzi is still wonderfully wild in many respects; the Gran Sasso d'Italia and Parco Nazionale d'Abruzzo are testament to what a lack of human habitation can achieve. The regions' economies are still based on agriculture, particularly sheep, corn, wheat and now a little bit of farro. If you visit in the late spring, Molise produces some very fine asparagus, and the wild onions and wild asparagus are very good.

REGIONAL VARIATIONS

DON'T MISS

- **Confetti** – Okay, so they're just sugared almonds, but the ones from Sulmona are considered the world's best
- **Brodetto** – A fish soup/stew, full of **frutti di mare** (seafood) eaten piping hot. It's usually served in a heavy terracotta pot to retain the heat
- **Maccheroni alla chitarra** – Hand-made egg pasta like a square spaghetti
- **Zafferano** – Locally grown saffron has an outstanding reputation and you can buy it here to take home

Shooting the breeze, Sulmona, Abruzzo

MINESTRONE DE TERAMO

Because seven is considered a lucky number with Christian signifi-cance, it plays a vital role in the soup of Teramo, often eaten at festivals. Teramo even hosts a whole festival around its soup, held on 1 May every year. There are 49 different things that must go into the making of **minestrone de Teramo**, otherwise known as **virtù**: seven kinds of fresh vegetables, seven legumes, seven meatballs, seven pig parts, seven dif-ferent seasonings and seven shapes of pasta. The last seven is the number of virgins who must prepare the dish. There is a theory that a gentleman who is served this soup will be too full (and satisfied) to com-promise a maiden's virtue. Another tale is that a suitor will win the favourable attentions of a virtuous lady if he offers her this dish.

The Abruzzi coast, while heavily frequented by tourists in summer, offers the sweet fish of the impossibly blue Adriatic, and any suggestion of a **frutti di mare** (seafood) meal should be accepted with unbridled enthu-siasm. Imagine a huge, steaming terracotta pot filled with brodetto, fish and seafood, including mussels, octopus, scampi, **cicale** (like a tiny crayfish) and any number of whole, yet small fish, scented with **peperone** (capsicum) and/or peperoncini (chillies) – you'll need a good lie down afterwards if the size of the portions resemble the ones we ate.

The pasta is also memorable. In fact, some of the best artisan-style, manufactured pasta in the country are made in Abruzzo, using copper or brass dies rather than the more common teflon ones. The difference is in the texture of the pasta and its ability to absorb and hold sauces.

The unique local pasta, called maccheroni by the locals, but known elsewhere as **maccheroni alla chitarra**, is significant. It looks like a kind of square spaghetti but is actually an egg pasta (spaghetti is usually made with water), rolled out to form a thin sheet and then rolled through a cutter. The cutter, a **chitarra**, has tightly strung wires, and it looks, with a little imagination, like a guitar, hence the name. Maccheroni is often eaten with a meat ragù, as opposed to spaghetti, which is more often served with a thinner sauce.

One Abruzzi speciality you may find all over the country is **confetti** (sugared almonds). Excellent local almonds from the town of Sulmona are sugared, coloured (or wrapped in coloured plastic), and shaped into almost anything. You may see bees, butterflies or stem after stem of flowers all made with fine material, bent wire and the occasional strategic almond. While these are good, the bitter-cocoa chocolates of Sulmona are just as good.

Campania

When most people think of Campania, they think of the wonderfully frenetic, seductively vibrant city, Napoli (Naples). Even just 20km from Napoli, locals have a different attitude, yet the whole of this densely populated region lives life as if Monte Vesuvio is just about to blow. Living for the minute comes naturally to the population, perhaps as a result of centuries of devastating earthquakes, or perhaps because it's too hot to be serious in summer. Whatever the reason, there's an infectious love of life and a corresponding love of good food.

Napoli has been a jewel in many crowns, from the time when Imperial Rome's hoi polloi used it as a holiday resort, to its consideration for the status as capital of the newly united Italy. And Napoli glitters still, as the harbour-playing backdrop to a place that is most easily defined by the deliciously outrageous nature of her people.

DON'T MISS

- **Mozzarella di bufala** – The ethereally perfumed, freshest-tasting cheese imaginable. The most memorable way to eat it (apart from on pizza) is in **insalata caprese**, with tomato, basil and just a touch of olive oil

- **Pizza** – Once you've tasted the best pizza, you'll never want to go home

- **Limoncello** – A sublime lemon liqueur to drink along the Costa Amalfi and on the isle of Capri

- **Napoli's Food Market** – Where the seething, voluptuous, life-engaging Neapolitans come together to chat, to check each other out, to argue about politics and love ... oh, and to buy food

- **Pompeii** – The unearthed town has a perfectly preserved bakery and kitchens so you get a real feel for how they cooked in the olden days

- **Spaghetti alla vongole** – The place that invented spaghetti is the best place to eat this classic dish of tiny clams with al dente spaghetti and garlic

But think of Campania's food and its history means little. This is the region that has given much of its cucina to the world: think spaghetti, pizza, mozzarella, eggplant parmigiana – the list goes on. To eat these dishes in Napoli is to live. **Mozzarella di bufala**, the real mozzarella cheese, puts any other cheese of the same name to shame (see the boxed text Making Mozzarella next). Spaghetti never tasted quite like this, and the pizze, if not to die for, are at least worthy of great pain.

The good food of the region comes from the tomatoes of San Marzano. Their sauce, **conserva di pomodoro**, is made from super-ripe tomatoes, cut and left to dry in the sun for at least two days to concentrate the flavour. This is the sauce that perfumes the world's best pizze, and makes the **parmigiana di melanzane** (baked eggplant with cheese) indecently good.

This port town has always had a close attachment to the sea, and the best **insalata di mare** (seafood salad) is found here, although versions exist all over the country. Besides a large variety of fish, the **aragoste** (crayfish) are highly regarded, as are the **cozze** (mussels) and **vongole** (clams).

Baccala display, Napoli, Campania   *Mollusc display, Napoli, Campania*

Despite the coast, many dishes are based on lamb, offal and grains. Rice is used in dishes such as **palle di riso** (rice balls), and polenta makes a guest appearance baked into things like **migliaccio 'e cigule** (baked polenta with sausages).

While the region is best known for its savoury food, one of the **dolci** (sweets) that you should try is the flaky pastry **sfogliatella**, like a Danish pastry filled with ricotta and candied fruit, and scented with cinnamon. Sfogliatelle come in a few forms: a softer, doughier one, a deep-fried version and the justifiably popular crispy version.

Puglia

In a nation dominated by mountains and hills, Puglia (Apulia) is the exception. It's the flattest region, stretching along the east coast, down and around the heel of the Italian 'boot'. It has a fair amount of rolling hills, and just a sprinkling of mountains. In parts it looks bleak and moon-like, its craggy rocks and little vegetation giving the impression of a barren landscape. But there are fertile pockets. In many areas olives dominate. Grape vines, grown over pergola-like trellises, stretch for hectare after hectare, and the unrelenting daylight and relative warmth imbue the vegetables of the region with a taste akin to edible sunshine.

While many foreign tourists only see the region as a pit-stop before leaving Bari and Brindisi by boat for Greece and beyond, Puglia has its own attractions which shouldn't be overlooked. Trani has the most wonderful harbour backed up by an incredible fish market just one block back from the sea. Martina Franca has a lively spirit, and the nearby **trulli** (conical-roofed houses) are truly remarkable.

Parts of Puglia were included in Magna Graecia, a collection of fairly autonomous city-states that (in theory) were ruled by Greece. Then came the usual array of conquerors: Romans, Swabians, Normans, Byzantines, Turks and the Spanish, to name a few. While these same rulers tended to leave Calabria and Basilicata to their own devices, the flatter land of Puglia invited a more invasive kind of rule. The countless wars and terrible massacres have left the locals with an insular nature. And while much of the influence of different empires can still be felt in the architecture, the food seems to be intrinsically local, with just a little input from outside.

Pugliese food, of any region in Italy, would probably be described as the most Italian, if it were possible to say such a thing. Pugliese food represents the essence of modern thought behind Italian food – take a single ingredient and try to capture its unique character, that special something, and bring it to the fore. You may eat the best meal of your life in Puglia.

Puglia's most famous pasta is the sublime **orecchiette**, the 'little ear'-shaped pasta often still made by hand and served with **cime di rapa**, bitter turnip tops tossed with anchovies. In fact, most of the pasta, including **cavatelli**, a flatter version of orecchiette, are served with vegetable-based sauces. Often, however, they are laced with a touch of something else, such as spiced lard, some stock, or even a meatball or two.

The **pane** (bread) of Puglia is legendary, and some of the best bakers in Roma and Milano are of Puglian descent. By far the best pane is cooked in a wood-fire. You may also come across **taralli**, which can be like tiny circular pretzels or as big as a doughnut. They can be crispy or just crusty, but they always have a hole in the middle.

Fresh fish at Trani market, Trani, Puglia

Chickpeas are also grown in the region, particularly around Nardo in the south, and like all Pugliese produce, seem to taste better than every other chickpea you've had.

Local sheep and cow's milk cheeses are very good and worth a taste. **Scamorza** is kind of like a firm mozzarella, the **provolone** is good, but it is the **burrata**, particularly from around Andria, that really astounds. Burrata is made by taking stretched cow's curd (mozzarella) and placing a bit of cream inside. The outside is pure white, impeccably smooth, and you cut it open to release strips of cheese encasing the cream.

DON'T MISS

- **Verdure** – The vegetables of Puglia have a taste that other regions' vegetables can only dream about. Must-tries are **peperone** (capsicum), **finocchio** (fennel), **melanzane** (eggplant) and **fave** (broad beans)

- **Burrata** – A cream-filled, cow's milk mozzarella with a dreamy texture and delectable taste. Drizzle with local olive oil and grind pepper over for an after-dinner snack

- **Olio di oliva** – Some of the biggest-flavoured and some of the most delicate oils come from Puglia, which produces 30% of Italy's olive oil

- **Olive di Cerignola** – Big, fleshy olives from a village of the same name. Sweet and linger in taste

- **Orecchiette** – The classic pasta, meaning 'little ears'

- **The fish market in Trani** – Fish straight from the boats being sold right near the most beautiful port just north of Bari

The local wine is abundant and cheap, but the standard is erratic, despite recent efforts to aim for quality rather than quantity. Much of the production used to be exported to other regions and countries, for use in their blends. That said, in Puglia there are many decent wines, both DOC and **vino da tavola** (table wines), so you should be able to find something you like.

Basilicata

So poor were the people from Basilicata that in particularly hard times – even within the last century – they only ate sheep that died of old age.

Thankfully, things have changed and markedly too. While this region is bordered by Calabria, Puglia and Campania, it has managed to retain its own character and sense of taste. Compared to the developed and wealthier Puglia, Basilicata has an infectious sense of purpose and identity, with enough character to carry off the impression of more affluence than it actually has. That's particularly true of the intriguing town of Matera, built into the side of cliffs.

Nearly half the region is mountainous, virtually all the rest is hills and in summer it bakes in the hot sun, looking desolate and barren. And a lot of it *is* desolate and barren after the extensive deforestation that has left the countryside eroded and scarred.

The harsh climes and the lack of easy access to the sea have left the area with a **cucina povera**, the cucina of the poor. But if you think cucina povera is something lacking taste, then think again. Local vegetables are densely flavoured, the pasta done well, gelati as good as just about anywhere, and the flagship wine, Aglianico del Vulture, is considered one of the best wines of the south.

The Sassi, Matera, Basilicata

MAKING MOZZARELLA

Asian water buffalo look kind of out of place in Italy. But the flavour of buffalo milk, and **mozzarella di bufala** in particular, suits Italy like a win in the football World Cup.

Mozzarella di bufala is made mostly in Campania, and the best is said to come from near Caserta and Battipaglia; the former is firmer, the latter more milky in texture. Like most farmhouse cheeses, the milk is heated every morning and culture is added to make a solid curd which is shredded. This is when the fascinating part of the cheese-making starts. Hot water is poured onto the curd, and it is spun around the base of the copper-lined tub. The cheesemaker has a stick in one hand, a scoop in the other, and ladles the whey/water mixture off as he stirs. The shredded curd becomes a solid mass, and when it's drained completely, is formed into the distinctive mozzarella balls.

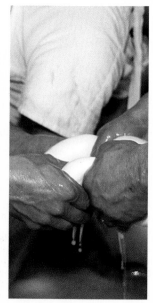

The old way to shape the cheese is by hand with three people working together. Two roll the cheese (still barely cool enough to handle) to leave an always smooth outer surface, while the other pinches off small orbs. The whole time, the cheese must be kept moving so it doesn't form a skin. A modern method is to tip the cheese into a roller that produces similar looking balls with a straighter, cleaner pinch mark.

Mozzarella di bufala is porcelain white, glossy and is formed as **bocconcini** (tiny mouthfuls), the classic ball (just a bit bigger than a golf ball), large balls, and **treccia** (plaits). It is at its best for about two days after making, should never be rubbery and by far the best flavoured cheese is unpasteurised.

Because of the expense of buffalo milk, a lot of mozzarella is now made with a percentage of cow's milk. **Fior di latte** is a 100% cow's milk cheese made in the same style. Anything but the proper mozzarella di bufala, though, is like a kiss from your brother. It's all very nice, but ...

Look out for the sign **'caseificio'** anywhere in Campania for fresh mozzarella that has been made on-site.

Although Basilicata shares many of the dishes of Calabria and Puglia, it also has its own cucina. The most renowned is the sausage **lucanica** (known as **luganega** in the north of Italy), a long, reddish-coloured pork meat sausage spiced with peperoncino, eaten fresh or dried. Because of the mountains, the region is particularly brilliant for wild mushrooms, most notably **cardoncelli**, the most commonly used mushroom in **agnello ai funghi**, a lamb stew with garlic and chilli.

You may well encounter **ciammotta**, a mixed selection of fried vegetables (including tomatoes, olives, capsicum, potatoes, onion and eggplant) that captures the essence of each ingredient and builds on it. There are quite a few offally bits in dishes such as **cazzmar**, lamb innards made into a sausage and baked, and there's a long, slow cooking method (needed for more, how do we say it ... more mature sheep) known as **cutturiddi**. Cutturiddi also gives its name to a relatively modern lamb stew that is cooked with chilli, tomatoes and celery. The **lampascioni**, slightly bitter wild onions, are widely liked and used to make **marmellata di lampascioni**, an onion marmalade scented with cinnamon.

DON'T MISS

see also entries for Calabria and Puglia in this chapter

- **Agnello ai cardoncelli** – Lamb stew scented with wild cardoncelli mushrooms
- **Lampascioni** – Bitter wild onions the size of a large marble
- **Lucanica** – The long pork and chilli sausage that the whole country tries to copy (but with less success)
- **Matera's market** – A refreshingly vibrant yet honest market on Via Cappelluti near the Stazione FAL

And despite the poverty, they've kept a sense of humour. **Strangolapreti lucani** are a shell-shaped pasta with eggs and lemon that translate directly as 'priest stranglers'. You will also find this dish in other regions nearby.

Calabria

The long, thin toe of Italy is often seen through a train or car window, as visitors shoot by on their way to somewhere else. More fool them, because the best Calabrese food isn't in Sicilia or Napoli but in Calabria. The hard part is to give it the credibility on paper that it has in real life. Even in Italian, the local **pomodori ripieni** just means stuffed tomatoes.

But the food is distinct and as good as, if not better than, many more trendy regions to the north. The **agrumi** (citrus fruit) is superb, the **fichi** (figs) are legendary, and Calabria makes a whole range of gorgeous **pastasciutta** (dry pasta). What's more, the locals can be as welcoming and friendly as Italians you'll find anywhere, once they decide that you're okay.

Calabria is fairly insular in its outlook, the result of being shafted by everyone from the ancient Greeks to the current snobbishness of the north. The Moors spent time here, as did most conquering nations, leaving a little of their cucina behind when they left. Because of this historic geographical vulnerability, anyone sailing by could drop by for a stoush and a bit of pillaging. So locals have always kept a wary eye on the sea, which brought invader after invader as well as creating marshy breeding grounds for malaria-carrying mosquitoes.

Nowadays, with **la mare** (the sea) posing less of a threat and more of an income from tourism, the food represents a mix of the hill-top history and the sea. You'll find **alici** (wonderful fresh anchovies, perhaps filled with herbs and breadcrumbs) alongside delicate lamb dishes and **carciofi ripieni**, artichokes stuffed with pecorino, breadcrumbs and herbs. The Calabrese have a penchant for **agrodolce**, matching sweet with sour. **Peperoni** (capsicum) is used extensively, reaching its peak cooked with local **caperi** (capers) in the stew **peperonata**.

The greatest **cedro** (citron, like a large lemon) in the world is reputed to come from Calabria, as do the finest **bergamotto** (bergamot, a citrus fruit, best known for scenting Earl Grey tea).

But for all its intense flavour and lingering taste, Calabrian cucina is built on just a few ingredients: good lamb, some mild cow's milk cheeses such as provolone and **caciocavallo**, pecorino as well as some fine vegetables. Anchovies are often seen, sometimes served **alici a crudo**, raw with just a drizzle of vinegar and oil, or as **acciughe**, preserved in salt.

Tropea is known for its **cipolla rossa** (red onion) and **bianchetti** (whitebait), the latter boasting a festival in its honour: the Sagra del Pesce Azzurroe della Cipolla Rossa, celebrated on 4 July.

Peperoncino, chilli, is dominant and used in everything from salumi to pasta. Dishes described elsewhere in the country as 'calabrese', particularly those with sausages, will have a certain amount of fire-power. Particularly common is the simply delicious **ciufftì**, a dish of spaghetti with olive oil, garlic and a dusting of ground peperoncino.

Before the advent of refrigeration, preserving food was important. Scalding summers and relatively mild winters in much of the south meant that some fresh food didn't keep for long. So the locals smoked some of the cheese to make it last longer; even ricotta was preserved. The preferred grating cheese is often a hard pecorino or **ricotta salata** (salted ricotta), as opposed to the parmigiano reggiano favoured further north.

DON'T MISS

- **Fichi** – Figs, fresh or dried, stuffed or unstuffed, any way you find them
- **Caciocavallo** – Large cow's milk cheeses tied around the middle and aged for up to one year, sometimes sold smoked. The unsmoked tends to be better
- **Cipolle di Tropea** – The famous red onions of Tropea particularly known in the soup **licurdia**, cooked with beetroot, carrot and potato
- **Cirò** – Sometimes referred to as the oldest wine in the world, Cirò is the most common Calabrian wine of quality. It's available in bianco, rosso and rosato
- **Fileja** – Home-made, water and semolina-based pasta, curled around wires
- **Provolone** – Super huge, pear-shaped cows' cheese usually eaten while still pale and sweet. Also available smoked

There is a hint of the Moors still evident in the dolci. Desserts are often based on **mosto cotto**, the cooked must (unfermented juice) from grapes also popular in Sardegna. **Crucetta** (stuffed figs) are common, both **fresca** (fresh) and **secco** (dried). The Calabrese also make **chinulille** (a sweet ravioli), which may have candied citrus fruit, dried chestnuts or, more likely, ricotta inside, scented with citrus zest.

Sicilia

Most first-time visitors to Sicilia (Sicily) come with expectations of the Mafia or the desolate countryside of movies like *Cinema Paradiso*. While the blistering summer sun lends a barren look to parts of Sicilia, much of the land is surprisingly fertile, bringing forth **agrumi** (citrus fruits), **caperi** (capers) and some of the best tomatoes you are ever likely to taste. And the Mafia is definitely something you are more likely to hear whispers about than actually experience.

The continuous invasions of the island have all had their impact, each conqueror taking as much from Sicilia as they could. But inadvertently each passing empire has left its own stamp. Tangible signs remain of Greek, Roman, Arab and Norman occupation, not least the use of almonds, couscous, sheep milk cheeses and rice.

This is food that really shouts rather than whispers. Most flavours aren't subtle, and some threaten to fight head-on. But when the balance is perfect, each ingredient adds to the whole.

Rice, seldom seen in central Italy, but a stalwart of the north, appears again here. Usually it is used in **arancini** (meaning 'little oranges' from their colour), deep-fried balls of rice traditionally flavoured with saffron, tomato, vegetables or perhaps a little meat. Wild fennel is used in dishes such as **paste con le sarde**, pasta with fresh sardines, pine nuts and raisins, and the artichoke is abundant.

Perhaps surprisingly for a region so blessed with such good ingredients and a rich culture, restaurant food in Sicilia can be disappointing, the result of no real restaurant culture until recently. Wealthy families always had the best private cooks, and everybody else ate at home. But good meals can be found when you eat out, usually prepared by female chefs who are cooking home-style meals for larger numbers.

Unlike the other large island, Sardegna, the fish from around the island has long been the backbone of the cucina. But overfishing and a drop in water quality mean that what was once a seemingly endless source of food is now running low. You'll still see plenty of seafood around, but it's not the staple it once was. Well-off visitors and locals alike can enjoy **aragoste** (lobsters) from Trapani or **pescespada** (swordfish) from Messina, while the cash-challenged among us can enjoy fresh and preserved anchovies and sardines.

Sicilian pasta is simply served – a mere sprinkling of fresh breadcrumbs and perhaps some chopped anchovies, or **alla norma**, tomato sauce, fried eggplant and some grated salted ricotta. One of the great ingredients of the region is caperi used sparingly in most dishes, but generously in **caponata**, a dish of browned vegetables doused in vinegar and given a punchy taste with anchovies and capers.

DON'T MISS

- **Frutti alla martorana** – Artisan Sicilian marzipan is made into the shape of fruits and other food and painted. Mushrooms may have 'dirt' on the bottom, bananas look like they are ripe, figs are often split. The best is incredible to behold. But no matter how much you may adore the look of them, if you don't like almond sweets, then it's better to look than eat. If you do like almond sweets, you'll love them

- **Arancini** – Deep-fried rice balls flavoured with meat or tomato, which you may find sold on the street

- **Dolci** – Anything sweet, from little bomba (like little rum baba) and **cannoli** (fried pastry tubes) to gelati and cassata

- **Granite** – Crumbly crushed ices served in bars everywhere when it's warm. A caffè granita usually comes with whipped cream on top and is often eaten with a **brioche** (pastry)

- **Pescespada** – Swordfish, often cooked with pine nuts, raisins and olives

- **Vini da dessert** – To match their sensational pastries, they've created at least two outstanding wines – **Marsala** and **Moscato**

Sicilians excel in everything sweet. The **paste di mandorle** (almond paste) is used to glorious excess in everything from tarts to the amazing **frutti alla martorana**, fruit-shaped and hand-painted sweets. These frutti may look like tiny prickly pears, figs, oranges, bananas and the like.

Other nuts are used too, such as **pistacchi** (pistachios). **Cassata siciliana**, a sponge cake filled with sweetened sheep's ricotta, chocolate, pistachios and candied fruit, is unlike versions sold elsewhere around the world (and it isn't frozen).

Perhaps not surprisingly (considering the heat) Sicilia is considered to be the home of Italian ice cream. Its soft gelati are some of the country's best, usually containing less dairy produce than those from further north. Another frozen food, **granita**, is sold in the warmer months, made from crushed ice flavoured with coffee, lemon or fresh almond milk.

Sardegna

The island of Sardegna (Sardinia), slung out well to the west of the Italian mainland, is a curious place. While most know of the Costa Smeralda on the north-east coast as the playground for the fabulously rich-if-not-famous, the true Sardegna is confronting. It's full of wonders, from its unforgiving mountains to the leathery-skinned locals descended from self-reliant, nomadic herdsmen. The food, too, has its own identity, and you can eat really well just about everywhere.

There's a reason for the island being so enigmatic. Centuries of invasions, matched with a rugged interior, have left the cucina with more than just a few far-flung influences. For thousands of years Sardegna has been inhabited by a race of shepherds, the Sardi, whose descendants can still be seen herding sheep along country roads. For a long time these **pastori** (shepherds) were organised into small autonomous groupings. But then the invasions began. Some were economic, some more physical, but almost everyone who passed through the Mediterranean, from the Phoenicians to the Austrians, had a go at Sardegna.

Thankfully for the Sardi, the interior of the island is tough country, inhospitable at times and impossible at others, at least before motorised transport. Even when Sardegna became part of a united Italy, malaria kept most people away from the coast until its eradication in the 1950s. So the Sardi developed a cucina that looked inland rather than out to sea.

Pecorino, the ever-present ewe's milk cheese, reaches its greatest heights here. The most famous bread is **pane carasau** (see also Bread in Staples & Specialities chapter) that the pastori could take with them for weeks at a time, and the pasta, such as **culingiones** (like a potato ravioli) tend to be on the heavy side. Everything is based on what is local, practical, and cost-effective. Even the **pane fresa**, a form of pane carasau, is made so that it can be folded into three and slid easily into backpacks.

While all who've dropped by have left their mark, it's the Spaniards and Arabs whose presence is most notable. **Impanadas** (baked dough filled with meat and herbs) is similar to the Spanish *empanada* and **fregola** (like couscous) is used in some soups and broths. Sardinians actually grow and use quite a bit of **zafferano** (saffron) on the island, and sweet almond pastries such as **tillicas**, crown-shaped pastries with almond meal, are a result of Moorish occupation.

While the sea hasn't shaped the food of the island as a whole, you can definitely find fresh seafood on the coast. Sardinians eat **brodetto** (fish soup/stew) as well as **burrida** (fish stew often thickened with nuts), while the **aragosta** (lobsters) of Alghero are justly famous. Most of the inspiration for seafood dishes comes from other regions, particularly Liguria.

Although you can eat well in the resort areas, if you want to see the real Sardegna (if such a thing exists), head for the area around Oliena near Nuoro in the central north. Here pane carasau is made, the locals are friendly, and the formaggi, wine and prosciutti are very good. Tours can be organised where you spend time walking with a pastoro before eating a traditional meal back in town.

DON'T MISS

- **Pane frattau (vrattau)** – The paper-thin mountain bread is soaked and topped with tomato, egg and pecorino. Simple and simply delicious
- **Bottarga** – Dried, pressed tuna roe. Try it finely grated over piping hot spaghetti in **spaghetti alla buttariga**
- **Culingiones** – Potato and wild mint 'ravioli' often made more like gnocchi. There seem to be nearly as many spellings (such as cullurgiones, culigiones) as there are cooks
- **Miele** – The honey is divine, particularly individual varietal honeys such as that made from pollen collected from **corbezzolo** (similar to a wild strawberry)
- **Pecorino sardo** – The semi-cooked cheese available as everything from **dolce** (sweet and fresh) to **stagionata** (aged)
- **Porcheddu** – Suckling pig scented with herbs and wood-roasted whole on a spit

Small sagre, festivals, are held throughout the region to celebrate the simple fare. Every November the tiny hill-based hamlet of Cavoi puts on a free feed of bread, potato, cheese and wine, while in Aritzo an October sagra celebrates the annual chestnut crop.

One of the greatest building blocks of Sardegna's cucina is pecorino. **Pecorino sardo** is the classic local cheese, a general term that, while used for many different cheeses, means a semi-cooked, nutty flavoured cheese sold at various ages. Keep an eye out for **fiore sardo**, the favoured cheese in Ligurian pesto, making a fine table cheese. The gently perfumed sheep's milk ricotta (labelled simply as 'ricotta') is sensational.

shopping
& markets

To shop in Italy is to be thrust, head reeling, heart pumping and mouth watering, into the heart of Italian life. A market is a heady experience that drips with vitality, and butchers' shops can be gruesome yet inspiring. The **caseificio** where you buy cheese can be the place where the cheese was made only hours before, and the person selling it to you may be the cheese-maker.

Italians love specialist shops, for meat, for cheese and for pastries. In fact, it seems that you can add the suffixes -icio or -eria to virtually any food product and open a shop. So if you sell lots of **prosciutto** (preserved ham) you may have a **prosciuttificio**. If someone makes a lot of **confetti** (coloured, sugared almonds) then their shop may be called a **confetteria** or **confettificio**. And a store that specialises in **grappa** (the high-octane digestive drink) may put up a sign saying **grapperia**. Thankfully most stores have names that are the same throughout the country.

Italy uses the decimal system (see the conversion guide on the inside back cover of the book) and so prices are usually by the **chilo** (kilogram), or very often by **l'etto** (the 100g). Most shops close early one day a week, and not many are open on Sundays. Expect just about every food shop to close for a few hours in the middle of the day outside of major cities for a siesta. The good thing is that they tend to stay open at least until you realise you're going to need some lunch.

Market in Oliena, Sardegna

Specialist Shops
Alimentari
Basically a shop that sells all sorts of food. A good alimentari is like a boutique supermarket with oils, cheeses, **salumi** (preserved meats) as well as
basics like water. Really good alimentari have lots of prepared **antipasti**
(mixed appetiser), including table olives and pickled vegetables.

Carne Equine
The horse butcher. Seen in most regions, you can buy all kinds of cuts
similar to beef. The meat is sweeter, and it's all for human consumption.

Caseificio
This is usually the place where cheese is made. Most cheese producers sell
direct to the public. Buying here means cutting out the middle man, low-
ering the cost, and even more importantly, cuts out the time lapse between
the production and the eating. Those near Napoli selling **mozzarella di
bufala** (buffalo milk mozzarella cheese) and those dotted around Emilia-
Romagna with **parmigiano reggiano** (parmesan cheese) signs should be
more than enough to entice you in.

Enoteca
Meaning 'place of wine', enoteca usually denotes a bottle shop although
they may serve glasses of wine, and good ones will always give tastings of
some wine.

Formaggeria/Latteria
Places selling milk and milk products such as cheese, cream and butter.
The most common name is the formaggeria, from **formaggio**, meaning
'cheese'.
   The range is usually enormous. They will always have parmigiano reggiano, mozzarella, ricotta and a selection of local cheeses. And they should
always give you an **assaggio** (a taste) before you buy.

Frutta e Verdura
Fruit and vegetable shops. They are found tucked into many small streets
and are often within striking distance of a macelleria, making shopping
relatively easy.

Macelleria
A butcher. Many sell just **vitello** (veal), **agnello** (lamb) and **manzo** (beef),
but they may sell poultry too.

SHOPPING

Mercato

The name means 'market' and could mean a fresh fruit and vegetable market. But if you ask Italians for **il mercato**, most of the time they will point you in the direction of a supermarket. This is a problem, as even tourist offices seem intent on directing you away from the real action (Italian markets can, and do, blow your mind), to a relatively antiseptic store.

View of Padova market, Veneto

Norcineria

The name of a specialist pork butcher named after the town of renowned pork butchers in Umbria, Norcia.

Pasticceria

A bakery. **Pasta** is anything with a pasty flour dough at some stage, so pastries, bread, biscuits and the like are all available here. Each city and region has its own specialities.

Pastificio

A specialist pasta (as we know it) shop, usually making **pasta fresca** (fresh pasta, often made with eggs) as well as **gnocchi** (potato dumplings).

Butcher shop, Padova

Pescheria

Specialist fish shop, selling all kinds of seafood.

Polleria

Specialist **pollame** (poultry) shop. Everything from guinea fowl and chicken to quail and pheasant.

Salumeria

Salumerie sell all kinds of salumi, meaning smallgoods – prosciutto, salami, **salsicce** (sausage), and the like. They will slice it to your needs.

Supermercato

The real name for a supermarket is **supermercato**, although it is often shortened to the confusing, yet simple, **mercato**. A good supermercato is fantastic, selling not just general groceries, but better salumi and formaggi than you'll find back home.

Tabacchi

Shops that sell tobacco as well as confectionery and salt. This was a way of enforcing an old-fashioned but effective salt-tax system by limiting who could sell the essential seasoning. Many bars are also Tabacchi.

SHOPPING

Torrefazione

Simply *the* place to buy coffee beans or grounds. Torrefazione means that it's a roasting house and the sooner you buy your coffee after it has been roasted (after the first week), the better. Don't let them grind it if you have a quality grinder yourself, as coffee's wonderful aroma will dissipate quicker once ground.

At the Market

Sheep-milk farmers selling ricotta out of the boot of cars; men with blackened hands biting the ends off ink-stained cuttlefish before preparing them for sale; spruikers yelling, open mouths full of chipped, stained teeth ... this is a **mercato** in full flight in Italy. Where Italians have a market, they have life, and the sheer liveliness of it defies the imagination.

You can hardly believe the freshness of the fish, the sweet smell of the herbs, the clamour and hubbub, the bustling, heaving humanity. **Vongole** (clams) may spray you with a fine thread of the seawater they're kept in, joke-telling stall holders jostle to have their photo taken, babies are clutched to hips, arguments are fought, lovers kiss, and all the while the buying and selling goes on.

When you decide to visit a market, you decide to become part of life at its most unadulterated, unbridled form. There's no pretension, no polite standing back to enjoy the view. It's all happening, and with a vengeance.

To be fair, the markets in Italy are different in every town. You won't see the vibrancy and sheer raunchiness of life in Bologna that you do in Napoli, but each is an expression of its people. Northern markets are more restrained, as life is more restrained. Things are more sure, more certain in the north than they are in the south.

Every region has its own attitude to markets. In Umbria they may be small, inconsequential even, while in Roma they're the lifeblood of a city-trapped populace. In Sardegna the market for fresh vegetables may be disappointing, as people mostly still grow what they need, but the scramble for seedlings is frenetic.

At most markets mobile formaggerie sell local cheese, as well as parmigiano and other national favourites. Meat could be for sale from a macelleria, or you may be able to buy your chickens still alive. Often there are seeds, flowers and tool stalls, with clothes and bag stalls parked around the edges.

Despite the feel of some markets, stall holders are highly unlikely to rip you off. It all comes down to their sense of pride, and the importance of not giving a **brutta figura**, 'a bad impression'. To an Italian, particularly market people who have the same stalls week after week, year after year, this is far more important than whether they can scam a few hundred lira from you. More likely is that they may slip a bruised apple in with the good ones if you don't keep your eye on them or tell them not to. That isn't giving brutta figura, of course, that is just running a smart business.

Good markets are a revelation. A good stall holder will not only tell you what fruit and vegetables are in season, but also how to cook them. And if they really care, they may even slip a little bundle of mixed herbs in with your purchases, something that will enhance a soup or lift a braise.

If someone tells you a market is open every day, that means every day except Sunday. Many markets close at about 1pm, and some don't re-open, although big ones do on most days. Saturday is usually the biggest shopping day of the week, because even workers can shop then. And a lot of extra shopping has to be done for that all-important Sunday lunch.

It doesn't matter how many times you visit an Italian market, there is always something new to see, someone new to meet, and something you can't believe going on.

Cheese stall at market in San Remo

PADOVA MARKET

The stallholder eyes me suspiciously. It's not that they are unfriendly, at Padova, but here it's the stallholder who does all the choosing.

The punters are well-behaved, unlike the sparkling chaos of somewhere like Sicilia's Messina. The Piazza delle Erbe, named, like so many markets, as the 'square of herbs', buzzes with a polite hum, as shoppers negotiate with stallholders over quality. Stalls in spring are groaning under the weight of asparagi, both green and white, displayed in plump bunches on tiered stands. Old, wizened men are cutting the stems and peeling the tough outer leaves off tight-headed **carciofi** (artichokes). To prevent discolouration, they are tossed into tubs of water with vinegar or lemon juice added. There are mounds of **fragole** (strawberries), wild and cultivated, fire-engine red and deliciously perfumed.

The Padova market stretches underneath a central palazzo to the Piazza delle Frutta, where – despite its name – clothes stalls dominate. All the meats, alimentari, formaggerie are inside the palazzo, along with a bakery which has been here since 1887.

Padovans seek out the country's best and tags indicate where the produce originated. A pasta shop sells **orecchiette fatto a mano**, Pugliese pasta 'made by hand'. **Speck** (smoked ham) from Alto Adige is described as 'Tirolo', prosciutto is the acclaimed Langhirano version, and **bresaola** (sliced dried meat) comes from Valtellina.

Outside, there's a man eating a pear in front of the fountain, having washed it there seconds before. He checked the prices of three stalls before he bought, and watched the quality of the pear as it was placed in a paper bag. He eats it while locals load their bikes with groceries, and swerve off up the narrow streets. Until tomorrow, when they'll be back for more fresh food. I look at the **fragole di bosco** (wild strawberries) I've bought. They taste extraordinary. I've been given the oldest punnet, but they're still fresher than anything I'd find at home. You may not be able to touch, but you always need to watch.

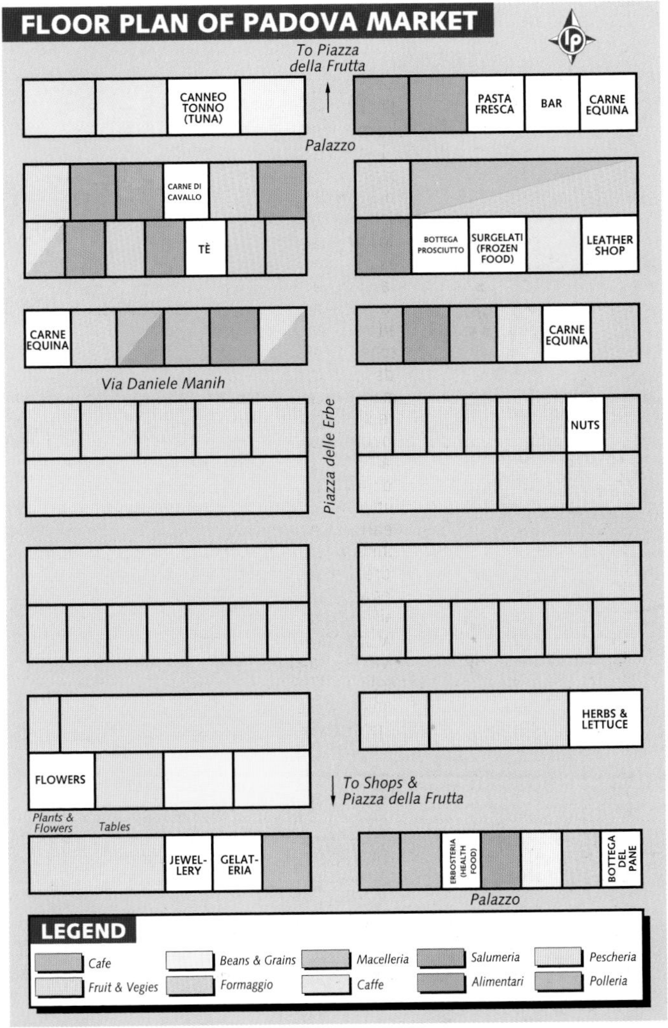

FLOOR PLAN OF PADOVA MARKET

To Piazza
della Frutta

CANNEO
TONNO
(TUNA)

PASTA
FRESCA

BAR

CARNE
EQUINA

Palazzo

CARNE DI
CAVALLO

TÈ

BOTTEGA
PROSCIUTTO

SURGELATI
(FROZEN
FOOD)

LEATHER
SHOP

CARNE
EQUINA

CARNE
EQUINA

Via Daniele Manih

Piazza delle Erbe

NUTS

HERBS &
LETTUCE

FLOWERS

To Shops &
Piazza della Frutta

Plants &
Flowers

Tables

JEWEL-
LERY

GELAT-
ERIA

ERBOSTERIA
(HEALTH
FOOD)

BOTTEGA
DEL
PANE

Palazzo

LEGEND

Cafe	Beans & Grains	Macelleria	Salumeria	Pescheria
Fruit & Vegies	Formaggio	Caffe	Alimentari	Polleria

SHOPPING

Insalata Caprese

This dish uses simple produce that you can buy at most alimentari. You'll need a sharp knife and plates. If you don't have plates, just put all the ingredients on really good white bread rolls.

Ingredients

2	large, fully ripe, vermilion-coloured tomatoes
100g	mozzarella di bufala
5–6	leaves fresh basil
	fine sea salt and freshly milled black pepper
	drizzle extra virgin olive oil

Core the tomatoes and cut into thin wedges. Slice the mozzarella as thinly as you can.

Arrange tomato and cheese slices, alternating between each, and slightly overlap them on the plate. Tear the basil leaves and scatter over the top. Sprinkle with salt and pepper, and drizzle generously with the olive oil. Serve with crusty white bread, then eat with the gusto of the Neapolitans.

Serves 2

Carpaccio

A dish of finely shaved raw beef, named after a painter whose palette the dish is supposed to emulate. It can be made with a mustard and egg yolk sauce, but the best is often a simple dressing of olive oil and lemon. To make the dish really provocative, add some of the balsamic vinegar you bought in Modena in the place of the lemon juice. To take it on a picnic, prepare the beef on a large plate and assemble the rest when you get to the destination.

For each serve, you will need

60g	prime beef fillet
½	tablespoon extra virgin olive oil
10	leaves **rucola** (rocket lettuce), washed well
5g	parmigiano reggiano, shaved with a potato peeler
½	lemon
	freshly milled black pepper
	fine sea salt

Freeze the fillet until very firm but not hard. Using a very sharp knife or a slicing machine, shave extremely thin slices of beef, laying each one on a plate as it is cut.

Allow the beef to warm to room temperature and drizzle with the oil, sprinkle with a little salt and pepper and garnish with the rocket and parmigiano.

Serve as an appetiser with the cut lemon for each guest to squeeze over the top as desired. If you use balsamic vinegar, allow 1 teaspoon per portion and sprinkle over the top before the oil.

SHOPPING

An Italian Picnic

Italians don't need an excuse to throw a picnic and can fully understand when you want to do the same. Basically any outdoor area, even sandwiched between an **autostrada** (motorway) exit ramp and a country road, can be fair game when it comes to public holidays, good weather and the need to eat outdoors.

Italian cucina is designed with the picnic in mind. Salumerie are overflowing with prosciutto, salame and **mortadella** (pork sausage), the kind of foods you can stuff into a bag, and pull out to create a fabulous meal in an instant. You can buy plain, unfilled **panini** (bread rolls) at just about any pasticceria; formaggerie sell all the finest cheeses, from the spreadable to the nutty. The best place for some preserved or prepared vegetables is often an alimentari, and a must-take is some ripe, red tomatoes.

An Italian roadside picnic, Lazio

Locals will take a football, a guitar, 20 of their best mates and all the kids on a picnic. But you can do it alone, if you like. Parks exist in every city, and offer perfect picnic spots. Some regions can be so overrun with picnickers on weekends and holidays that public picnic tables in the woods may need to be booked and paid for in advance. Rocks and grass, however, tend to come for free.

If you're really doing an authentic Italian picnic, you'll need one thing for sure and it has no substitute – the corkscrew. It is also a great social gate-opener as there are always more people wanting to open bottles outside on a sunny day than there are ways to open the bottles.

SHOPPING

Things to Take Home

You can take domestic quantities of just about every food out of Italy. The problem is where you want to take them to. Within a united Europe there are no restrictions at all, but North America and Australasia pose a problem (see the boxed text below).

QUARANTINE RULES

Australia and New Zealand have justifiably strict quarantine rules to protect their unique wildlife, and every single item of food or plant matter must be declared, even holy water. Declaring them doesn't mean they're banned, but items that won't be allowed in include: milk and milk products; raw and unroasted nuts; eggs and egg products; fresh fruit and vegetables; salmon and trout products (conditions apply); live plants (although many seeds are acceptable); and most pork and pig products. You usually won't have trouble with dried foods if they are dirt-free, so a bag of porcini secchi (dried mushrooms) should definitely find its way into your bag.

North America can pose the same difficulties as Australasia. Some fruit, vegetables and plants may be acceptable but must be declared and be free of pests. Most meat products are banned, while fresh mushrooms and truffles are okay if free of dirt. Breads and baked goods are okay, so too most confectionery, and dried foods such as rice, tea and roasted coffee. Some seeds and plant matter require permits.

SHOPPING

Food stall on the roadside in Calabria

The things you should try to take home are those that are either hard to buy where you are from or are overpriced. So **porcini** mushrooms are a must, perhaps in a dried form, or preserved in oil. Truffles (if you can bring them into your home country) are so much cheaper in Italy. A great, rare wine or olive oil may be worth carrying home, particularly those from small producers whose product would be hard to find anywhere. If you visit Modena and you're cashed up, buy up big on **aceto balsamico tradizionale di Modena**, the real balsamic vinegar, as it is very addictive, and prices can double when you leave Italy.

Many good importers now exist all over the world, importing the best, often artisan-made, Italian goods. But if you fall in love with an item while you're away, it's safer to buy it then and there.

If you don't know whether an ingredient is available at home, the best thing to do is to take a bit back so at least you can cook a favourite holiday dish once. And remember that while it's great to bring back a few choice items, if your bags are already fairly full, very little is worth paying exorbitant excess baggage rates on.

where to
eat & drink

You won't be hard pushed to find somewhere to eat in Italy. Step onto virtually any street and you'll encounter the ubiquitous bar/caffè for a snack and a drink. It's all part of the mentality of a nation that thinks of food as part of life's journey, not the end point, and not as some highlight.

Italians eat out often, mostly in cheaper places like a bar, **pizzeria** (pizza restaurant), or **osterie** (eating houses). They love to dine in **ristoranti** (restaurants) too, if they can afford it. Because most city dwellers live in fairly confined surrounds, dining out is often the best way to socialise, and if there's one thing that matters more than the meal, it is social interaction.

Lone diners are commonplace, although most are male, and it's not unusual, even for couples, to be seated at a table with others. Make the most of this, as the locals do, to get to know another soul, even if it's only briefly.

Don't be surprised if everybody smokes – there's not much you can do to stop them. A self-righteous comment to other diners is unlikely to endear you to them, or to anybody else in the restaurant for that matter. If you don't like smoke, choose your restaurants carefully.

Many, if not most, eateries don't take credit cards, although Visa is most widely accepted. There's no space to tip on credit card slips, so if you're a tipper, it's best to carry some cash in small notes. Italians don't tip too much, but it's good to pop a coin on the bar with your receipt when you go for coffee, and a few hundred lira in cash on a restaurant table when you leave. The **pane e coperto** ('bread and cover', a cover charge) is not considered part of a tip (see the boxed text Coperto).

Mobile (cellular) phones have caught on in a big way in Italy, and there is a corresponding lack of etiquette; playing with the phone, phoning friends while dining companions sit idly at the restaurant table – you know the scene. As a visitor it's good to be polite so, unless you are expecting an important call, switch off the blasted phone. And when you take that really important call in the middle of your meal, it's good manners to leave the table to talk.

COPERTO

When in restaurants, visitors occasionally find themselves in disputes over the **pane e coperto**. This is the charge you incur just for sitting down for a meal in most restaurants. Basically it's a set, nominal charge you're going to have to pay regardless of what you eat. Coperto means 'cover' and doesn't necessarily include **servizio**, the service charge, which can be an extra 15% again. While we all know that things such as bread and linen cost money, it would seem logical to include them as overheads in the prices of dishes. But that's simply not the way it's done and you won't change it by arguing that you didn't eat the bread or order any copertos.

Places to Eat & Drink

Rule number one, and the only rule worth remembering if you don't have time to read the rest of this section, is don't judge a restaurant by its decor. It's as simple as that. The most brilliant food can be served in the ugliest of surroundings.

If you want to know more, the variety, the quality, and the sheer depth and range of eating are something most countries can only dream about. While there are plenty of options on where to eat throughout Italy, the beauty is that most eateries have clearly defined roles. So all bars will serve coffee and **brioche** (pastries) as well as drinks. All osterie will provide you with a reasonable meal in unpretentious surroundings, and all pizzerie will sell you a pizza.

Because of this focus, there is a huge number of places where you can find something to eat and drink. Thankfully, each establishment doesn't try to be all things to all people, but rather concentrates on doing their (often simple) thing well.

Outdoor table, Como, Lombardia

No matter where you go, the first thing to do is show you're human and be civil. A "Buongiorno" or "Buonasera" is the basic greeting in any shop, bar or restaurant.

In a bar/caffè, you'll probably have to pay for what you want even before you order it. Look around for a cash register (often away from the bar) and keep your receipt to take to the bar with you.

In a restaurant, the usual first offer of the waiter is "**Cosa vuole da bere?**" meaning "Do you want a drink?". No matter how it sounds, it doesn't mean do you want a beer.

WHERE TO EAT & DRINK

Always keep your receipt when you pay for anything, including a meal in a restaurant, until you have left the premises. The much feared **guardia di finanzia** (financial police) are very strict and you can be charged if you don't have a receipt when you leave. So make sure you are given one ("**Ricevuta, per favore**" or "A receipt, please") and hang on to it. The business can also be fined, so it's in their interests for them to give you one.

Agriturismo

All over Italy, working farms are set up as what are known as **agriturismi**. While many sell their goods and offer a unique, very worthwhile option for accommodation, many also serve meals (some serve meals for lodgers only). Look for the characteristic green and gold signs in the country, marked with a knife and fork, and you could be eating the kind of food that the farmer's wife has been cooking for her family for years. Agriturismi are generally quite cheap, usually unrefined (but sometimes awesome), and tend to typify what is actually eaten by locals. Most are open for **cena** (dinner) only.

Bar/Caffè

The single most common place to find something to eat and drink is the bar (sometimes called a caffè bar). Bars are tremendously popular hangouts, mostly serving coffee, soft drinks, juices and alcohol. They're open from early (some from about 6am) until quite late (about 10pm). The food is essentially simple – including brioche, pre-made **panini** (bread rolls) with light fillings, and **tramezzini** (crustless sandwiches). They also serve **spuntini** (snacks) to have with drinks, such as olives, potato crisps or little slices of **frittata** (like an omelette) that you eat with toothpicks. A good bar usually has very professional staff.

Some **pasticcerie** (see the Shopping chapter) also sell coffee, but their focus is firmly on bread and pastries.

Birreria

A birreria is a bar that specialises in selling beer, usually seen in central and northern regions and often in conjunction with another title such as Caffè. In the far north, don't be surprised to see someone – okay, it'll be a man – leaning on the bar and drinking a beer for breakfast.

Frasca/Locanda

Friulian wine producers open their doors and provide a place to drink (see the Regional Variations chapter) and often sell food to fire the engine. Most are open in the evenings only, many until quite late.

SLOW FOOD

As the rest of the world has rushed to embrace fast food, Italy began to follow suit, albeit at a much slower pace. There are hamburger joints creeping into cities as there are in most countries, although we can't imagine Pizza Hut taking off. The difference with Italy is that a hamburger from a multinational actually takes far longer to serve than most of the other food you can buy. What's more, foreign chain restaurants are reputed to serve the worst coffee in the land.

Fast food as a concept doesn't sit easily with Italians and it was here that the first organised, politically active group decided to tackle the issue head on. The movement spawned Slow Food, symbolised by the snail (slow, as well as good to eat), which now has chapters worldwide. The volunteer-run chapters organise feasting and frivolity, as well as social programmes to promote good food and good wine to be consumed (slowly, of course) in good company. Slow Food Arcigola can be contacted at Via della Mendicità Istruita, 45, 12042 Bra (Cn) Italy. Phone (0172) 41 9611, fax (0172) 41 1218, or on the web at **http://www.slowfood.it**

Osteria

This is the classic eating house that in many ways epitomises Italy. Osterie (occasionally spelt hostarie) were originally family-run places for locals to drop by and have a drink, a snack and perhaps a little gamble at the end of the day. Typically this would have been a drinking hole for men. Over the years the osterie started serving food, as their customers craved more than just good company and local wine to satisfy their souls.

These days, many osterie will still serve you just a drink but their focus is on simple food relevant to their region, usually with a verbal menu.

Many osterie are open at nights only, but most open for **pranzo** (lunch) from 12.30 until 3pm, and again for cena (dinner) from 7pm until late. You can push all these times back the farther south you travel. While a few flashy (and flashily priced) ristoranti have used the name osteria to give an impression of rustic beginnings, most osterie are still relatively cheap and one of the absolute joys of dining out in Italy.

Paninoteca

Roughly translated as bread roll (panino) place (-teca), the paninoteca is really a specialist sandwich shop. Even the simplest of fillings (for example, **prosciutto**, preserved ham, with no other spreads) can be a joy to eat. Most paninoteche are open during normal daytime hours.

Pizzeria
It's self explanatory – a pizzeria sells pizze. Many pizzerie also act as **trattorie** (reasonably priced eating houses) during the day, and light the wood-fired oven for evening trade only. **Pizza a(l) taglio** means pizza by the slice, the style popularised in Roma (see Pizze in the Staples & Specialities chapter). No-one, no matter what they have visited Italy for, should miss eating real Italian pizza at least once.

Polentaria
Not often seen, it's the name of a specialist restaurant for making **polenta** (see Grains in the Staples & Specialities chapter). As polenta is a northern dish you will only see a polentaria north of Emilia-Romagna.

Ristorante beside the Canale Grande, Venice, Veneto

Ristorante
A **ristorante** (restaurant) implies an eating establishment that is more sophisticated than a trattoria or an osteria, with correspondingly higher prices. Printed menus take the place of verbal ones and flowers could be – but probably won't be – fresh instead of plastic. By definition the food should be more refined, served with more care and be matched with an equally decent wine list. As the name implies, a ristorante should also restore the body, although a mere name is no guarantee of any of this.

Outdoor tables at Piazza del Campo, Siena, Toscana

TELEPHONE ORDERS (of a different kind)

"My father is happy for you to eat here," says Giuseppe Pedroni, "but there's one problem."

We're very tired, very, very hungry, and can't believe we've made it to this brilliant osteria, out in the country near Modena, without too many navigational nightmares. But any problem now, at 8.30pm, is a big problem for us.

"You see," continues Giuseppe, "my father hates mobile phones."

We heave a sigh of relief. Yes, we do have a mobile, but it can't ring while we're in Italy. Regardless, Giuseppe will take it and put it behind the counter until we leave. In a country where mobile (cellular) phones are prolific, and the restaurant etiquette regarding them is appalling, it's nice to see someone who doesn't lower his standards.

Italo Pedroni, Giuseppe's father, is a gruff old man with a heart of gold. We'd already asked if he spoke English after he grunted instructions in a language we couldn't understand.

"No," was his answer in rough Italian, "do you speak dialect?" We don't, of course, and that is that, as far as communication is concerned, until Giuseppe appears to explain about the phone. When that's sorted, he disappears and never comes back, leaving us to his father's mutterings in dialect.

There's no menu, no wine list, no explanation of what will happen. The wine is Italo's own lambrusco, the food – some of the most memorable anywhere – just appears one dish after another, and the tension dissipates quickly as we eat. There's handmade tortellini with butter and local parmigiano reggiano cheese (made about 5km away), **tagliatelle** (pasta) with beef and liver **ragù** (sauce), caramelised roast pork, chicken simmered in lambrusco and some fried veal.

It seems we're almost too relaxed. At one point Italo's eyebrows knot as he clears the plates, and he points angrily at Alan, our photographer, gesturing that he should leave. It turns out that the light meter in a case on Alan's belt looks remarkably similar to a mobile phone. Italo thinks we've betrayed his trust.

The light meter is exposed, and Italo lets rip with a small (but significant) smile. The rest of the meal goes down as easily as the **aceto di balsamico** (balsamic vinegar) that is made in Italo's attic.

Spaghetteria

Originating from the former street-stalls of Napoli that sold bowls of spaghetti, spaghetteria are good for no-frills, delicious pasta and **secondi** ('second' or main course) at low prices. They keep normal restaurant hours but, despite the good value, they are slowly falling out of favour in Italy.

Tavola Calda

Literally a 'hot table', a tavola calda serves mostly pre-made food that you queue for, usually with a tray, cafeteria style. It isn't, however, anything like the cafeteria that most English-speaking nations know, full of drying casseroles and deep-fried food. The tavola calda is usually a showcase for the local foods, some of which are reheated to order (rarely in microwaves), along with pizza a taglio, **carni arrosti** (roasted meats) and **insalata** (salads). Most are open all day from about 11am.

FOREIGN FOOD

While Italian-style restaurants seem to have found a place in just about every other country in the world, Italians themselves seem quite content with what they have. You don't see many foreign restaurants in the country, except in the bigger cities of the north, particularly Milano. Italians are still getting to know their regions, so you're more likely to see a Sicilian restaurant than a French one, or a Tuscan grill than a Brazilian one. The most common foreign restaurant is **Cinese** (Chinese), which many younger, urban Italians visit on occasion. Their verdict is that on a good day, Cinese restaurants are pretty ordinary. Things are changing ever so slowly with immigration. The increasing African population is having some effect, so if you're after Ethiopian food, the area south of the station in Milano is quite good.

Trattoria

A trattoria is often family run, and very similar to osterie in many respects, including the reasonable prices. The cucina is less complex than in ristoranti, the service less aloof and usually more amiable, and things like finesse take a back seat to the honest and heart-warming. Really great food cannot always be guaranteed, but you'll be impressed by how often it is.

Trattoria Antichi Cancelli Via Faenza, Florence

STREET EATS

Compared to many other countries, Italy's street food is underwhelming, probably due to the number of fantastic low-cost eateries. The street food they do have absolutely everywhere is gelati, the ubiquitous Italian ice-cream that is a favourite snack food, especially in the warmer months.

In Napoli you might find the local **sorbetteria**, a mobile cart offering a refreshing, slushy drink of iced fresh lemon juice tempered with sugar. Also in Napoli the street-eating theme reaches new heights when you find the **trippa** (tripe) carts selling unbleached, fragrant trippa with slices of **testa di vitello** (slow-cooked, gelatinous veal cheeks). It seems that tastes are slowly changing and these carts are gradually disappearing. Nowadays most people can be seen eating pizza on the streets of Napoli. When you have tasted how good it is, you can fully understand.

In Sicilia, you may find roasted **fave** (broad beans) and **ceci** (chickpeas), or **arancini**, deep-fried rice balls scented with tomato and herbs. Mobile rosticcerie (rotisserie grill) vans can be found in markets, sometimes offering food on the side of the road, particularly in (but not confined to) Sardegna and central Italy. Often it is **porchetta/porceddu**

Vegetarians & Vegans

Vegetarians, at least at first glance, are abundantly catered for in Italy. Vegetarianism was unheard of until the early 1980s, probably because frequent consumption of meat was mainly for the rich anyway. But as the trend has spread, more on more restaurants provide vegetarian options. In larger cities, such as Roma and Milano, there are specialist vegetarian restaurants, although they are still a rarity.

While menus around the country carry a bounty of vegetarian food, you need to be aware of misleading names. **Cavatelli con pomodoro**, while translated as pasta with tomato, can just as easily have a meatball snuggled into it or sausage crumbled through. The simple **spaghetti alla puttanesca** may be laced with anchovies. Even the seemingly harmless **panna cotta**, the cooked cream dessert popular around the nation, is set with gelatine. Cheese, too, is virtually always made with animal rennet, so if that's on your list of no-nos, then cheese is also out.

To be sure you're only eating what you choose, see the Useful Phrases section at the beginning of the Eat Your Words chapter. Look for the word **magro** (lean) on menus, which usually implies without meat.

Vegans are in for a much tougher time. Cheese is used in small amounts everywhere, so you have to say "**senza formaggio**" (without cheese) if you

(young pig stuffed with liver, garlic and herbs) and **pollo** (chicken) that are being roasted on spits over burning wood. The meats are often sold sliced to eat at home, but the rosticceria owner will sometimes fill a panino with the fragrant morsels. Anytime that you see a van with the sign **Porchetta - cotto a legna** (pork cooked over wood), you'll not regret stopping.

In Liguria the staple street food is **farinata** (a large flat chickpea pancake). It is broken into pieces and sold on the streets, although, out of the peak tourist season, it's easier to find this wonderful nibble in restaurants.

In autumn and winter keep an eye (and a nose) out for **castagne** (chestnuts) being roasted slowly in the open. Vendors make cute paper cones and dish up split, piping-hot chestnuts to gleeful punters.

Chestnut seller, Roma, Lazio

don't want any. Virtually all **dolce** (sweets), including **gelati** (ice cream), contain eggs, milk or both, and **pasta fresca**, the fresh pasta used abundantly in some regions, including in bean soups, usually contains eggs.

In the north, olive oil, sometimes considered inherently Italian, is usually replaced with butter or lard. The south is much more vegan-friendly: pasta is usually based on water instead of eggs, and the vegetables are some of the best you will eat anywhere. A simple **pizza marinara** (see Pizza in the Staples & Specialities chapter), reaching its most perfect form in Napoli, shouldn't have a single thing from a beast.

Selecting peaches at market stall, San Remo, Liguria

Children

You'd be hard-pressed to find a children's menu in most Italian restaurants. It's not that kids aren't welcome; it's because they are *so* welcome. Local children are treated very much as adults and are taken out to dinner from a very tender age, and may even have a taste of wine while they're there. Before long, kids know most of the foods offered on an adult menu and parents tend to negotiate with their kids as to what they would like. You'll often see families order a **mezzo piatto** ('half-plate') off the menu for the smaller guests. Virtually all restaurants are perfectly comfortable tailoring a dish to meet your kid's tastes.

High chairs are available in many restaurants. The sort that attaches to the table is most practical for smaller **bambini** (babies). While children are often taken out, and the owner's kids may be seen scrambling about the room, it's expected that kids be well behaved, and disciplined if they are not.

Drinking from water fountain, Milano, Lombardia

If you're invited to someone's house, the usual thing is to ask if the children are welcome. While the presence of all generations is essential at large family gatherings, children are not always going to be comfortable at an adult meal at someone's home. Small babies are expected to come with the parents, but wildly energetic ankle-biters less so. As with all cultures, ask when you're invited and respect your host's wishes.

understanding
the menu

If you don't know your **contorni** (side dishes) from your **dolci** (desserts), ordering a meal can take a little getting used to. When you first arrive, it'll probably be only a matter of minutes before you're hungry. At least you'll be in the right place at the right time but the menu won't look like the one from your favourite Italian restaurant back home.

An Italian menu is usually displayed outside the door of the restaurant. Often, but not always, this written menu will be offered to you when you are seated. But in many cheaper, more friendly **osterie** (eating houses), you may be given a verbal list based on the written one. The staff will recommend things that are particularly good that day, and add some specials that the chef may have made because an ingredient is currently in season. While ordering verbally can seem like a financially daunting way to go, prices are based on those on the printed list that must be made available on your request. Particularly proud owners, however, can be justifiably offended if you don't trust their recommendations. Pride means that it's highly unlikely you will be ripped off most of the time.

Types of Menus
Most menus are à la carte, so you order from a standard, long list. There are also fixed-price menus known variously as **menu fisso** (fixed menu), **menu turistico** (tourist menu) and **menu di lavoro** (workers' menu). Most of the time you will have a choice of one or two dishes within a set-priced meal. The most popular term is menu turistico, which doesn't necessarily mean it's just for tourists.

There's very rarely any such thing as a separate children's menu (see Children in the Where to Eat & Drink chapter).

Reading the Menu
Numerous sections, a seemingly endless list of choices and all written in Italian – menus here can be disconcerting. (If your menu is in English, you're in a touristy area and the quality of food will falter accordingly.) Even with allowance for the language barrier, Italian waiters – who are usually helpful, courteous and understanding – are often bewildered by the way travellers order.

The best way to choose your dishes is to only pick one dish, at most, from each section. If the waiter suggests you've chosen two similar meals, say spaghetti from the primi section, and tortellini in brodo from the zuppa section, take their advice and change your order.

The Courses
The following courses are seen on menus in Italy.

Stuzzicherie
From **stuzzicare**, meaning to 'whet the appetite', this basically means antipasti, although it could imply snacks. The term is only seen occasionally on menus, but variations may be used on advertising boards outside, along with the common expression **spuntini**, meaning snacks.

Antipasti

This is the first course in a lengthy meal, and shouldn't be confused with pasta, as an antipasto *never* includes pasta. The word actually means 'before the pasta' and includes all the **salumi** (smallgoods) such as **prosciutto** or **salame**. It could be **pecorino** cheese with **fave** (broad beans), grilled **peperone** (capsicum), perhaps melted smoked **scamorza** cheese, sun-dried tomatoes with a drizzle of fine olive oil, and the like. **Bruschetta**, basically a grilled bread appetiser, is an antipasto. Antipasti appear on virtually every menu you will see in Italy.

Primi

This is the actual 'first' course of the meal proper (as opposed to the antipasti that are intended more as appetite stimulants). The classic primi for most of the country is pasta, although it could quite easily be soups. Traditionally, at home, many Italians would be fed a really large primo in the hope that they wouldn't want a secondo, because pasta is cheap. You can expect to eat pasta every day in Italy, and the hundreds of shapes and numerous sauces turn what could be monotonous into a brilliant journey of discovery. Pasta is cooked to order in virtually every restaurant so be prepared to wait the 9–10 minutes or so that it takes to cook.

Zuppe/Minestre

These are the soups, and most of the time they'll be placed under the primi heading on menus. But on occasion they are separated out. Toscana, in particular, often uses the term minestre as an alternative to primi. That's because the dominant first course in Toscana was traditionally the soup. But these soups are no slouches – they are more like stews, and usually thickened with bread. Keep an eye out for the Tuscan **ribollita**, the reboiled soup with black cabbage.

The word zuppa is used more in the south, and minestra more in the north, but both terms have travelled. Many of the other terms can be quite confusing. Pasta can mean pasta, but it can also be used in the name of a soup, such as **pasta e fagioli**, **pasta e ceci** (soups with pasta and beans and chickpeas respectively), while in Emilia-Romagna, pasta is actually called minestra. **Tortellini in brodo**, small pasta parcels in a clear broth, can often be a thoroughly filling dish with more pasta than soup.

Secondi

Here, at the business end of the menu, you'll find all the meaty, fishy things including braised meats, roasted poultry and the like. Sometimes the secondi are separated into sections such as **griglia** (the grills), **carne** (the meats) and **pesce** (fish and seafood). The most popular of these names on menus is carne, implying the meat course, even if it's seafood.

Most secondi come devoid of anything except the items listed on the menu. For example, **ossobuco con polenta** means you'll receive wonderful braised veal shin with a cornmeal paste, but there won't be a vegetable in sight. If you need something to break up the protein then you'll need a separately listed, and separately priced, contorno.

Contorni

Contorni are side-dishes. Usually they are vegetables or salad. Because a meat dish in Italy is a MEAT dish, if you want anything from a plant then you'll need to order a contorno. The most popular are **patate arrosto** (roasted potato), **spinaci** (spinach), **insalata** (salad) and **verdure miste** (mixed vegetables). Generally the vegetables will come camouflage-green in colour, cooked until they are very, very soft.

Insalata will usually come undressed and restaurants will supply the oil and vinegar to dress it. Use the vinegar first, because if you dress it with oil first the vinegar won't be able to coat the leaves, and they'll tend to be unpalatable. You will rarely, if ever, find American-style salad dressings, except in flash hotels.

Dolci/Frutta

The most popular sweet in restaurants isn't very sweet at all. Italians love to eat **frutta** (fruit) after a meal, and they're so adept they can use a knife and fork to peel and eat an orange without you so much as noticing them do it. The fruit you receive in a restaurant is rarely exotic, and tends to consist of an apple, an orange, some melon (in season) and, if you're really lucky, a piece of pineapple. In parts of Puglia they actually use the term 'frutta' to refer to all the dolci on a menu.

While frutta is a fabulous way to end an Italian meal, the dolci are often worth a look. **Panna cotta**, a gelatine-thickened, cooked cream dessert, is everywhere, usually served with caramel or chocolate sauce. **Tiramisù** (liqueur and coffee-soaked sponge with mascarpone) is also a good national sweet but even these are often bought in.

Many **trattorie** (local restaurants) offer commercial sweets which are bought frozen and kept in refrigerators you can see from the dining room. They aren't terrible, especially compared to other countries, but neither are they inspiring.

The best dolci are those made in-house.

Carte dei Vini

The wine list is something of a curiosity in a restaurant. Most often it won't be offered unless you ask for it, as most Italians still drink the **vino da casa**, the house wine. And most of the time there's nothing wrong with that.

Red capsicum

Glasses of sparkling wine

If you do see a list, often the wines are broken up into sections: **frizzante/spumante** (fizzy wines); **vini bianchi** (white wines); **vini rosati** (rosè-style wines); **vini rossi** (red wines); and **vini da dessert** (dessert wines). As well as those, some very fancy restaurants may also have other lists, including **aperitivi** (aperitifs), **liqueri** (liqueurs), **digestivi** (digestives), **grappa** (the strong, ubiquitous digestive) and **vini da contemplazione** (wines of contemplation). Local wines, of which most Italians are particularly proud, might be listed under a heading **nostrano**, meaning ours. **Esteri** refers to foreign wines, rarely seen except in the most expensive restaurants.

an italian
banquet

Nothing beats the pleasure of the communal table, especially if you're sharing your new-found culinary love affair with friends. And face it, many people would admit to knowing how to whip up some aspect of 'Italian food', such is its popularity.

Minestrone

Minestrone has more versions than cooks. Modern cooks add each vegetable at a different stage, while older cooks tend to boil everything for an eternity. But the soup should always be thick. You can change the vegetables with the seasons and always make enough to have the next day, as it only gets better.

Ingredients

300g	dried white **cannellini** beans
2	tablespoons olive oil
3	medium-sized onions, peeled and diced
2	cloves garlic, crushed
2	large carrots, peeled and diced
4–5	courgettes (zucchini), peeled and diced
3	medium-sized potato, peeled and diced
1/4	small cabbage, finely chopped
1	piece parmigiano skin, about 3cm x 5cm
2	medium-sized peeled tomatoes (tinned Italian tomatoes are okay)
2 1/2	litres chicken stock
100g	green beans, topped, tailed and cut into 1cm lengths
50g	finely broken spaghetti
	salt and pepper

Soak the white beans in water for as long as possible, up to 24 hours.

Heat the oil and gently fry the onion until a very pale gold. Add the garlic, carrot and zucchini and gently fry for about 5 minutes more.

Throw in the potato, cabbage, parmigiano skin, tomato and chicken stock. Add some salt and pepper and simmer very gently for about 1 1/2 hours.

Toss in the drained cannellini beans and cook for an hour longer or until the beans are soft.

Add the green beans and spaghetti, simmer for a further 10 minutes and serve. If you have pesto, a dob on top makes it more Ligurian.

Serves 10 as a primo

To reproduce the *authentic* Italian experience at home, switch on the fluorescent lights, buy some plastic flowers, and put the television on in the corner, just loud enough to interrupt the free-flow of conversation.

Sound horrific? Well, that's the typical **trattoria** (eating house) in Italy, and when you're there it all seems so life-affirming and extraordinary. At home, however, it's another story. The key is to turn all the good things from Italy into something special, if not exactly authentic. The beauty of doing it yourself is that you can give the experience your own stamp, make it an expression of your personality.

A LOVER'S MENU

Antipasto	Fresh figs filled with gorgonzola, wrapped in **prosciutto** (preserved meat) and grilled (to be eaten with the fingers); **Bruschetta** (grilled bread) with tomato and basil; Beef carpaccio
Primo	**Spaghetti puttanesca** (a sauce of anchovy, garlic and tomato)
Secondo	**Saltimbocca** (veal with sage and prosciutto)
Dolci	**Cantucci e vin santo** (hard biscuits with sweet wine)
Vino	Prosecco (bubbly)/Soave (white)/Amarone della Valpolicella (red)

The music could well be Luciano Pavarotti, if opera is your thing. Have the lights on low. Candles are essential, and if you're serving one of the great Italian red wines, such as Barbaresco or Amarone, open it at breakfast (just don't drink it then!). They really do need the time.

A GROUP MENU

Antipasto	Prosciutto **Pecorino e fava** (sheep milk cheese and broad beans) **Carciofi all giudea** (deep-fried artichokes)
Primo	**Tagliatelle con ragù** (pasta with meat sauce)
Secondo	Ossobuco
Dolci	Panna cotta
Vino	Lambrusco (bubbly red)/Pinot Grigio (white)/Montepulciano d'Abruzzo (red)

Ossobuco

A lipsmacking dish of slow-cooked veal shanks scented with parsley and lemon.

Ingredients

8–12	pieces ossibuchi (slices from small veal shanks including bones)
	plain flour, for dusting
30g	butter
¹/₂	tablespoon olive oil
2	medium-sized onions, finely diced
2	medium-sized carrots, diced
250ml (1 cup) dry white wine	
8	sprigs fresh thyme
1	400g tin Italian peeled tomatoes, chopped, including juices
1–2	teaspoons salt
500ml (2 cups) water or veal stock	
1	teaspoon grated lemon zest
2	tablespoons chopped parsley
2	cloves garlic, finely crushed

Dust the ossibuchi with flour, and fry in the butter and oil in a large, deep frying pan until brown. Remove and set aside.

In the same pan, gently fry the onion, then add carrot and when starting to colour, add the wine and thyme.

Reduce until nearly dry, add the meat, tomatoes, salt and water or veal stock. Cover and simmer very gently until tender, 1¹/₂–2 hours.

Five minutes before serving, add the mixed lemon, parsley and garlic. Serve with polenta or parmigiano risotto.

Serves 6

Panna cotta

Panna cotta literally means 'cooked cream'. A good panna cotta is soft and tender, innocently white and as gentle as a mother's kiss. This is the gelatine dessert that tastes too good to be this easy.

Ingredients
600ml cream (35% fat)
1½ teaspoons gelatine, dissolved in 2 tablespoons cold water
90g castor (superfine) sugar

Bring the cream to the boil, stir in the sugar and simmer for 3 minutes until the sugar dissolves.

Add the gelatine, allow to cool slightly, and strain into six individual dariole or cylindrical moulds. Allow to set in the fridge.

To serve, dip the moulds into hot water briefly to loosen, and up-end the panna cotta onto serving plates. Serve with a drizzle of caramel or chocolate sauce, or perhaps some berries.
Serves 6

If you're trying to fully reconstruct a meal the way it would happen in an Italian home, then guests will be late, but they'll bring flowers or wine. And they won't go home until the wee hours. They also won't help with the washing up, just as you won't at their house.

Keep it simple. Cook dishes that don't demand constant attention. Risotto is great for the family or a lover, so you can stir it slowly while you talk and think about life, travel and poetry. But unless you have a big kitchen, risotto isn't a good move if six of your nearest and dearest want to hear about your trip.

Maybe it'd be better to stick with a hearty soup, followed by some **ossobuco** (see recipe earlier in this chapter). In summer, try the **carpaccio** and make the **minestrone** soup with lots of fresh beans and peas, and less carrot and potato. Serve it at room temperature.

The simplest dessert would be a great **Vin Santo** wine from Toscana with a bag of **cantucci** biscuits. You dunk the cantucci in your glass and suck the wine from them, which is as much fun in a group as for two. For something a little less debauched, you could try a slippery, wobbly little **panna cotta** (see recipe).

fit & healthy

The first rule when you travel to Italy is to avoid anything that looks or smells like it'll make you sick. The intrepid traveller within doesn't need a challenged digestive system. Italians believe that the best way to avoid an upset stomach is to slurp a good dose of **grappa** or a similar fire-water after dinner. A good way to get an upset stomach, on the other hand, is to slurp too much grappa.

From the look of things, the most dangerous thing that can happen to you in Italy will happen in a shower, if all those emergency cords in bathrooms are anything to go by. Compared to that, the food is positively safe.

In fact, it's far more dangerous catching a taxi to dinner in Roma or Napoli than anything dinner can dish up. That said, here are a few tips that can keep you fighting-fit for the meals ahead.

Water

Just about all the tap water in Italy is fine to drink, but locals don't drink it, and don't recommend it to outsiders either. This is a throwback to a time when its safety couldn't be guaranteed. These days that's being over cautious. But the main reason they use bottled spring water is that it's absolutely delicious and cheap. To save money, buy your water in a supermarket rather than at a bar. It's worth carrying a litre every day, and you will be sure to drink it. If you really need to buy a drink of water outside the Colosseo on a stinking hot day, expect to be ripped off by touts.

Heat

A real concern during summer is the heat. While the sun isn't as hot as in the southern hemisphere, temperatures can soar over 40°C (100°F) in the south, particularly in August. The best approach is to do what the locals do: spend a fair amount of time sheltering indoors having a late lunch that begins about 2pm, then grab some shut-eye. If you must be out during the heat of the day, drink plenty of bottled water and always wear sunscreen.

Seafood

Seafood can bring out unexpected allergies in anybody, and the range of seafood in Italy may be a problem for some. The fish in restaurants is amazingly fresh, and there is little to fear from food poisoning if you cook it properly. Raw seafood, however, has been blamed for a few cholera outbreaks within the last two decades, and its consumption has been banned.

Safety on the Streets

Italy is, thankfully, one of the countries where women can still walk home alone after dark, though it always pays to be careful. Big towns like Napoli and Genova have seedy areas that may be fine during the day, but which shouldn't be trodden at night – just ask the locals. Because Italians are always out walking, you can regard anywhere that has many people strolling around as relatively safe. As for taxis, the fares are completely out of control, so include them when you work out how much you want to spend on meals so you can enjoy a worry-free night out.

Allergies

There are a few things to watch with Italian food when it comes to allergens. While you can usually see what's in the food you're eating, some ingredients are hidden. You can expect onion in most dishes, garlic in many. Anchovies and nuts are often crushed into sauces, and milk products are used when you wouldn't think they are. For instance, bolognese ragù can be cooked in milk, and risotti finished with cream. If you think you may be allergic to some seafood, definitely don't eat it raw, and avoid molluscs (shellfish). Nuts are also used extensively in chocolates and sweets.

Many migraine sufferers find that certain foods, such as red wine, mushrooms, or cheese can bring on an attack. If this is you, go easy on the parmigiano, note that red wine is cooked into many dishes, and those delectable black and white truffles you've been dreaming about are, sadly, virtually certain to trigger a reaction.

Diabetes

There's not much you can't tell from looking at the food on the plate. However there's a lot of hidden fat in some foods, and fat is one of the reasons why Italian food tastes so good. Despite what dietitians from around the world say about the Mediterranean diet, that ideal isn't the food eaten in many parts of modern Italy.

Pasta sauces can be quite rich, ragùs are often finished with butter, and salami are laced with lard or the like. However, meals tend to balance themselves out if you order with the fat content in mind. Perhaps go easy on the amount of parmigiano you use on top.

Many Italian beers and wines are lower in alcohol content than the New World – just check the bottle to be sure. Italians typically eat fruit after dinner, a much healthier alternative to something sickly sweet.

FIT & HEALTHY

No guide such as this can be written without the resources of the many hundreds of authors who have gone before. The following books represent some of the reading the author found most useful.

Agriturismo Guida alle Vacanze in Campagna. Annual publication by Touring Club Italiano, in Italian. A comprehensive guide to rural, working farm accommodation.

Burton Anderson's Guide to the Wines of Italy. Brilliant, compact guide to regions, varieties and producers.

Burton Anderson, *The Wine Atlas of Italy*. The very big brother (coffee table size) to Anderson's pocket guide, with pictures, maps and more information.

Pellegrino Artusi, *The Art of Eating Well*. Recent translation from the Tuscan who was considered the father of Italian middle-class gastronomy in the 19th century.

Bruno Battistotti, *Cheese: A Guide to the World of Cheese and Cheesemaking*. Good, comprehensive cheese text.

Nicolas Belfrage, *Life Beyond Lambrusco (Understanding Italian Fine Wine)*. A handy guide to wines, with a lot of cultural and social comment.

Antonio & Priscilla Carluccio, *Carluccio's Complete Italian Food*. From the owners of a London restaurant, the recipes are good as are the descriptive sections, such as on mushrooms. Comprehensive.

Carol Field, *Celebrating Italy*. A truly remarkable book celebrating the celebrations of Italy.

Marcella Hazan, *The Essentials of Classic Italian Cooking*. The must-have on any English-speaking cooks' shelf. Recipes are inspired, and Italy virtually springs to life from the pages.

Edizioni Mida (ed), *La Cucina delle Regioni d'Italia*. A series of 21 books that celebrate in dialect and Italian (and in some books English) the cooking of each region according to real cooks.

Osterie d'Italia. Annual publication by **Slow Food Editore**. The essential guide to the entrancing, casual, regional osterie of Italy. In Italian.

Renato Ratti, *Consoscere I Vini d'Italia*. Superb coverage of Italian wines from the ground to the vine and beyond. In Italian.

Ristoranti d'Italia. Annual publication by the **Accademia Italiana della Cucina**. The essential guide to more up-market restaurants, with reliable ratings and useful pointers to local delicacies. In Italian.

Maguelonne Toussaint-Samat, *History of Food*. Everything you wanted to know about the history of western food, in which Italy is totally immersed.

Italia (Yearly). Annual publication by **Gambero Rosso Editore**. The national version of a series of individual city guides to the eating in Italy. Includes shops, all levels of restaurants, etc. In Italian.

Barbara Santich, *The Original Mediterranean Cuisine*. What did Italians and others of the Mediterranean eat before tomatoes and potatoes? This book tells it all.

eat your words
language guide

Pronunciation

As transliterations give only an approximate guide to pronunciation, we've included this guide for those who want to try their hand at pronouncing Italian more like a native speaker.

Vowels

a   as the 'a' in 'art'
e   as the 'e' in 'tell'
i   as the 'i' in 'bin', but slightly longer
o   as the 'o' in 'hot' or in 'port'
u   as the 'oo' in 'book'

Consonants

c   as the 'k' in 'kick' before a, o and u;
     cas the 'ch' in 'choose' before e or i
ch   as the 'k' in 'kick'
g   as the 'g' in 'get' before a, o or u;
     as the 'j' in 'job' before e or i
h   always silent
r   a rolled sound
s   as the 's' in 'mouse' or in 'pose'
sc   as the 'sc' in 'scooter' before a, o, u and h;
     as the 'sh' in 'sheep' before e and i
z   as the 'ts' in 'its';
     as the 'dz' in 'beds'

Double Consonants

Double consonants are pronounced longer than single consonants. The vowel that precedes a double consonant is shortened and clipped.

papa   pah-pah   Pope
pappa   pup-pah   baby food

Combined Letters

gli   as the 'lli' in 'million'
gn   as the 'ny' in 'canyon'

When ci, gi and sci are followed by 'a', 'o' or 'u', the i isn't pronounced unless it has an accent (ì). Thus the name Giovanni is pronounced jo-vahn-nee.

Stress

Any syllable with an accent is stressed, as in ci-tà, otherwise stress usually falls on the second last syllable, as in spa-ghet-ti

Useful Phrases
Eating Out

restaurant
  un ri-sto-rahn-te

un ristorante

Do you speak English?
  pahr-lah ingleze?

Parla inglese?

Can you help me, please?
  pwo ah-yoo-tahr-mee, per fah-vo-re?

Può aiutarmi, per favore?

Could you speak a bit more slowly, please?
  po-tre-be par-lah-re un po pyoo
  len-tah-men-te, per fah-vo-re?

*Potrebbe parlare un pò più
  lentamente, per favore?*

Table for ..., please.
  un tah-vo-lo per ... per fah-vo-re.

Un tavolo per ..., per favore.

Just Try It!

What are they eating?
  kozah stah-no mahn-jahn-do?

Cosa stanno mangiando?

I'll try what she's/he's having.
  vo-ray kwe-lo ke stah
  mahn-jahn-do ley/loo-ee

*Vorrei quello che sta mangiando
  lei/lui.*

What's the specialty of this region?
  kwah-le e lah spe-chah-lee-tah
  dee kwes-tah re-jo-ne?

*Qual'è la specialità
  di questa regione?*

What's the speciality here?
  kwah-le lah vos-trah spe-chah-lee-ta?

Qual è la vostra specialità?

What are today's specials?
  kwah-lee so-no ee pee-yah-tee
  del jorno?

Quali sono i piatti del giorno?

What do you recommend?
  ko-zah mi kon-seel-yah?

Cosa mi consiglia?

What's that?
  ko-ze?

Cos'è?

What's in this dish?
  kwah-lee so-no lyee in-gred-yen-tee
  in kwes-to pee-yah-to?

*Quali sono gli ingredienti
  in questo piatto?*

The Menu

May I see the menu?
  po-tray ve-de-re il me-noo?

Potrei vedere il menù?

Do you have a menu in English?
  ah-ve-te un me-noo skri-to
  in in-gle-ze?

Avete un menu scritto in inglese?

I'd like the set lunch, please.
vo-ray il me-noo (del jor-no;
tu-rees-tee-ko), per fah-vo-re

Vorrei il menù (del giorno; turistico), per favore.

What does it include?
ko-zah e kom-pre-zo?

Cosa è compreso?

Does it come with salad?
lin-sah-lah-tah e kom-pre-zah?

L'insalata è compresa?

Is service included in the bill?
il ser-vit-see-yo e kom-pre-zo
nel kon-to?

Il servizio è compreso nel conto?

What is the soup of the day?
kwah-le e lah tsoo-pah/
mi-nes-trah del jor-no?

*Quale è la zuppa/
minestra del giorno?*

I'd like the set lunch, please.
vo-ray il me-noo tu-rees-ti-ko,
per fah-vo-re

Vorrei il menu turistico, per favore.

Throughout the Meal

Not too spicy please.
non tro-po pi-kahn-te, per fah-vo-re

Non troppo piccante, per favore.

I'd like ...
vo-ray ...

vorrei ...

Is that dish spicy?
kwel pee-yah-to e pi-kahn-te?

Quel piatto è piccante?

It's not hot (temperature).
non e kahl-do

Non è caldo

I didn't order this.
non o or-dee-nah-to kwes-to

Non ho ordinato questo.

I'd like something to drink.
vo-ray kwahl-ko-zah dah be-re

Vorrei qualcosa da bere.

Can I have a (beer) please?
po-so ah-ve-re oo-nah bi-rah,
per fah-vo-re?

Posso avere una birra per favore?

Please bring me ...	mi por-tah ... per fah-vo-re?	*Mi porta ... per favore?*
some water	del-ah-kwah	*dell'acqua*
some wine	del vi-no	*del vino*
some salt	del sah-le	*del sale*
some pepper	del pe-pe	*del pepe*
some bread	del pah-ne	*del pane*
an ashtray	un por-tah-che-ne-re	*un portacenere*
a cup	oo-nah that-sah	*una tazza*

a fork	oo-nah for-ke-tah	*una forchetta*
a glass	un bik-ye-re	*un bicchiere*
a knife	un kol-te-lo	*un coltello*
a napkin	un to-vahl-yo-lo	*un tovagliolo*
a plate	un pee-yah-to	*un piatto*
a spoon	un kook-yah-yo	*un cucchiaio*
a teaspoon	un kook-yah-ee-no	*un cucchiaino*
a toothpick	oo-no stoot-si-kah-den-tee	*uno stuzzicadenti*

Thank you, that was delicious.
grahts-ye, e-rah skwee-zee-to/   *Grazie, era squisito/delizioso.*
delitsyozo

Please pass on our compliments
to the chef.
por-tee per fah-vo-re i nos-tri   *Porti per favore i nostri*
kom-pli-men-tee ah-lo chef   *complimenti allo chef.*

This food is	kwes-to chee-bo e	*questo cibo è*
brilliant	e-che-len-te	*eccellente*
cold	fre-do	*freddo*
stale	stahnt-yo/vek-yo	*stantio/vecchio*
burnt	broo-chah-to	*bruciato*
undercooked	po-ko ko-to	*poco cotto*
spoiled	ah-vahr-yah-to	*avariato*

The bill, please.
il kon-to, per fah-vo-re   *Il conto, per favore.*

Let's (not) give her/him a tip.
(non) dee-yah-mo-le lah mahn-chah   *(Non) Diamole la mancia.*

You May Hear
Do you want anything to drink?
ko-zah (vwo-le/vo-le-te) dah bere?   *Cosa (vuole (sg)/volete (pl)) da bere?*

Would you like ...?
(vwo-le/vo-le-te) del...?   *(Vuole (sg)/Volete (pl)) dell'/del ...?*

Enjoy your meal!
bwon ah-pe-tee-to   *Buon appetito!*

Family Meals
You're a great cook!
say (oon kwo-ko; oo-nah kwo-kah)   *Sei (un cuoco; una cuoca)*
e-chets-yo-nah-le!   *eccezionale!*

This is brilliant!
e e-che-len-te!   *È eccellente!*

If you ever come to (Australia)
I'll cook you a local dish.
se ve-ray in (a-hu-strahlyah) ti
koo-chi-ne-ro un pee-yah-to lokahle

Se verrai in (Australia) ti
cucinerò un piatto locale.

Do you have the recipe for this?
ay lah ri-che-tah dee kwes-to
pee-yah-to?

Hai la ricetta di questo piatto?

Is this a family recipe?
kwes-tah e oo-nah ri-che-tah
dee fah-mil-yah?

Questa è una ricetta di famiglia?

I've never had a meal like this before.
non o may goos-tah-to un
pee-yah-to si-mi-le pri-mah do-rah

Non ho mai gustato un
pasto simile prima d'ora.

Could you pass the (salt) please?
pwoy pah-sahr-mee il (sah-le)
per fah-vo-re?

Puoi passarmi il (sale) per favore?

Thanks very much for the meal.
mol-te graht-sye per il pahs-to

Molte grazie per il pasto.

I really appreciate it.
lo ah-pret-sah-to mol-to

L'ho apprezzato molto.

Special Needs

I'm a vegetarian, (I don't eat meat or
dairy products).
so-no ve-je-tahr-yah-nah/o,
(non mahn-jo ne kahr-ne ne
lah-ti-chee-nee)

Sono vegetariana/o,
(non mangio nè carne nè latticini).

Do you have any vegetarian dishes?
ah-ve-te pee-yah-tee
ve-je-tahr-yah-nee?

Avete piatti vegetariani?

Does this dish have meat?
che kahr-ne in kwes-to pee-yah-to?

C'è carne in questo piatto?

Does this dish have gelatin?
kwes-to pee-yah-to kont-ye-ne
je-lah-tee-nah?

Questo piatto contiene gelatina?

Can you recommend a vegetarian dish,
please?
chi po-tre-be kon-sil-yah-re un
pee-yah-to ve-je-tahr-yah-no?

Ci potrebbe consigliare un
piatto vegetariano?

Could you cook this without meat?
po-tres-te pre-pah-rah-re kwes-to
pee-yah-to sent-sah kahr-ne?

Potreste preparare questo piatto
senza carne?

I don't eat ...	non mahn-jo	Non mangio ...
meat	lah kahr-ne	la carne
poultry	il po-lah-me	il pollame
fish	il pe-she	il pesce
seafood	i froo-tee dee mah-re	i frutti di mare
pork	il mah-yah-le	il maiale
cured meats	i sah-loo-mee	i salumi

I'd like a kosher meal.
vo-ray un pahs-to kah-sher — *Vorrei un pasto kasher.*

Is it ...?	e sent-sah ...	È senza ...?
gluten-free	gloo-ti-ne	glutine
lactose-free	lah-toz-yo	lattosio
wheat-free	froo-men-to/grah-no	frumento/grano
salt-free	sah-le	sale
sugar-free	zoo-ke-ro	zucchero
yeast-free	lee-ye-vee-to	lievito

Does it contain eggs/dairy products?
kont-ye-ne wo-vah o lah-ti-chee-nee? — *Contiene uova o latticini?*

I'm allergic to (peanuts).
so-no ah-ler-jee-ko ah (ah-rah-kee-dee) — *Sono allergico a (arachidi).*

Is this organic?
e bee-yo-lo-jee-ko? — *È biologico?*

Self Catering

Where is the nearest (market)?
do-ve il mer-kah-to pee-yoo vi-chee-no — *Dov'è il mercato più vicino?*

When does this shop open?
kwahn-do ah-pre kwe-sto ne-got-syo? — *Quando apre questo negozio?*

How much?
kwahn-to kos-tah? — *Quanto costa?*

Can I pay by credit card?
po-so pah-gah-re kon lah kahr-tah dee kre-dee-to? — *posso pagare con la carta di credito?*

Where can I find ...?
do-ve tro-vo ...? — *Dove trovo ...?*

I am looking for ...
sto cher-kahn-do ... — *Sto cercando ...*

Can I have a ...?	po-so ah-ve-re ...?	Posso avere ...?
bottle	oo-nah bo-teel-yah	una bottiglia
box	oo-nah skah-to-lah	una scatola

can	oo-nah lah-tee-nah	*una lattina*
packet	un pah-ke-to	*un pacchetto*
bag	oo-nah borsah	*una borsa*
tin of ...	un bah-rah-to-lo dee ...	*un barattolo di ...*

Can I taste it?
lo po-so ah-sah-jah-re

Lo posso assaggiare?

Where/What is the expiry date?
do-ve/kwah-le lah dah-tah dee
skah-dent-sah?

Dov'è/qual'è la data di scadenza?

How much is a kilo of (cheese)?
kwahn-to kos-tah un kee-lo-grah-mo
dee (for-mah-jo)?

*Quanto costa un kilogrammo
di (formaggio)?*

Do you have anything cheaper?
ah kwahl-ko-zah dee me-no
kos-to-zo?

Ha qualcosa di meno costoso?

Is this the best you have?
kwes-to e il mil-yo-re ke ah?

Questo è il migliore che ha?

What is the local speciality?
kwah-le lah spe-chahl-ee-tah
lo-kah-le?

Qual'è la specialità locale?

Give me (half) a kilo, please.
me ne dyah (meddso) un
kilograhmmo, per fahvore

*me ne dia (mezzo) un
kilogrammo per favore*

I'd like (six) slices of (ham).
vo-ray (say) fe-te dee (pro-shoo-to)

vorrei (sei) fette di (prosciutto)

Can I taste it?
lo po-so ah-sah-jah-re?

Lo posso assaggiare?

Can you give me a discount?
mi fah lo skon-to?

Mi fa lo sconto?

Making Your Own Meals
Where can I find ...?
do-ve po-so tro-vah-re ...?

Dove posso trovare ...?

The ingredients of this recipe are ...
lyee in-gred-yen-tee dee
kwes-tah ri-che-tah so-no ...

*Gli ingredienti di
qusta ricetta sono ...*

At the Bar
Shall we go for a drink?
ahnd-yah-mo ah pren-de-re
kwahl-ko-zah dah be-re?

*Andiamo a prendere
qualcosa da bere?*

Can I buy you a coffee?
ti off-ro kah-fe?

Ti offro caffè?

I'll buy you a drink.
ti off-ro oo-nah be-vahn-dah

Ti offro una bevanda.

It's on me.
pah-go/off-ro ee-yo

Pago/Offro io.

It's my round.
mi o-koo-po ee-yo dee kwes-te

Mi occupo io di queste.

You can get the next one.
lah pro-si-mah lah pah-gee too

La prossima la paghi tu.

Okay.
dah-kor-do; ok-ay; vah bene

D'accordo; Okay; Va bene.

Thanks, but I don't feel like it.
grahts-ye mah) non mi vah

Grazie, ma non mi va.

What would you like?
ko-zah pren-dee?

Cosa prendi?

No ice.
nee-yen-te/sent-sah gee-yah-cho

niente/senza ghiaccio

Can I have ice, please
po-so ah-ve-re del gee-yah-cho
per fah-vo-re?

*Posso avere del ghiaccio,
per favore?*

Same again, please.
fah-chah-mo il bis; un ahl-tro
per fah-vo-re

*Facciamo il bis; Un altro,
per favore.*

Cheers!
chin chin

Cin cin!

I don't drink (alcohol).
non be-vo (ahl-ko-lee-chee)

Non bevo (alcolici).

This is hitting the spot.
kwes-to e kwe-lo ke chee vwo-le

Questo è quello che ci vuole!

I'm a bit tired, I'd better get home.
so-no un po stahn-kah/o, e mel-yo
ke vah-dah ah kah-zah

*Sono un po' stanca/o, è meglio
che vada a casa.*

Where is the toilet?
do-ve so-no i ser-veet-see

Dove sono i servizi?

So, do you come here often?
vee-ye-ne/i kwee spe-so?

Vieni/e qui spesso?

I'll have a ...
pren-do oo-nah ...

Prendo una ...

I don't drink.
non be-vo

Non bevo.

Getting Attention In The Bar

I'm next!
do-po to-kah ah me! — *Dopo tocca a me!*

Excuse me!
skoo-zee — *Scusi!*

One Too Many?

Is food available here?
ser-vi-te chee-bee kwah? — *Servite cibi qua?*

I'm feeling tipsy.
mi sen-to un po bri-lah/o — *Mi sento un po' brilla/o*

I'm feeling drunk.
mi sen-to un po oo-bree-yah-kah/o — *Mi sento un po' ubriaca/o.*

I think I've had one too many.
sen-to dah-ver be-voo-to tro-po — *Sento d'aver bevuto troppo.*

I'm pissed.
so-no chu-kah/o — *Sono ciucca/o.*

I feel ill.
non mi sen-to be-ne — *Non mi sento bene.*

I feel like throwing up.
mi vee-ye-ne dah vo-mi-tah-re — *Mi viene da vomitare.*

She/He's passed out.
e sve-noo-tah/o — *È svenuta/o.*

I'm hung over.
o lah sbor-nee-yah — *Ho la sbornia.*

What did I do last night?
ko-zah o fah-to lah skor-sah no-te? — *Cosa ho fatto la scorsa notte?*

Wine

May I see the wine list, please?
mi fah ve-de-re lah lees-tah day vi-ni per fah-vo-re? — *Mi fa vedere la lista dei vini, per favore?*

What is a good year?
kwah-le oo-nah bwo-nah ah-nah-tah? — *Qual è una buona annata?*

May I taste it?
po-so de-goos-tahr-lo? — *Posso degustarlo?*

Which wine would you recommend with this dish?
kwah-le vee-no e kon-sil-yah-bee-le kon kwes-to pee-yah-to — *Quale vino è consigliabile con questo piatto?*

Can you recommend a good local wine?
chi pwo kon-sil-yah-re un
bwon vee-no lo-kah-le?

*Ci può consigliare un
buon vino locale?*

May I taste it?
lo po-so ah-sah-jah-re?

Lo posso assaggiare?

I'd like a glass of ... wine.	vo-ray un bik-ye-re dee vee-no ...	*Vorrei un bicchiere di vino ...*
red	ro-so	*rosso*
white	bee-yahn-ko	*bianco*
rosé	ro-zah-to	*rosato*

This is brilliant!
e e-che-len-te

È eccellente!

This wine has a nice/bad taste.
kwes-to vee-no ah un bwon/
kah-tee-vo sah-po-re

*Questo vino ha un buon/
cattivo sapore.*

This wine has a nice/bad colour.
kwes-to vee-no ah un bel/
broo-to ko-lo-re

*Questo vino ha un bel/
brutto colore.*

This wine is corked.
kwes-to vee-no sah dee tah-po

Questo vino sa di tappo!

very dry	mol-to se-ko	*molto secco*
dry	se-ko	*secco*
semi-dry/full	ro-ton-do	*rotondo*
fruity	ah-mah-bee-le	*amabile*
lightly sweet	dol-cheen-yo	*dolcigno*
sweet	dol-che	*dolce*
very sweet	mol-to dol-che	*molto dolce*

The definite articles (la or il, corresponding to 'the' in English) or indefinite articles (una or un, corresponding to 'a' or 'one' in English) are included with each noun. Either the definite or indefinite article has been chosen according to the way the word is most likely to be used. Just remember, la becomes una, while il becomes uno.

A

abalone	lo-re-kyah dee mah-re	l'	orecchia di mare
air-conditioning	lahr-yah kon-dits-yon-aht-ah	l'	aria condizionata
alcohol	lahl-kol	l'	alcol
ale	lah bee-rah	la	birra
almond	lah mahn-dor-lah	la	mandorla
almond milk	lord-sah-tah	l'	orzata
anchovies	le ah-choo-ge	le	acciughe
anise	lah-nee-che	l'	anice
aniseed	i se-mi dee ah-nee-che	i	semi di anice
appetiser	lahn-ti-pah-sto	l'	antipasto
apple	lah me-lah	la	mela
apricot	lahl-bi-ko-kah	l'	albicocca
arrowroot	lar-oon-do	l'	arundo
artichoke	il kahr-cho-fo	il	carciofo
asparagus	lyee ahs-pah-rah-jee	gli	asparagi
ATM	il bahn-ko-maht; lah kahs-sah ow-to-mah-tee-kah	il	Bancomat; la cassa automatica
aubergine	lah me-lahn-zahn-a	la	melanzana
au gratin	grah-tee-nah-tah/o		gratinata/o
avocado	lah-vo-kah-do	l'	avocado

B

baby's bottle	il bi-be-ron	il	biberon
bacon	lah pahn-che-tah	la	pancetta
bad	mah-le		male
to bake	kwo-che-re ahl for-no		cuocere al forno
bakery	il for-nah-yo; lah pah-ne-ter-ee-yah	il	fornaio; la panetteria
banana	lah bah-nah-nah	la	banana
to barbeque	ah-ros-ti-re ah-lah gril-yah		arrostire alla griglia
barbeque grill	lah grah-tee-ko-lah	la	graticola
barley	lor-zo	l'	orzo
basil	il bah-zee-lee-ko	il	basilico
bass	il pe-she per-see-ko	il	pesce persico
to baste	un-jere		ungere
bathroom	il bahn-yo	il	bagno
batter	lah pah-ste-lah	la	pastella
bay leaf	lah fol-yah dah-lo-ro	la	foglia d'alloro
beans	i fa-jol-ee	i	fagioli

bechamel	*lah besh-ah-me-lah*	la	besciamella
beef	*il mahn-zo*	il	manzo
beer	*lah bir-rah*	la	birra
beetroot	*lah bahr-bah-bee-ye-tol-ah*	la	barbabietola
berries	*le bah-ke*	le	bacche
best	*lah/il mil-yo-re*	la	/il migliore
better	*mil-yo-re*		migliore
bib	*il bah-vah-lee-yi-no*	il	bavaglino
big	*grahn-de; gro-sah/o*		grande; grossa/o
bill (check)	*il kon-to*	il	conto
bird	*un oo-che-lo*	un	uccello
biscuits	*i bis-ko-tee*	i	biscotti
bite	*un mor-so*	un	morso
bitter	*ah-mah-rah/o*		amara/o
black	*ne-rah/o*		nera/o
blackberries	*le mo-re*	le	more
blackcurrant	*il ri-bes ne-ro*	il	ribes nero
black olive	*lo-lee-vah ne-rah*	l'	oliva nera
black pudding	*il sahng-gwee-nah-cho*	il	sanguinaccio
black truffle	*il tahr-too-fo ne-ro*	il	tartufo nero
blanched	*sko-tah-tah/o*		scottata/o
blender	*il froo-lah-to-re*	il	frullatore
blueberry	*il mir-tee-lo*	il	mirtillo
to boil	*bo-lee-re*		bollire
boiled water	*lah-kwah bo-len-te*	l'	acqua bollente
boiling	*bo-len-te*		bollente
bone	*lo-so*	l'	osso (m)
to book	*pre-no-tah-re; ri-ser-vah-re*		prenotare; riservare
bottle	*un-ah bot-teel-yah*	una	bottiglia
bottle opener	*un ah-pri-bo-teel-ye*	un	apribottiglie
bowl	*un pee-yah-to fon-do*	un	piatto fondo
brains	*le cher-vel-lah*	le	cervella
to braise	*stu-fah-re/brah-zah-re*		stufare/brasare
braised	*brah-zah-tah/o*		brasata/o
bran	*lah kroos-kah/se-mo-lah*	la	crusca/semola
brandy	*il bren-dee*	il	brandy
brazil nut	*lah no-che del brah-zee-le*	la	noce del Brasile
bread	*il pah-ne*	il	pane
breadroll	*il pah-nee-no; lah pahn-yo-te-lah*	il	panino; la pagnottella
breadstick	*il fi-lon-chee-no*	il	filoncino
breakfast	*lah (pree-mah) ko-lahts-yo-ne*	la	(prima)colazione
bream	*lah-brah-mee-de*	l'	abramide
breast	*il pet-to*	il	petto
brisket	*lah poon-tah dee pe-to*	la	punta di petto
broad bean	*lah fah-vah*	la	fava
broth	*il bro-do*	il	brodo
to brown	*ro-zo-lah-re*		rosolare
browned	*ro-zo-lah-tah/o*		rosolata/o

English	Pronunciation		Italian
brown loaf (bread)	il pah-ne skoo-ro	il	pane scuro
Brussels sprouts	i kah-vo-li-ni dee brook-sel	i	cavolini di Bruxelles
buckwheat	il grah-no sah-rah-che-no	il	grano saraceno
to burn	broo-chah-re		bruciare
butter	il boo-ro	il	burro
buttery	boo-ro-zah/o		burrosa/o
to buy	kom-prah-re		comprare

C

English	Pronunciation		Italian
cabbage	il kah-vo-lo	il	cavolo
café	un kah-fe/bahr	un	caffè/bar
cakes	le tor-te; le pahs-te; i pahs-tee-chee-nee	le	torte; le paste; i pasticcini
calamari	i kah-lah-mah-ree	i	calamari
can (tin)	oo-nah skah-to-lah; oo-nah laht-tee-nah	una	scatola; una lattina
can opener	lah-pree-skah-to-le	l'	apriscatole (m)
candle	oo-nah kahn-de-lah	una	candela
cantaloupe	il kahn-tah-loo-po	il	cantalupo
capers	i kah-pe-ree	i	capperi
capon	il kah-po-ne	il	cappone
capsicum	il pe-pe-ro-ne	il	peperone
caramel	il kah-rah-me-lo	il	caramello
carrot	lah kah-ro-tah	la	carota
cashew	lah-kah-joo	l'	acagiù
cashier	lah kahs-ye-rah; il kahs-sye-re	la	cassiera; il cassiere
casserole	lah kah-ser-wo-lah	la	casseruola
cauliflower	il kah-vol-fee-yo-re	il	cavolfiore
caviare	il kah-vee-yah-le	il	caviale
celery	il se-dah-no	il	sedano
cereal	i che-ree-ah-lee	i	cereali
chamois	il kah-mosh-o	il	camoscio
chamomile	lah kah-mo-mee-lah	la	camomilla
to change	kahm-bee-yah-re		cambiare
change (coins)	lyee spee-cho-lee	gli	spiccioli
chanterelle	il gah-lee-nah-cho	il	gallinaccio
chard	il kahr-do	il	cardo
cheap	ah bah-so pret-so; e-ko-no-mi-kah/o	a	basso prezzo; economica/o;
check (bill)	il kon-to	il	conto
cheese	il for-mah-jo	il	formaggio
blue	bloo		blu
goat's	dee kah-prah; kah-pree-no		di capra; caprino
hard	doo-ro		duro
semi-firm	se-mee-doo-ro		semi-duro
soft	mor-bee-do		morbido
chef	il kah-pok-wo-ko	il	capocuoco/chef

English	Pronunciation		Italian
cherries	le chil-ye-je	le	ciliegie
cherry tomatoes	ee po-mo-do-ree pee-ko-lis-see-mee	i	pomodori piccolissimi
chestnut	lah kah-stahn-yah	la	castagna
chestnut flour	lah fah-ree-nah dee kah-stahn-ye	la	farina di castagne
chickpea	il che-che	il	cece
chicken	il po-lo	il	pollo
chicory	lah chi-ko-ree-yah	la	cicoria
chilli	il pe-per-on-chee-no ros-so	il	peperoncino rosso
chips	le pah-tah-tee-ne frit-te	le	patatine fritte
chocolate	il cho-ko-lah-to	il	cioccolato
to choose	shel-ye-re		scegliere
chop (meat)	lah brah-cho-lah	la	braciola
chopped (cut)	tahl-yah-tah/o		tagliata/o
chopping board	il tahl-ye-re	il	tagliere
Christmas Day	il nah-tah-le	il	Natale
Christmas Eve	lah vi-jeel-yah dee nah-tah-le	la	Vigilia di Natale
chump	il tal-yo ahl-to (kon los-so)	il	taglio alto (con l'osso)
cider	il si-dro	il	sidro
cigar	il see-gah-ro	il	sigaro
cigarette papers	le kahr-tee-ne (per see-gah-ret-te)	le	cartine (per sigarette)
cigarettes	le see-gah-ret-te	le	sigarette
cinnamon	lah kah-nel-lah	la	cannella
citrus	lah-groo-me	l'	agrume
clams	la von-go-le	le	vongole
clean	pu-lee-tah/o		pulita/o
cocktail	il kok-tail	il	cocktail
cocoa	il kah-ka-ho	il	cacao
coconut	lah no-che dee ko-ko	la	noce di cocco
cod	il bah-kah-lah	il	baccalà
coffee	il kah-fe	il	caffè
coffee grinder	il mah-chi-nah-kah-fe	il	macinacaffè
coffee machine	lah mah-ki-nah dah kah-fe	la	macchina da caffè
coin change	lyee spi-cho-lee; le mo-ne-tee-ne	gli	spiccioli; le monetine
coke (drink)	lah ko-kah	la	coca
cold (temperature)	fre-dah/o		fredda/o
–water	lah-kwah fre-dah		l' acqua (f) fredda
condiments	i kon-dee-men-tee	i	condimenti
consomme	il bro-do ri-stre-to	il	brodo ristretto
cookies	i bi-sko-tee	i	biscotti
cooking	lah ko-too-rah	la	cottura
copper pot	il pah-yo-lo	il	paiolo
corn	il grah-notoor-ko	il	granoturco
–bread	il pah-ne dee mays		pane di mais
–flakes	i fee-yo-kee dee mays		i fiocchi di mais
–meal	lah fah-ree-nah jah-lah		la farina gialla
courgette flowers	i fee-yo-ree dee zoo-kah		i fiori di zucca
courgettes	lyee zoo-kee-nee	gli	zucchini
cover charge	il ko-per-to	il	coperto

English	Pronunciation		Italian
cow	*lah moo-kah; lah vah-kah*	la	mucca; la vacca
crab	*il grahn-kyo*	il	granchio
crackling	*i chi-cho-lee*	i	ciccioli
crayfish	*lah-rah-go-stah*	l'	aragosta
cream	*lah pah-nah/kre-mah*	la	panna/crema
cress	*il kre-sho-ne*	il	crescione
croissant	*il kor-net-to*	il	cornetto
crops	*il rah-kol-to*	il	raccolto
crumb	*lah mo-lee-kah*	la	mollica
cucumber	*il che-tri-o-lo*	il	cetriolo
cup	*un-ah kop-ah/that-sah*	una	coppa/tazza
curd	*lah kahl-yah-tah*	la	cagliata
cured ham	*il pro-shoot-to kroo-do*	il	prosciutto crudo
currant	*loo-vah sool-tah-nee-nah*	l'	uva sultanina
custard	*lah kre-mah in-gle-ze*	la	crema inglese
to cut	*tahl-yah-re*		tagliare
cutlery	*le po-zah-te*	le	posate
cutlets	*le ko-to-le-te*	le	cotolette
cuttlefish	*le sep-ye*	le	seppie

D

English	Pronunciation		Italian
date (fruit)	*il dah-te-ro*	il	dattero
decaffeinated	*de-kah-fe-nah-to*		decaffeinato
to deep-fry	*fri-je-re in ah-bon-dahn-te ol-yo*		friggere in abbondante olio
deer	*un cher-vo*	un	cervo
delicatessen	*lah pit-see-ke-ree-ya/ sah-loo-me-ree-yah*	la	pizzicheria/ salumeria
delicious	*de-lit-see-yo-zah/o*		deliziosa/o
dental floss	*il fi-lo in-ter-den-tah-le*	il	filo interdentale
dessert	*il dol-che*	il	dolce
dill	*lah-ne-to*	l'	aneto
dining car	*lah kah-rot-sah ree-sto-rahn-te*	la	carrozza ristorante
dinner	*lah che-nah*	la	cena
dinner time	*lo-rah dee che-nah*	l'	ora di cena
dirty	*spor-kah/o*		sporca/o
discount	*lo skon-to*	lo	sconto
dishwashing	*lah-vah-re i pee-yah-tee*		lavare i piatti
dough	*lah pah-stah*	la	pasta
dozen	*oo-nah dod-see-nah*	una	dozzina
dressing	*il kon-dee-men-to*	il	condimento
dried	*se-kah/o; e-see-kah-tah/o*		secca/o; essiccata/o
to drink	*be-re*		bere
drink	*oon-ah be-vahn-dah*	una	bevanda
drinkable (water)	*lah-kwa po-tah-bee-le*	l'	(acqua) potabile
dry	*se-kah*		secca
duck	*un ah-nah-trah*	un'	anatra

E

each	chah-skoo-nah/o		ciascuna/o
Easter Sunday	lah do-me-ni-kah dee pas-kwah	la	Domenica di Pasqua
to eat	mahn-jah-re		mangiare
economical	ah bwon mer-kah-to		a buon mercato
eel	lang-wil-lah	l'	anguilla
eggplant	lah lah me-lahn-zah-nah	la	melanzana
... eggs	le wo-vah ...	le	uova ...
beaten	zbaht-toote		sbattute
fried	frit-te		fritte
poached	in kah-mee-chah		in camicia
scrambled	strah-paht-sah-te		strapazzate
soft-boiled	ah-lah kok		alla coque
eggs Benedict	le wo-vah ah-lah be-ne-dikt	le	uova alla Benedict
eggs florentine	le wo-vah ah-lah fee-yo-ren-tee-nah	le	uova alla fiorentina
egg white	il byahn-ko dwo-vo	il	bianco d'uovo
endive	lin-dee-vee-yah	l'	indivia
enough	ah-bah-stahn-zah		abbastanza
Enough!	bah-stah!		Basta!
excellent	bri-lahn-te; mahn-yee-fee-kah/o		brillante; magnifica/o
expensive	kah-rah/o		cara/o

F

farm	oo-nah fah-to-ree-ah	una	fattoria
farmer	un ah-gree-kol-to-re	un	agricoltore
to fast (not eat)	dee-joo-nah-re		digiunare
fat	grah-sah/o		grassa/o
fennel	il fi-nok-yo	il	finocchio
fennel seed	il se-me dee fi-nok-yo	il	seme di finocchio
fermentation	lah fer-men-taht-see-yo-ne	la	fermentazione
fig	il fee-ko	il	fico
fillet	il fi-le-to	il	filetto
first course	il pri-mo pee-yah-to	il	primo piatto
fish	il pe-she	il	pesce
—merchant	un pe-shee-ven-do-lo		un pescivendolo
—shop	lah pes-ke-ree-yah		la pescheria
—soup	lah zoo-pah dee pe-she		la zuppa di pesce
fishing	lah pes-kah	la	pesca
flank	lah no-che; il so-ko-sho	la	noce; il soccoscio
flavour	lah-ro-mah; il sah-po-re	l'	aroma; il sapore
flour	lah fah-ree-nah	la	farina
food	il chee-bo	il	cibo
—poisoning	lin-to-see-ka-zee-yo-ne		l' intossicazione
	ah-lee-men-tah-re		alimentare
—processor	il tri-tah-tu-to		il tritatutto
—scraps	lyee ah-vahn-zee dee chee-bo		gli avanzi di cibo
fork	lah for-ke-tah	la	forchetta

241

frankfurter	*il ver-stel*	il	würstel
free (of charge)	*grah-tis*		gratis
free-range	*roos-pahm-te*		ruspante
fresh	*fres-kah/o*		fresca/o
fridge	*il free-go-ree-fe-ro*	il	frigorifero
fried	*fri-tah/o*		fritta/o
frog	*lah rah-nah*	la	rana
frozen foods	*i sur-je-lah-tee*	i	surgelati
fruit	*lah froo-tah*	la	frutta
–bread	*il pahn dee froo-tah*		il pan di frutta
–cake	*lah tor-tah dee froo-tah*		la torta di frutta
–juice	*il soo-ko dee froo-tah*		il succo di frutta
–salad	*lah mah-che-don-yah*		la macedonia
to fry	*fri-je-re*		friggere
frying pan	*lah pah-de-lah*	la	padella
full	*pye-nah/o; kom-ple-tah/o*		piena/o; completa/o

G

game (wildlife)	*lah sel-vah-jee-nah/ kahch-yah-jo-ne*	la	selvaggina/ cacciagione
garlic	*lahl-yo*	l'	aglio
–press	*lah pre-sah per ahl-yo*		la pressa per aglio
garnished	*gwahr-nee-tah/o*		guarnita/o
gelatin	*lah je-lah-tee-nah*	la	gelatina
gherkin	*il che-tree-yo-lo verde; il che-tree-yo-lee-no so-tah-che-to*	il	cetriolo verde; il cetriolino sottaceto
giblets	*le ri-gahl-ye/in-ter-yo-rah*	le	rigaglie/interiora
ginger	*lo zen-ze-ro*	lo	zenzero
glass (drinking)	*un bik-ye-re*	un	bicchiere
goat	*un-ah kah-prah*	una	capra
good	*bwo-nah/o/i/e*		buona/o/i/e
goose	*lo-kah*	l'	oca
gooseberry	*loo-vah spee-nah*	l'	uva spina
grapefruit	*il pom-pel-mo*	il	pompelmo
grapes	*loo-vah*	l'	uva
to grate	*grah-too-jah-re*		grattugiare
grater	*lah grah-too-jah*	la	grattugia
gravy	*il soo-go (dee kahr-ne)*	il	sugo (di carne)
grease	*il grah-so; loon-to*	il	grasso; l'unto
green beans	*i faj-yo-lee-nee*	i	fagiolini
greengrocer	*il froo-ti-ven-do-lo*	il	fruttivendolo
greens	*le ver-doo-re*	le	verdure
grill	*lah grah-tee-ko-lah*	la	graticola
to grill	*kwo-che-re ah-lah gril-yah*		cuocere alla griglia
grocery store	*un ne-go-ze-yo dee ah-lee-men-tah-ree*	un	negozio di alimentari
grouper	*lah cher-nee-ah*	la	cernia
guinea-fowl	*lah fah-rah-o-nah*	la	faraona

| guts | le frah-tah-lee-ye | le | frattaglie |

H

hake	il nah-ze-lo	il	nasello
half done	ko-to ah me-ta		cotto a metà
halibut	lahl-ee-boot	l'	alibut
ham	il pro-shoo-to	il	prosciutto
hamburger	il me-dahl-yo-ne dee kahr-ne; lah zveet-se-rah	il	medaglione di carne; svizzera
hangover	lah choo-kah/pee-yom-bah/stop-ah	la	ciucca/piomba/stoppa
hare	lah le-pre	la	lepre
haricot bean	il faj-o-lo bee-yan-ko	il	fagiolo bianco
harvest	il rah-kol-to	il	raccolto
haunch	lah kosh-ah ;il kwahr-to	la	coscia; il quarto
to have	ah-ve-re		avere
hazelnut	lah noch-o-lah	la	nocciola
health	lah sah-loo-te	la	salute
health shop	ler-bo-ris-te-ree-yah	l'	erboristeria (f)
heart	il kwo-re	il	cuore
herbal	ahl-le er-be		alle erbe
herring	lah-reen-gah	l'	aringa
highchair	il se-jo-lee-no	il	seggiolino
honey	il mee-ye-le	il	miele
horse meat	lah kahr-ne e-kwee-nah	la	carne equina
horseradish	il rah-fah-no te-desk-o	il	rafano tedesco
hot	kahl-do		caldo
—water	lah-kwah kahl-dah		l' acqua (f) calda
hunger	lah fah-me	la	fame
to be hungry	ah-ve-re fah-me		avere fame

I

ice	il gee-yah-cho	il	ghiaccio
icecream	un je-lah-to	un	gelato
icing (frosting)	lah glah-sah	la	glassa
icing sugar	lo zoo-ke-ro ah ve-lo	lo	zucchero a velo
to infuse	fah-re un in-foo-zo	fare	un infuso
ingredient	un in-gre-dee-yen-te	un	ingrediente

J

jam	lah mahr-me-lah-tah	la	marmellata
jelly	lah jel-ah-tee-nah	la	gelatina
juice	il soo-ko	il	succo
juicer	lo sprem-yah-groo-mi	lo	spremiagrumi
juniper	il jin-e-pro	il	ginepro

K

| kebabs (skewers) | lyee spee-ye-dee-nee | gli | spiedini |

keg	un bah-ri-lot-o	un	barilotto
kettle	il bo-lee-to-re	il	bollitore
kid (goat)	il kah-pre-to	il	capretto
kidney	il re-ne	il	rene
kitchen	lah koo-chee-nah	la	cucina
kiwifruit	il ki-wi	il	kiwi
knife	un kol-te-lo	un	coltello
knuckle	lo zahm-pe-to; il pee-ye-dee-no	lo	zampetto; il piedino

L

ladle	il mes-to-lo	il	mestolo
lager	lah bee-rah kee-yah-rah	la	birra chiara
lamb	lan-yel-o	l'	agnello
lard	il lahr-do; lo stroo-to	il	lardo; lo strutto
leek	il por-o	il	porro
leg	lah zahm-pah/gahm-bah; il ko-sho-to	la	zampa/gamba; il cosciotto
legumes	i le-goo-mee	i	legumi
lemon	il li-mo-ne	il	limone
lemonade	lah lee-mo-nah-tah	la	limonata
lentil	lah len-tik-yah	la	lenticchia
lettuce	lah lah-too-gah	la	lattuga
lime	lah li-me-tah	la	limetta
liqueur	il li-kwo-re	il	liquore
liquorice	lah li-kwee-reet-see-yah	la	liquirizia
a little	un po-ko/po	un	poco/po'
liver	il fe-gah-to	il	fegato
loaf (of bread)	lah pahn-yo-tah	la	pagnotta
lobster	lah-rah-gos-tah	l'	aragosta
loin	lah lom-bah-tah; il lom-bo	la	lombata; il lombo
lunch	il prahn-zo	il	pranzo
lunchtime	lo-rah dee prahn-tso	l'	ora di pranzo
lung	il pol-mo-ne	il	polmone

M

macadamia	lah mah-kah-dah-mee-yah	la	macadamia
macaroon	lah-mah-re-to	l'	amaretto
mace	il mah-chis	il	macis
mackerel	lo sgom-bro	lo	sgombro
main course	il pee-yaht-o prin-chee-pah-le	il	piatto principale
maize	il mah-iz	il	mais
mandarin	il mahn-dah-ree-no	il	mandarino
many (a lot)	tahn-te/i		tante/i
margarine	lah mahr-gah-ree-nah	la	margarina
to marinate	mah-ri-nah-re		marinare
marjoram	lo-ree-gah-no	l'	origano
market	il mer-kah-to	il	mercato

marrow	*il mi-do-lo*	il	midollo
marzipan	*il mar-zah-pah-ne*	il	marzapane
mayonnaise	*lah mah-yo-ne-ze*	la	maionese
meal	*il pahs-to*	il	pasto
meat	*lah kahr-ne*	la	carne
–sauce	*il rah-goo*		il ragù
meatball	*lah pol-pet-ah*	la	polpetta
meatloaf	*il pol-pet-o-ne*	il	polpettone
medium rare	*non tro-po ko-tah/o*	non	troppo cotta/o
melon	*il mel-o-ne*	il	melone
menu	*il me-noo; lah lees-tah*	il	menu; la lista
meringue	*lah me-reen-gah*	la	meringa
milk	*il lah-te*	il	latte
millet	*il mil-yo*	il	miglio
mince	*lah kahr-ne tree-tah; tree-tah-re*	la	carne trita; tritare
to mince	*tree-tah-re*		tritare
mincer (meat/ vegetable)	*il tri-tah-kahr-ne/ tri-tah-ver-doo-rah*	il	tritacarne/ tritaverdura
mineral water	*la-kwah mi-ne-rah-le*	l'	acqua minerale
mint	*lah men-tah*	la	menta
mixing bowl	*il froo-lah-to-re*	il	frullatore
morel	*lah spoon-yo-lah*	la	spugnola
mortar	*il mor-tah-yo*	il	mortaio
muesli	*il mooz-lee*	il	müesli
mushrooms	*i foon-gee*	i	funghi
mussels	*le kot-se*	le	cozze
mustard	*lah sen-ah-pe/mos-tahr-dah*	la	senape/mostarda
mutton	*il mon-ton-e*	il	montone

N

napkin	*il tov-ahl-yo-lo*	il	tovagliolo
neck	*il ko-lo*	il	collo
nectarine	*lah pes-kah-no-che*	la	pescanoce
nougat	*il to-ro-ne*	il	torrone
nutcracker	*lo skee-ya-chah-no-chee*	lo	schiaccianoci
nutmeg	*lah noch-e mos-kah-tah*	la	noce moscata

O

oat	*lah-ve-nah*	l'	avena
oatmeal	*lah fah-ree-nah dah-ve-nah*	la	farina d'avena
octopus	*il po-li-po*	il	polipo
off (food)	*gwah-stah/o*		guasta/o
offal	*le in-te-ree-yo-rah*	le	interiora
oil	*lol-yo*	l'	olio (m)
olive oil	*lol-yo dee o-lee-vah*	l'	olio di oliva
extra virgin	*ek-strah ver-jee-ne*		extravergine
... olives	*le o-lee-ve ...*	le	olive ...

green	*ver-dee*		verdi
black	*ne-re*		nere
stuffed	*ri-pye-ne*		ripiene
omelette	*lah fri-tah-tah*	la	frittata
onion	*lah chee-po-lah*	la	cipolla
to open	*ah-pree-re*		aprire
orange	*un-ah-rahn-chah*	un'	arancia
–juice	*il soo-ko dah-rahn-chah*		il succo d'arancia
oregano	*lo-ree-gah-no*	l'	origano
organic	*nah-too-rah-le*		naturale
oven	*il fŏr-no*	il	forno
overcooked	*strah-ko-tah/o*		stracotta/o
ox	*il boo-we*	il	bue
oxtail	*lah ko-dah dee boo-we*	la	coda di bue
oysters	*le os-tree-ke*	le	ostriche

P

paprika	*lah pah-pree-kah*	la	paprika
parmesan	*il par-mi-jah-no*	il	parmigiano
parsley	*il pret-se-mo-lo*	il	prezzemolo
parsnip	*lah pahs-ti-nah-kah*	la	pastinaca
pastry shop	*lah pah-stee-che-ree-yah*	la	pasticceria
to pay	*pah-gah-re*		pagare
peach	*lah pes-kah*	la	pèsca
peanut	*lah-rah-kee-de*	l'	arachide
pear	*lah pe-rah*	la	pera
peeled	*pe-lah-tah/o*		pelata/o
peeler	*lah pe-lah-tree-che*	la	pelatrice
pepper	*il pe-pe*	il	pepe
pepper mill	*i mah-chee-nah-pe-pe*	i	macinapepe
perch (fish)	*il pesh-e per-see-ko*	il	pesce persico
persimmon	*il kah-kee*	il	cachi
pestle	*il pes-te-lo*	il	pestello
pheasant	*il fah-jah-no*	il	fagiano
to pickle	*me-te-re so-tah-che-to*		mettere sott'aceto
pickled	*in sah-lah-mo-yah*	in	salamoia
pickled vegetables	*i so-tah-che-tee*	i	sottaceti
pie	*il pah-sti-cho*	il	pasticcio
piece	*un pet-so*	un	pezzo
pig	*un mah-yah-le*	un	maiale
pigeon	*il pi-cho-ne*	il	piccione
pike	*il looch-o*	il	luccio
pine nuts	*ee pi-no-lee*	i	pinoli
pineapple	*lah-nah-nahs*	l'	ananas
pistachio	*il pi-stahk-yo*	il	pistacchio
pizza maker	*il pit-sah-yo-lo*	il	pizzaiolo
plain chocolate	*il chok-o-lah-to fon-den-te*	il	cioccolato fondente

plain flour	*lah fah-ree-nah*	la	farina
plate	*il pyah-to*	il	piatto
plum	*oo-nah su-zee-nah*	una	susina
to poach (eggs)	*kwo-che-re (wo-vah) in cah-mee-chah*		cuocere (uova) in camicia
pork	*il mah-yah-le*	il	maiale
–sausages	*le sahl-seech-e dee mah-yah-le*		le salsicce di maiale
–spareribs	*le kos-tee-ne dee mah-yah-le*		le costine di maiale
pot	*lah pen-to-lah*	la	pentola
potato	*lah pah-tah-tah*	la	patata
–masher	*lo skee-yah-chah-pah-tah-te*		lo schiacciapatate
poultry	*il pol-ah-me*	il	pollame
to pound	*bah-te-re*		battere
prawns	*i gahm-be-ro-nee*	i	gamberoni
preservative	*il kon-ser-vahn-te*	il	conservante
pressure cooker	*lah pen-to-lah ah pres-yo-ne*	la	pentola a pressione
price	*il pret-so*	il	prezzo
prune	*lah proon-yah*	la	prugna
public toilet	*un gah-bee-net-o; un bahn-yo*	un	gabinetto; un bagno
pudding	*il boo-dee-no*	il	budino
puff pastry	*lah pah-tah sfol-yah*	la	pasta sfoglia
pulp	*lah pol-pah*	la	polpa
pulses (vegetable)	*ee le-goo-mee*	i	legumi
pumpkin	*lah zoo-kah*	la	zucca
pure	*poor-ah/o*		pura/o

Q

quail	*lah kwahl-yah*	la	quaglia
quality	*lah kwah-lee-tah*	la	qualità

R

rabbit	*un ko-neel-yo*	un	coniglio
radish	*il rah-vah-ne-lo*	il	ravanello
raisins	*loo-vah se-kah*	l'	uva secca
rare (cooked)	*po-ko kot-o; ahl sahng-we*		poco cotto; al sangue
raspberries	*i lahm-po-nee*	i	lamponi
raw	*kroo-dah/o*		cruda/o
receipt	*lah ri-che-voo-tah*	la	ricevuta
recipe	*oo-nah ri-che-tah*	una	ricetta
to recommend	*rah-ko-mahn-dah-re; kon-seel-yah-re*		raccomandare; consigliare
red cabbage	*il kah-vo-lo ros-o*	il	cavolo rosso
red capsicum	*i pe-pe-ro-ni*	i	pepperoni
red mullet	*lah tril-yah dee skol-yo*	la	triglia di scoglio
to reserve	*fah-re oo-nah pre-no-taht-see-yo-ne*	fare	una prenotazione
reservation	*oo-nah pre-no-tat-see-yo-ne*	una	prenotazione
restaurant	*un ri-sto-rahn-te*	un	ristorante

ribs	*le kos-to-le-te*	le	costolette
rice	*il ri-zo*	il	riso
arborio	*ahr-bor-yo*		arborio
brown	*ro-zo-lah-re*		rosolare
wild	*sel-vah-tee-ko*		selvatico
ripe	*mah-too-rah/o*		matura/o
roast	*lah-ro-sto; ah-ros-tee-re*	l'	arrosto; arrostire
rocket (salad)	*lah roo-ko-lah*	la	rucola
roll	*il ro-to-lo*	il	rotolo
rolled oats	*i che-re-ah-lee pah-sah-tee*	i	cereali passati
rolling pin	*il mah-te-rel-o*	il	matterello
root	*lah rah-deech-e*	la	radice
rosemary	*il roz-mah-ree-no*	il	rosmarino
roulade	*lin-vol-tee-no*	l'	involtino
rump	*lah ku-lah-tah; il ko-do-ne*	la	culatta; il codone
rye	*lah se-gah-le*	la	segale

S

saffron	*lo zah-fe-rah-no*	lo	zafferano
sage	*la sahl-vee-yah*	la	salvia
salad	*lin-sah-lah-tah*	l'	insalata
–bowl	*lin-sah-laht-ye-rah*		l' insalatiera
salami	*il sah-loo-me*	il	salume
salmon	*il sahl-mo-ne*	il	salmone
salt	*il sah-le*	il	sale
salt mill	*il mah-chee-nah-sah-le*	il	macinasale
salty	*sah-lah-tah/o*		salata/o
sardine	*lah sahr-dee-nah/sahr-dah*	la	sardina/sarda
sauce	*lah sahl-sah*	la	salsa
saucepan	*il te-gah-me; lah kah-ser-wo-lah*	il	tegame; la casseruola
sausage	*lah sal-see-chah*	una	salsiccia
sautéed	*ro-zo-lah-tah/o in pah-del-ah*		rosolata/o in padella
savoury	*sah-po-ro-zo*		saporoso
to scald	*sko-tah-re*		scottare
scales (weighing)	*lah bi-lahn-chah*	la	bilancia
scallop	*lah kah-pah-sahn-tah*	la	cappasanta
scampi	*lyee skahm-pee*	gli	scampi
scissors	*le for-bee-chee*	le	forbici
sea	*il mah-re*	il	mare
seafood	*i froo-ti dee mah-re*	i	frutti di mare
seasoned	*kon-dee-tah/o*		condita/o
seasoning	*il kon-dee-men-to*	il	condimento
seat (chair)	*oo-nah sed-yah; un se-dee-le*	una	sedia; un sedile
second course	*il se-kon-do pee-yah-to*	il	secondo piatto
semolina	*il se-mo-lee-no*	il	semolino
service charge	*il ser-vit-see-yo*	il	servizio
sesame seed	*il se-me dee se-sah-mo*	il	seme di sesamo

shallots	*le skah-lon-ye*	le	scalogne	
shallow-fry	*fri-je-re le-je-ro*		friggere leggero	
shank	*lo steen-ko*	lo	stinco	
shark	*il pe-she-kah-ne*	il	pescecane	
sharpening stone	*lah pee-ye-trah per ah-fi-lah-re*	la	pietra per affilare	
sheep	*oo-nah pe-ko-rah*	una	pecora	
shellfish	*i mo-loos-kee/kros-tah-chay*	i	molluschi/crostacei	
sherry	*lo she-ree*	lo	sherry	
shin	*lo steen-ko*	lo	stinco	
shoulder	*lah spah-lah*	la	spalla	
shrimp	*lyee skahm-pee*	gli	scampi	
shut	*kee-yoo-zah/o*		chiusa/o	
side dishes	*i kon-tor-nee*	i	contorni	
sieve/sifter	*il se-tah-cho*	il	setaccio	
silverbeet	*lah bye-to-lah*	la	bietola	
simmer	*len-ta e-bo-lit-see-yo-ne*		lenta ebollizione	
sirloin	*il kon-tro-fee-le-to*	il	controfiletto	
skewer	*lo spee-ye-do/spee-ye-dee-no*	lo	spiedo/spiedino	
skin	*lah pe-le*	la	pelle	
–of fruit	*lah boo-chah*		la buccia	
slice	*oo-nah fet-ah*	una	fetta	
sliced	*tahl-yah-tah/o*		tagliata/o	
smell	*oon o-do-re*	un	odore	
smoke	*il foo-mo*	il	fumo	
to smoke (food)	*ah-foom-i-kah-re*		affumicare	
smoked	*ah-foo-mi-kah-to*		affumicato	
snacks	*lyee stoot-see-kee-nee*	gli	stuzzichini	
snap peas	*il pi-ze-lo ah skyo-ko*	il	pisello a schiocco	
soda water	*lah so-dah*	la	soda	
soft drink	*lah bee-bee-tah*	la	bibita	
sole (fish)	*lah sol-yo-lah*	la	sogliola	
sourdough bread	*il pah-ne ah lee-ye-vi-to nah-too-rah-le*	il	pane a lievito naturale	
soup	*lah zoo-pah*	la	zuppa	
–spoon	*il kook-yah-yo*		il cucchiaio	
sparerib	*lah kos-to-le-tah dee mah-yah-le*	la	costoletta di maiale	
sparkling wine	*lo spu-mahn-te*	lo	spumante	
spicy	*pi-kahn-te*		piccante	
spider crab	*lah grahn-che-o-lah*	la	granceola	
spinach	*lyee spee-na-chee*	gli	spinaci	
spirits (liquor)	*i li-kwo-ree*	i	liquori	
spoon	*oon koo-kyah-yo*	un	cucchiaio	
spoonful	*oo-nah ku-kyah-yah-tah*	una	cucchiaiata	
spring lamb	*lah-bahk-yo*	l'	abbacchio	
squid	*il kah-lah-mah-ro*	il	calamaro	
stale	*stahn-tee-yah/o*		stantia/o	
starch	*lah-mee-do*	l'	amido	
steak	*lah bis-te-kah*	la	bistecca	

medium rare	*non tro-po ko-tah/o*		non troppo cotta/o
rare	*po-ko kot-o; ahl sahng-we*		poco cotto; al sangue
well done	*ben ko-to*		ben cotto
to steam	*kwo-che-re ah vah-po-re*		cuocere a vapore
steep	*lin-foo-zee-yo-ne*	l'	infusione
stew	*lo stu-fah-to*	lo	stufato
stock (liquid)	*il bro-do ris-tre-to*	il	brodo ristretto
stout (beer)	*lah bi-rah skoo-rah*	la	birra scura
stove	*il for-ne-lee-no*	il	fornellino
straw	*lah kah-noo-chah*	la	cannuccia
strawberries	*le frah-go-le*	le	fragole
string beans	*i faj-yo-lee-nee*	i	fagiolini
stuffed	*fahr-chee-tah/o*		farcita/o
stuffing	*il rip-ye-no; lah fahr-chah*	il	ripieno; la farcia
sturgeon	*lo stori-yone*	lo	storione
sugar	*lo zoo-ke-ro*	lo	zucchero
–coated almonds	*i kon-fe-tee*		i confetti
sultana	*loo-vah sul-tah-nee-nah; loo-ve-tah*	l'	uva sultanina; l' uvetta
sun-dried	*i po-mo-do-ri*	i	pomodori
tomatoes	*ess-ee-kah-tee ahl sole*		essiccati al sole
sunflower oil	*lol-yo dee ji-rah-so-le*	l'	olio di girasole
supermarket	*il soo-per-mer-kah-to*	il	supermercato
sweet	*dol-che*		dolce
sweetcorn	*il grah-no-toor-ko*	il	granoturco
syrup	*lo shi-ro-po*	lo	sciroppo

T

table	*lah tah-vo-lah*	la	tavola
–companions	*i ko-men-sah-lee*		i commensali
tablecloth	*lah to-vahl-yah*	la	tovaglia
tail	*lah ko-dah*	la	coda
tarragon	*il drah-gon-che-lo*	il	dragoncello
tart (dessert/cake)	*lah kro-stah-tah*	la	crostata
taste (flavour)	*il sah-po-re*	il	sapore
tasty	*sah-po-ree-tah/o*		saporita/o
tea	*il te*	il	tè
chamomile	*lah kah-mo-mee-lah*		la camomilla
decaffeinated	*de-kah-fay-nah-to*		decaffeinato
herbal	*de-le er-be*		delle erbe
lemon	*il li-mo-ne*		il limone
milk	*il lah-te*		il latte
peppermint	*lah men-tah pi-pe-ree-tah*		la menta piperita
teaspoon	*il ku-kyah-ee-no*	il	cucchiaino
thick	*den-so; spe-so*		denso; spesso
to thicken	*le-gah-re*		legare
thirst	*lah se-te*	la	sete
thyme	*il tee-mo*	il	timo

English	Pronunciation		Italian
tin (can)	*lah skah-to-le-tah*	la	scatoletta
tin opener	*lah-pree-skah-to-le*	l'	apriscatole (m)
tip (gratuity)	*lah mahn-chah*	la	mancia
toast	*il pah-ne tos-tah-to*	il	pane tostato
toaster	*il tos-tah-pah-ne*	il	tostapane
toilet	*il gah-bi-ne-to*	il	gabinetto
−paper	*lah kahr-tah i-je-nee-kah*		la carta igienica
tomato	*il po-mo-do-ro*	il	pomodoro
−purée	*lah pah-sah-tah dee po-mo-do-ro*		la passata di pomodoro
tongs	*le mo-le*	le	molle
tongue	*lah ling-wah*	la	lingua
tonic water	*la-kwah to-nee-kah*	l'	acqua tonica
toothpicks	*lyee stoot-si-kah-den-tee*	gli	stuzzicadenti
tripe	*lah tri-pah*	la	trippa
trout	*lah tro-tah*	la	trota
truffles	*i tahr-too-fee*	i	tartufi
tuna	*il to-no*	il	tonno
turkey	*il tah-kee-no*	il	tacchino
turnip	*lah rah-pah*	la	rapa

U

| undercooked | *po-ko ko-tah/o* | | poco cotta/o |

V

vanilla	*lah vah-nil-yah*	la	vaniglia
veal	*il vi-te-lo*	il	vitello
vegetable	*la ver-doo-rah*	la	verdura
−garden	*lor-to*		l' orto
−oil	*lol-yo ve-je-tah-le*		l' olio vegetale
vegetarian	*ve-je-tahr-yahn-o*		vegetariano
venison	*il cher-vo*	il	cervo
vine	*lah vee-te*	la	vite
vinegar	*lah-che-to*	l'	aceto
balsamic	*bahl-sah-mi-ko*		balsamico
cider	*dee see-dro*		di sidro
malt	*ahl mahl-to*		al malto
wine	*dee vi-no*		di vino

W

waiter	*un-ah/un kah-mer-ye-rah/e*	una /un	cameriera/e
walnut	*lah no-che*	la	noce
warm	*tee-ye-pi-dah/o*		tiepida/o
water	*lah-kwah*	l'	acqua
−bottle/flask	*lah bo-rah-chah*		la borraccia
−no gas	*lah-kwah nah-too-rah-le*		l' acqua naturale

English	Pronunciation	Italian
–(from tap)	*lah-kwah dee roo-bee-ne-to*	l' acqua di rubinetto
–with gas	*lah-kwah gah-sah-tah*	l' acqua gassata
watermelon	*il ko-ko-me-ro*	il cocomero
wedding cake	*lah tor-tah noot-see-yah-le*	la torta nuziale
well done (cooked)	*ben ko-to*	ben cotto
wheat	*il grah-no/froo-men-to*	il grano/frumento
–germ	*il jer-me dee grah-no*	il germe di grano
to whip cream	*mon-tah-re lah pah-nah*	montare la panna
whisk	*il fru-lee-no*	il frullino
whisky	*lwis-kee*	l' whisky
white	*bee-yahn-ko*	bianco
–pudding	*il boo-dee-no bee-yahn-ko*	il budino bianco
–truffle	*il tahr-too-fo bee-yahn-ko*	il tartufo bianco
whiting	*il mer-lah-no*	il merlano
whole	*in-te-rah/o; tu-tah/o*	intera/o; tutta/o
wholemeal bread	*il pah-ne in-te-grah-le*	il pane integrale
wholewheat	*in-te-grah-le*	integrale
–flour	*lah fah-ree-nah in-te-grah-le*	la farina integrale
wild boar	*il ching-yah-le*	il cinghiale
wild greens	*ly or-tah-jee sel-vah-tee-chee*	gli ortaggi selvatici
wine	*il vee-no*	il vino
dry	*se-ko*	secco
fruity/medium	*ah-mah-bee-le*	amabile
lightly sweet	*dol-cheen-yo*	dolcigno
red	*ro-so*	rosso
semi-dry/full	*ro-ton-do*	rotondo
sweet	*dol-che*	dolce
white	*bee-yahn-ko*	bianco
very dry	*mol-to se-ko*	molto secco
very sweet	*mol-to dol-che*	molto dolce
wine tasting	*lah de-goo-staht-see-yo-ne*	la degustazione
wood	*il len-yo*	il legno
wooden spatula	*oo-nah spah-to-la dee len-yo*	una spatola di legno

Y

English	Pronunciation	Italian
yeast	*il lee-ye-vee-to*	il lievito

Z

English	Pronunciation	Italian
zucchini	*ly tsu-kee-nee*	gli zucchini
–flowers	*i fee-yo-ree dee zoo-kah*	i fiori di zucca

Italian Culinary Dictionary

In Italian, nouns always have a feminine or masculine form. With various exceptions, there are some ways to tell which form a word should take. Generally speaking, masculine forms end in 'o' and are preceded by the definite article il (the) or the indefinite article un/uno (a). Feminine forms end in 'a' and are preceded by the definite article la (the) or the indefinite article una (a).

Italian plurals are easy to spot: in general nouns and adjectives that end in o in the singular end in i in the plural while nouns and adjectives that end in a in the singular end in e in the plural. Thus il coltello (the knife) becomes i coltelli (the knives).

A

abbacchio *ah-bahk-yo* lamb – most often young, milk-fed and around two months old
–alla cacciatora *ah-lah kah-chah-to-rah* lamb casserole with garlic, rosemary, white wine, anchovies & chilli – sometimes roasted (Roma, Lazio)
–a scottadito *ah sko-tah-dee-to* lamb cutlets, covered with breadcrumbs and fried in oil (Lazio)

acciughe *ah-choo-ge* anchovies – the most popular fish in Italy – often preserved in salt (*see also* **alici**)
–a beccafico *ah be-kah-fi-ko* anchovies stuffed with parsley, garlic, grated sheep's cheese, salt, oregano, crumbled crumb and oil. They are floured and fried. (Calabria)
–ripiene *rip-ye-ne* a fish-based dish, prepared with anchovies stuffed with cheese, breadcrumbs, garlic, parsley & eggs, breaded then fried. (Liguria)

aceto *ah-che-to* vinegar – almost always wine-based
–balsamico (di Modena) *bahl-sah-mee-ko (dee mo-de-nah)* special aged vinegar (*see* the **Balsamic Vinegar** section in **Staples** for more details)

acqua *ah-kwah* water
–fredda *fred-dah* cold water
–minerale *mi-ne-rah-le* mineral water
–potabile *po-tah-bi-le* drinkable (water)

acquacotta *ah-kwah-ko-tah* a soup prepared with tomato sauce, peppers, artichokes, oil, eggs, onion, celery and bread. It's eaten with slices of bread sprinkled with beaten egg. (Grosseto, Toscana) There is a version from Siena with mushrooms.

acquapazza *ah-kwah-paht-sah* 'crazy water' – fish soup, with stale bread, tomatoes and sweet herbs (Lazio)

acqua vite *ah-kwah vee-te* (*see* **grappa**)

agghiotta di pesce spada *ahg-yo-tah dee pesh-e-spah-dah* swordfish cooked with a sauce prepared with tomatoes, potatoes, olives, capers and celery (Messina, Sicilian)

aglio *al-yo* garlic

aglio e olio *al-yo e ol-yo* simple garlic and olive oil pasta sauce (Lazio)

agnello *ahn-ye-lo* lamb
–a cutturo *ah koo-too-ro* lamb with lard, oil, sage, pasley and chilli, served on slices of bread (Abruzzo)
–ai funghi *ay foon-gi* lamb baked with oil, garlic, chilli and **cardoncelli** mushrooms served on large slices of home-made bread. (Basilicata)

–al forno *ahl for-no* tender lamb baked with garlic, potatoes, olive oil (Puglia)

–al rosmarino *ahl roz-mah-ree-no* lamb cooked with salt, garlic, leeks, olive oil, rosemary and white wine (Ciociaria, Lazio)

–alla romagnola *ahn-ye-lo ah-lah ro-mahn-yo-lah* little pieces of lamb in a sauce prepared with tomato sauce and fresh peas (Emilia-Romagna)

–da latte *dah lah-te* milk-fed very young lamb

agnoli mantovani *an-yo-li mahn-to-vah-nee* pasta stuffed with capon (game bird), and served in capon stock (Mantua, Lombardia)

agnolini *ahn-yo-lee-ni* round pasta stuffed with stewed beef, eggs, cheese, nutmeg and other ingredients, served in broth or with meat sauce (Lombardia)

agnolotti ripieni *ahn-yo-lo-ti rip-ye-ni* stuffed pasta filled with meat (braised veal, roast pork, rabbit, sausage, brain), cooked herbs, eggs and parmesan, cooked in broth but served with sauce (Piedmont)

agriturismo *ah-gree-too-riz-mo* organised farm tours, meals and accommodation

agro *ah-gro* tart, sour

agro, all' *ah-gro, ahl* oil and lemon dressing

al dente *ahl den-te* 'to the tooth' – used to describe cooked pasta and rice still slightly hard

al sangue *ahl sahng-we* rare (cooked)

albana di romagna *ahl-bah-nah dee ro-mahn-yah* dry or medium sweet white wine – the dry goes well with soups and fish-based dishes while the medium sweet with fruit and desserts (Emilia-Romagna)

albicocca *ahl-bee-ko-kah* apricot

alborella *ahl-bo-re-lah* common fresh-water fish

alcol *ahl-kol* alcohol

alici *ah-lee-chi* anchovies (*see also* **acciughe**)

–a crudo *ah kroo-do* anchovies macerated in oil, vinegar, garlic and parsley. Served with a sauce of lemon juice, oil, salt and bay leaf. (Calabria)

–all'arancia *ahl-lah-rahn-chah* anchovies arranged in layers with lemon, olives, pine nuts and baked with orange juice (Sicilia)

–all'origano *ahl-o-ree-gah-no* anchovies fried in oil with garlic, oregano, vinegar and salt (Calabria)

–arraganate *ah-lee-chi ah-rah-gah nah-te* anchovies with breadcrumbs, garlic, mint & capers, sprinkled with oregano and oil and baked (Puglia)

–'mbuttunate *m-bu-too-nah-te* fried anchovies with breadcrumbs, garlic, oil and parsley (Napoli, Campania)

alimentari *ah-lee-men-tah-ree* grocery shop

aliotide *ah-lee-o-tee-de* limpet – small shellfish

all'... *ahl* ... in the style of

alla ... *ah-lah* ... in the style of

alle ... *ah-le* ... in the style of

allo ... *ah-lo* ... in the style of

alloro *ah-lo-ro* bay leaf

amabile *ah-mah-bee-le* °in-between' – wine that is not dry or sweet

amaretti *ah-mah-re-ti* almond biscuits/cookies (macaroons)

–di San Geminiano *dee sahn je-min-yah-no* soft almond biscuits (Modena, Emilia-Romagna)

–di Sassello *dee sah-se-lo* delicious almond biscuits (Sassello, Liguria)

–sardi *sahr-dee* big almond biscuits made with almonds, egg whites and honey (Sardegna)

amaretto *ah-mah-re-to* almond flavoured liqueur

amaro *ah-mah-ro* bitter; also herbal drinks (alcoholic or non-alcoholic) taken after meals to aid digestion (**digestivo**). Some are also taken before meals as **aperativi**.

amatriciana, all' *ah-mah-tree-chah-nah, ahl* pasta sauce with a salami, tomato, capsicums and cheese base (Lazio)

ampanad *ahm-pah-nahd* pie prepared with mashed dried broad beans, boiled green vegetables and stale home-made bread (Puglia)

ananas *ah-nah-nahs* pineapple

anatra *ah-nah-trah* duck (*also* **anitra**)
 –al sale *-ahl sah-le* roast duck cooked in a crust of coarse salt. From Emilia-Romagna. (Piacenza)

angiulottus *ahn-joo-lo-tus* stuffed square pasta served with meat sauce or tomato sauce (Sardegna)

anguilla *ahn-gwi-lah* eel
 –alla fiorentina *ah-lah fyo-ren-tee-nah* baked eel (Firenze, Toscana)

anice *ah-ni-che* aniseed

anisetta *ah-ni-se-tah* aniseed; also an aniseed liqueur

anitra *ah-ni-trah* duck (*also* **anatra**)
 –all'arancia *ah-lah-rahn-chah* roasted duck sprinkled with orange juice and grappa (Toscana)

annoglia *ah-nol-yah* dry-cured pork sausage with chilli, garlic and salt (Campania)

anolini *ah-no-lee-nee* stuffed round pasta with braised beef sauce, cheese, parmesan and breadcrumbs served in broth (Emilia-Romagna)

antipasto *ahn-ti-pahs-to* appetiser which can include numerous varieties of cured meats, pickled vegetables, cheeses, etc.
 –pasquale *pah-skwah-le* Easter dish prepared with green salad, hard-boiled eggs, salted and smoked ricotta, dry-cured pork sausage or capocollo (Campania)

aperitivo *ah-pe-ree-tee-vo* an alcoholic drink taken before a meal to stimulate the appetite

aprire *ah-pree-re* to open

apribottiglie *ah-pri-bot-teel-ye* bottle opener

apriscatole *ah-pri-skah-to-le* can opener

aragosta *ah-rah-go-stah* lobster/crayfish

arancia *ah-rahn-chah* orange

arancini *ah-rahn-chee-nee* large rice-balls stuffed with a rich meat sauce, usually eaten as a starter (Sicilia)

aranzada *ah-rahnt-sah-dah* almond nougat (Sardegna)

arborio *ahr-bo-ree-yo* short grain rice ideal for **risotto**

aringa *ah-ring-ga* herring

arista *ah-ri-stah* loin – generally pork
 –alla fiorentina *ah-lah fyo-ren-tee-nah* loin baked with rosemary, fennel seed and garlic (Firenze, Toscana)

aroma *ah-ro-mah* aroma

aromatico *ah-ro-mah-tee-ko* aromatic

aromi *ah-ro-mee* herbs

arrabbiata, all' *ah-rah-bee-yah-tah, ahl* 'angry-style', spicy tomato and chilli sauce

arrosticini *ah-ros-tee-chee-nee* skewered and roasted meat – often lamb

arrostire *ah-ros-tee-re* to roast

arrostire alla griglia *ahr-ros-ti-re ahl-gril-yah* to barbeque

arrosto *ah-ro-sto* roasted

artigianale *ahr-ti-jah-nah-le* home-made

asiago *ahz-yah-go* hard white cheese (Veneto)
 –d'Allevo *dah-le-vo* sweet, medium-fat
 –mezzano *med-sah-no* matured for three to eight months
 –pressato *press-ah-to* delicate cheese matured for 20 to 40 days

–stravecchio *strah-vek-yo* matured for at least two years

–vecchio *vek-yo* matured for nine to 18 months

asino *ah-zee-no* donkey – not very common meat

asparago/i *ah-spah-rah-go/jee* asparagus

–alla bassanese *ah-spah-rah-jee ah-lah bah-sah-ne-ze* white asparagus steamed and served with hard-boiled eggs; each diner prepares their own sauce by mixing eggs, salt, pepper, olive oil, lemon and vinegar, and dips the asparagus into it. The white asparagus of Bassano are a specialty and have a **DOC**.

aspretto/aspro *ah-spre-to/ah-spro* sour

assaggio *ah-sah-jo* a taste

avanzi *ah-vahn-zee* left-overs

B

babà *bah-bah* traditional sweet made with flour, sugar, salt, milk and sultanas (Campania)

baccalà *bah-kah-lah* dried salted cod used extensively throughout Italy

–alla napoletana *ah-lah nah-po-le-tah-nah* dried cod stew (Campania)

–alla pizzaiola *ah-lah pit-sah-yo-lah* with a tomato sauce (Lazio)

–alla romana *ah-lah ro-mah-nah* with a tomato sauce, raisins and pine nuts (Lazio)

–alla vicentina *ah-lah vich-en-tee-nah* cooked in milk and served with polenta (Vicenza, Veneto)

–mantecato *mahn-te-kah-to* puréed cod boiled and stewed – usually served with polenta (Veneto)

baci *bah-chee* 'kisses'; type of chocolate; can also be a pastry or biscuit

bagna caòda *bahn-yah ka-o-dah* fondue-style dish where diners dip cooked and raw vegetables into a central pot of sizzling oil, butter, garlic and melted anchovies sometimes a glass of red wine is added. Often each diner has their own sizzling pot. (Piedmonte)

bagnet (piemontese) *bahn-yet (pye-mon-te-ze)* sauce served with boiled meat (Piemonte)

–ross *ross* cooked sauce with garlic, carrots, onion, tomato, red wine, sugar, salt and chilli

–vert *vert* cold sauce parsley, garlic, anchovies, breadcrumbs, vinegar and olive oil

bagnetto verde *bahn-ye-to ver-de* parsley and garlic sauce

bagnomaria *bahn-yo-mah-ree-ah* bain-marie, method of double boiling

balsamico *bahl-sah-mee-ko (see* aceto balsamico)

barbabietola *bahr-bah-bee-ye-tol-ah* beetroot

Barbaresco *bahr-bah-res-ko* popular dry red wine made from **nebbiolo** grapes, suits roasts and ripe cheeses (Piemonte)

Barbera *bahr-be-rah* dark red grapes; also an excellent red wine (Piemonte)

Bardolino *bahr-do-lee-no* light red wine – excellent with light meals and soft cheeses (Veneto)

Barolo *bah-ro-lo* the most respected, and often expensive, Italian red wine, made from **nebbiolo** grapes (Piemonte)

basilico *bah-zee-lee-ko* basil

batsoà *baht-so-ah* boned, boiled and fried pig's trotters (Piedmont)

battuto *bah-too-to* soup or meat seasoning prepared with lard, celery, onion, garlic, carrots and parsley

bavetta *bah-ve-tah* long, thick pasta

bel paese *bel pah-ye-ze* soft creamy cheese

ben cotto *ben ko-to* well done (cooked)

bere *be-re* to drink

besciamella *besh-ah-mel-lah* bechamel sauce

bescó'cc *besk-och* boiled and baked biscuits almond biscuits soaked in grappa (Lombardia)

bevanda *be-vahn-dah* drink

bianchetti *byahn-ke-ti* whitebait; very small and delicate white fish, such as anchovies or sardines, fried in oil – can be served hot or cold (Liguria)

bianco *byahn-ko* white

bianco d'uovo *byahn-ko dwo-vo* egg white

bicchiere *bik-ye-re* glass (drinking)

biferno rosso *bee-fer-no ros-o* red wine – goes well with salami, first courses, lamb and pork (Molise)

bigné *bin-ye* cream puff
  –di San Giuseppe *dee sahn joo-ze-pe* fried cream puffs with custard and sprinkled with icing sugar (Lazio)

bigoli *bi-go-li* thick wholemeal flour spaghetti
  –con l'anatra *kon lahn-ah-trah* cooked in duck broth and served with a sauce prepared with duck's giblets (Vicenza, Veneto)

birra *bir-rah* beer
  –alla spina *ahl-spee-nah* tap beer

biscló'la *bish-o-lah* cake similar to **panettone** studded with nuts, hazelnuts, dried figs and raisins

biscotti *bis-ko-ti* biscuits
  –di Prato *dee prah-to* tasty almond and pine-seed biscuits soaked in **vin santo** (Prato, Toscana)

biscó'cc *bisk-och (see* **bescó'cc***)*

bisi *bi-zi* peas (Veneto)

bistecca *bis-te-kah* steak
  –alla fiorentina *ah-lah fyo-ren-tee-nah* very tasty and thick loin steak with its bone – must be hung for 5 days before cooking and is usually grilled and eaten rare (Firenze, Toscana)

bitto *bi-to* cheese produced in limited quantities from cow's milk. Buttery, pleasing and delicate-tasting. The more mature variety (two to three years) is used as a seasoning. (Valtellina)

blanc manger *blahnk mahn-je* a sweet white dessert made with milk, sugar and vanilla (Valle d'Aosta)

bocconcini *bo-kon-chee-nee* can refer to anything bite-sized – usually meat or cheese
  –di carne alla genovese *dee kahr-ne ah-lah jen-o-ve-ze* beef stew prepared with onion, oil and white wine – also used as a pasta sauce. This dish comes from Campania but has Ligurian origins – it seems that Ligurian seafarers prepared this speciality on the quays of the port of Napoli.

boghe in scabescio *bo-ge in skah-besh-o* floured fish marinated in vinegar with onion, garlic, sage and parsley, and browned in oil (Liguria)

boleto *bo-le-to* large family of mushrooms

bollente *bo-len-te* boiling

bollire *bo-lee-re* to boil

bollito *bo-lee-to* boiled

bollito (Bú'ì) *bo-lee-to (boo-ee)* mixed boiled meat served with various sauces – usually seven kinds of meat are used: veal, chicken, beef, capon, cotechino, sausage and rump, although other types of meat can be added (Piedmont)
  –misto *mis-to* selection of boiled meats cooked in broth and served with various sauces
  –misto modenese *mis-to mo-de-ne-ze* prepared with beef, pig's trotter, calf's tongue, capon, **cotechino** and other kinds of boiled meat – usually served with **salsa verde**, **Mostarda di Cremona** or **peperonata**

bomba di riso *bom-bah dee ri-zo* baked rice with stewed pigeon, eggs, mushrooms, truffles and sausage (Emilia-Romagna) bomba di riso alla lunigianese *bom-bah dee ri-zo ah-lah loo-nee-jah-ne-ze* rice **timballo** stuffed with pigeon meat wrapped in chards (Toscana)

bombas *bom-bahs* meatballs prepared with veal, parsley, eggs, garlic, breadcrumbs and stewed in tomato, onion and oil (Sardegna)

bonèt *bo-net* baked pudding made with milk, eggs, macaroons, sugar, cocoa, coffee, **Marsala** and rum (Piedmonte)

borlotti *bor-lo-tee* (see **fagioli**)

bosco *boss-ko* forest; wild

bostrengo *bo-streng-go* a cake prepared with boiled rice, chocolate, sugar, spices and pine nuts (Pesaro, Marche)

bottega *bo-te-gah* shop

bottiglia *bot-teel-yah* bottle

boudin *boo-den* blood sausage made with potatoes, lard and pig's blood, (Valle d'Aosta)

bra *brah* mild cheese

bracioloa *brah-cho-lah* chop/cutlet

braciolone napoletano *brah-cho-lo-ne nah-po-le-tah-no* large steak rolled and filled with bacon, **provolone**, hard-boiled eggs, raisins, pine nuts, parsley, marjoram & pepper, cooked in a tomato sauce (Napoli, Campania)

branzi *brahn-zee* delicious soft table cheese

branzino *brahn-zee-no* sea bass

brasare *brah-zah-re* to cook slowly

brasato *brah-zah-to* beef marinated in red wine and spices and stewed for a long time (Lombardia)
  –al barolo *ahl bah-ro-lo* local beef marinated in an aged **Barolo** wine and spices then slowly cooked with tomatoes, onion, carrots, celery, meat stock and the marinade – served with the sauce and either polenta or mashed potatoes (Piedmonte)

bresaola *bre-zah-o-lah* traditional starter made with beef (but also horse meat) which is pickled, air-dried and matured. It's sliced and seasoned with oil, lemon and pepper. (Valtellina, Lombardia)

brioche *bree-osh* breakfast pastry

broccoli *bro-ko-li* broccoli
  –nera *ne-ra* dark purple broccoli

brochat *brosh-ah* sweet, thick cream made with milk, wine and sugar – eaten with rye bread (Valle d'Aosta)

brodetto *bro-de-to* fish soup – the most common fish soup is prepared with Adriatic fish cooked with onion and herbs (Veneto)
  –all'anconetana *ah-lahn-ko-ne-tah-nah* fish soup made with many kinds of Adriatic fish, and tomato, prepared in a casserole (Ancona, Marche)
  –gradese *grah-de-ze* fish dish with angler and scorpion fish cooked with oil, garlic, vinegar and pepper (Friuli)

brodo *bro-do* broth

brôs *bross* an unusual creamy and cheesy paste made by putting older cheese with oil, vinegar, pepper, salt, **grappa**, garlic, herbs and spices into a terracotta jar and fermenting it for a month (Piedmont)

brunello di Montalcino *broo-ne-lo dee mon-tahl-chee-no* type of grape; also a popular red wine (Toscano)

bruscandoli *broo-skan-do-lee* hops

bruschetta *bru-ske-tah* stale bread sliced, toasted, sprinkled with garlic, and flavoured with salt, pepper and olive oil. Sometimes tomatoes, wild fennel and oregano are added.

bruscitt *bru-shit* lean beef cut into pieces, cooked with lard, butter, fennel seeds and red wine, and served with fresh polenta or mashed potatoes (Varese, Lombardia) brut *broot* dry, of wine

brutti ma buoni *broo-tee mah bwon-ee* 'ugly but good' – hazelnut macaroons

bucatini *boo-kah-tee-nee* long hollow tubes of pasta

buccellato di Lucca *bu-che-lah-to dee lu-kah* traditional ring-shaped cake made with sultanas, candied citrus and aniseed (Lucca, Toscana)

buccia *boo-chah* peel, rind

budellaccia vergini su la gratella *bu-de-lahch-ah ver-jee-nee su lah grah-te-lah* smoked pig's giblets flavoured with spices, fennel seed, salt and then grilled (Umbria)

budino *boo-dee-no* pudding
 –del prete *del prete* pudding prepared with chopped candied almonds and eggs (Trentino Alto-Adige)
 –di ricotta *dee ri-ko-tah* pudding made of lemon-flavoured **ricotta** cheese, eggs and sugar (Lazio)

bugie *boo-jee-ye* 'lies', small ribbons of sweet pastry covered with sugar

buono/a *bwo-no/nah* good

buongustaio *bwon-goo-stah-yo* connoisseur/gourmand

burrata *boo-rah-tah* fresh **mozzarella** cheese filled with other fresh cheese and fresh cream, wrapped in green asphodel leaves

burrida *bu-ree-dah* fish-soup served with an oil, minced nut, vinegar and spice sauce (Sardegna)
 –di pesce alla ligure *dee pesh-e ah-lah lee-gu-re* stewed fish with tomatoes, oil, garlic, celery, carrots, anchovies and dried mushrooms (Liguria)

burro *boo-ro* butter

burtléina *boort-le-ee-nah* little omelette prepared with water, flour, lard and onion, served with salami (Piacenza, Emilia-Romagna)

busecca *bu-ze-kah* tripe – generally cut into thin strips and stewed with beans (Milano, Lombardia)

busechina *bu-ze-kee-nah* dessert of boiled chestnuts cooked in white wine, milk and cream – prepared for All Souls' Day (Milano, Lombardia)

bussolà vicentino *bu-so-lah vi-chen-tee-no* dessert prepared with chocolate, pine nuts, candied citron, pepper, cinnamon and nutmeg (Vicenza, Veneto)

bustrengo *bu-streng-go* sweet pastry with pine nuts, apples, nuts, lemon peel and sugar (Emilia-Romagna)

C

cacao *kah-ka-ho* cocoa

cacciagione *kahch-yah-jo-ne* large game

caciotta *kah-cho-tah* semi-soft mild cheese

cacciucco (alla livornese) *kah-choo-ko (ah-lah li-vor-ne-ze)* fish soup prepared with at least five kinds of fish cooked with onion, oil, red pepper, tomato, garlic and red wine (Livorno, Toscana)

cachi *kah-ki* persimmon

cacio *kah-cho* name for cheese in general; also a creamy cheese

caciocavallo *kah-cho-kah-vah-lo* hard cow's milk cheese (Campania)

cacioricotta *kah-cho-ree-kot-ah* home-made cake prepared with sheep's milk curd, coffee & lemon peel (Abruzzo)

caciotta *kah-cho-tah* sheep's milk cheese; also can refer to any cheese

caciuni *kah-choo-ni* like big **ravioli** stuffed with egg-yolks, sheep's cheese, other cheese, sugar and lemon peel (Marche)

caffè *kah-fe* coffee (*see* also the **Coffee** section in the **Drinks** chapter)
 –alla valdostana *ah-lah vahl-do-stah-nah* coffee prepared with **grappa**, lemon peel and spices (Valle d'Aosta)
 –americano *ah-me-ri-kah-no* long and black

–corretto *ko-re-to* coffee with a dash of liqueur – usually taken after meals

–doppio *dop-yo* long and black

–espresso *es-pre-so* very strong black coffee served in small cups and drunk at any time of the day

–macchiato *mahk-yah-to* strong coffee with a drop of milk

–ristretto *ri-stre-to* very concentrated coffee – the strongest!

caffellatte *kah-fe-lah-te* coffee with milk – only drunk for breakfast

calamari *kah-lah-mah-ree* calamari, squid

caldo *kahl-do* hot

calhiettes tradizionali *kahl-yet trah-dits-yo-nah-lee* mixture of raw grated potatoes, left-over meat, minced lard, onion, flour and eggs mixed and boiled – normally used to prepare dumplings and omelettes (Piedmont, Turin)

calzone *kahl-zo-ne* small flat bread made with two thin sheets of pasta stuffed with any number of ingredients, fried or baked. Commonly stuffed with minced pork, eggs and cheese or tomatoes and anchovies. (Puglia)

–di scarole *dee skah-ro-le* small tasty fried **calzoni** stuffed with prickly lettuce, salt, vinegar, oil, anchovies and olives (Napoli, Campania)

–di verdura *dee ver-doo-rah* stuffed with boiled and sautéed chards or endive, chilli and black olives and then baked (Basilicata)

–mbuttunato *m-bu-too-nah-to* stuffed with grated cheese, **ricotta**, **provola**, sausage and crackling

–napoletano *nah-po-le-tah-no* this variety is a kind of pizza stuffed with **mozzarella**, ham, **ricotta** and parmesan, then baked (Napoli)

camomilla *kah-mo-mil-lah* chamomile

camoscio *kah-mosh-o* chamois – type of venison

–in salmì *in sahl-mee* chamois' leg cooked in **salmì** – a marinade prepared with spices and sometimes wine (Lombardia)

campari *kahm-pah-ree* herb-based alcoholic drink normally mixed and used as an **aperitivo**

canederli *kah-ne-der-li* big dumplings made with stale bread, **speck** and other ingredients such as cheese, liver or dried prunes. Served in broth or in stews. (Trentino Alto-Adige)

cannaroni *kah-nah-ro-nee* long and quite big pasta tubes

cannella *kah-ne-lah* cinnamon

cannellini *kah-ne-lee-nee* (see **fagioli**)

cannelloni *kah-ne-lo-ni* stuffed tubes of pasta filled with spinach, minced roast veal, ham, eggs, parmesan, salt, pepper and nutmeg baked with meat sauce, butter, bechamel sauce and grated parmesan (Cuneo, Piedmont)

–alla Barbaroux *ah-lah bahr-bah-roo* crêpes filled with minced roast veal, ham, cheese and eggs baked with bechamel (Piedmont)

cannoli (ripieni) *kah-no-li (rip-ye-nee)* sweet pastry tubes with a rich filling made with sugar, candied fruit, sweet **ricotta** and other ingredients (Sicilia)

Cannonau *kah-no-now* type of grape; also a dry or sweet red wine (Sardegna)

canonsei *kah-non-sey* (see **casoncelli**)

cantarello *kahn-tah-re-lo* chanterelle mushrooms – very popular

cantina *kahn-tee-nah* cellar

cantucci *kahn-tu-chee* crunchy hard biscuits made with aniseed and almonds and, by tradition, served with **Vin Santo** (Toscana)

capasante *kah-pah-sahn-te* scallops

capocollo *kah-po-ko-lo* dry-cured pork sausage made with pork neck and shoulder, salted and washed with red wine. It's flavoured with pepper and chilli and matured for at least three months. It can also be smoked, before maturing. (Calabria and Puglia)

caponata *kah-po-nah-tah* starter, prepared with vegetables (celery, cauliflower, spinach, aubergines, onions, tomatoes, peppers, endive, olives) cooked in oil and vinegar, served with olives, anchovies and capers (Sicilia)

cappellacci di zucca *kah-pe-lah-chi dee tsoo-kah* stuffed small pasta, filled with pumpkin and parmesan (Ferrara, Emilia-Romagna)

cappelletti *kah-pe-le-tee* similar to **tortellini**, only larger. Stuffed with sheep's cheese, **ricotta**, breadcrumbs, eggs, nutmeg, lemon peel and cloves and served with meat stock. (Emilia-Romagna) They can also be stuffed with roast pork, capon, ox marrow, cinnamon and other spices (Marche)

cappelli d'angelo *kah-pe-lee dahn-je-lee* 'angel's hair', long thin strands of pasta

cappello da prete *kah-pe-lo dah pre-te* lower part of the pig's trotter, boiled and served with **salsa verde** or mustard (Parma, Emilia-Romagna)

capperi *kah-pe-ri* capers

cappon magro *kah-pon mah-gro* salad prepared with vegetables (carrots, potatoes, cabbage, French beans and celery), fish and shellfish, dressed with a rich green sauce prepared with hard-boiled eggs, olives, garlic, pine nuts, parsley, oil and vinegar (Liguria)

cappone *kah-po-ne* capon (game bird)

cappuccino *kah-pu-chee-no* coffee prepared with milk, served with a lot of froth and sprinkled with cocoa – considered a morning drink by Italians. It's named after the Capuchin monks who wore robes of chocolate and cream colours.

capra *kah-prah* goat; also goat's cheese

caprese *kah-pre-ze* salad with tomato, basil and **mozzarella**

capretto *kah-pre-to* kid (goat)
–alla piacentina *ah-lah pyah-chen-tee-nah* kid cut into pieces cooked with broth, white wine, garlic and parsley (Piacenza, Emilia-Romagna)

caprino *kah-pree-no* tart goat cheese often mixed at the table into a paste with oil, pepper and sweet vinegar

caramellare *kah-rah-me-lah-re* to caramelise

carbonada *kahr-bo-nah-dah* sliced salted beef cooked in red wine with onion, salt and pepper (Valle d'Aosta)

carbonara, alla *kahr-bo-nah-rah, ah-lah* pasta sauce, normally with raw egg, cheese and **pancetta** – sometimes cream is added

carciofi *kahr-cho-fee* artichokes – used throughout Italy and can be stuffed, fried or pickled
–alla giudia *ah-lah joo-dee-yah* whole artichokes, fried (Lazio)
–alla matticella *ah-lah mah-ti-che-lah* artichokes roasted on a wood fire, flavoured with an olive oil, garlic, salt and mint sauce (Velletri, Lazio)
–alla romana *ah-lah ro-mah-nah* artichokes stuffed with their own stalks, garlic, salt and pepper, cooked in water and olive oil (Roma, Lazio)
–ripieni *rip-ye-ni* artichokes stuffed with breadcrumbs, parmesan, cheese, parsley, garlic, capers, olives and oregano, cooked in a pan (Calabria)
–selvatica *sel-vah-tee-kah* wild artichokes

cardoncelli *kahr-don-che-lee* type of mushroom, similar to oyster mushrooms

carnaroli *kahr-nah-ro-lee* short grain rice ideal for **risotto**

carne *kahr-ne* meat
–equina *e-kwee-nah* horse meat
–suina *soo-ee-nah* pork
–trita *tree-tah* mince meat

carota *kah-ro-tah* carrot

carpa *kahr-pah* carp

carpaccio *kahr-pah-cho* very thin slices of raw meat, normally served with mayonnaise

carpione *kahr-pyo-ne* fried floured fish preserved in a marinade of vinegar, oil, sage, fennel seeds, sweet marjoram, salt and pepper – served as a starter (Lake Como, Lombardia)

carta da musica *kahr-tah dah moo-zi-kah* thin and very crunchy bread (Sardegna)

carteddate *kahr-te-dah-te* Christmas sweets – little strips of pastry rolled-up and sprinkled with honey or **vino cotto**, fried and covered with honey, icing sugar and cinnamon (Puglia)

cartoccio *kahr-to-cho* cooking method where fish, chicken or game are tightly wrapped in tinfoil and baked

casadinas *kah-zah-dee-nahs* Easter specialty consisting of little pastry baskets filled with fresh cheese, mint and saffron (Sardegna)

casata *kah-zah-tah* cake prepared for Easter where puff pastry is stuffed with cheese, eggs, cinnamon, vanilla, sugar, chocolate, citron and liqueur

cascà di carloforte *kah-skah dee kahr-lo-for-te* couscous with various vegetables (peas, cauliflower, etc.), minced meat and spices (Sardegna)

casó'la *kah-so-lah* this dish is a real calorie bomb! A stew prepared with pork, sausage and lard cooked with tomato sauce, carrots, celery, onion and abundant savoy cabbage, cooked for hours and served with polenta. (Lombardia)

càsonséi *kah-zon-say* rectangles of pasta usually stuffed with parmesan, vegetables and sausage (Lombardia)

cassa *kah-sah* cashier – in many bars you have to pay the cashier not the barperson

cassata *kah-sah-tah* ice cream or sponge cake stuffed with sweet **ricotta**, vanilla, chocolate, pistachios, candied fruit and liqueur (Sicilia)

–sulmonese *sool-mo-ne-ze* very sweet cake made with sponge cake dunked in liqueur and stuffed with almond nougat and chocolate cream, covered with cream (Sulmona, Abruzzo)

cassola *kah-so-lah* rich fish-soup with tomato sauce, garlic, oil, parsley, basil and chilli (Cagliari, Sardegna)

casoncelli *kah-zon-che-li* pasta stuffed with sausage, spinach, eggs, raisins, almond biscuits, cheese and breadcrumbs, served with melted butter and sage (Lombardia)

castagnaccio *kahs-tahn-yah-cho* baked cake made with chestnut flour and sprinkled with pine nuts and rosemary (Toscana)

castagne *kahs-tahn-ye* chestnuts
–al latte *ahl lah-te* simple soup made with dry chestnuts cooked in milk (Lombardia)

castelmagno *kahs-tel-mahn-yo* nutty blue cheese (Piedmonte)

casumarzo *kah-zu-mahr-zo* rarely seen sheep cheese with small maggots inside! (Sardegna)

casunzei *kah-zoon-say* kind of **ravioli** stuffed with pumpkin or spinach, ham and cinnamon – served with melted butter and smoked **ricotta**. (Belluno, Veneto)

caulada *ka-hoo-lah-dah* cabbage-based soup, with sausage, lard, pork, veal, mint and garlic (Sardegna)

cavallo *kah-vah-lo* horse

cavallucci *kah-vah-loo-chi* rustic white sweets made with candied orange, nuts and spices (Siena, Toscana)

cavatelli *kah-vah-te-li* home-made small round pasta – often served with tomato sauce, oil and rocket (Molise)

–al ragù *ahl rah-goo* **cavatelli** served with a lamb **ragù** (Molise)

cavolata *kah-vo-lah-tah* (*see* **caulada**)

cavolo *kah-vo-lo* cabbage
  –nero *ne-ro* dark cabbage (Toscana)

cazzimperio *kaht-sim-per-ee-yo* fresh and crunchy vegetables (such as fennel, carrot, etc) are dunked into a tasty sauce prepared with oil, salt and pepper (Lazio)

cazzmar *kaht-smahr* dish prepared with lamb's entrails, liver and giblets, made into sausage, baked and served sliced (Basilicata and Puglia)

cecenielli *che-chen-ye-li* very small fish which can be fried or put on pizzas (Napoli, Campania)

ceci *che-chee* chickpeas

cefalo *che-fah-lo* mullet

cena *che-nah* dinner

cenci *chen-chee* traditional carnival sweets made with sweet pastry sprinkled with icing sugar (Siena, Toscana)

ceriole *che-ree-yo-le* (*see* **umbrici**)

cernia *cher-nee-yah* grouper

cervello *cher-ve-lo* brain
  –fritto *free-to* ox brain floured and fried, served hot with artichokes in batter (Siena, Toscana)

cervo *cher-vo* venison
  –alla panna *ah-lah pah-nah* haunch of deer cooked with vegetables, spices, vinegar, pepper and cream (Lombardia)

cevapcici *che-vahp-chee-chee* spicy fresh sausages of Slavic origin made with pork, beef or lamb, normally grilled and cut into pieces (Friuli)

chenella *ke-ne-lah* meatballs (sometimes made with fish) served in broth or with a sauce

chiacchiere *kyah-ke-re* (*see* **bugie**)

Chianti *kyahn-tee* most famous Italian red wine, made mainly from san-giovese grapes. The best of these are wonderful. (Toscana)

chifferi *ki-fe-ree* curved pasta tubes

chilo *kee-lo* kilo

chinulille *ki-noo-li-le* round or square **ravioli** stuffed with sugar, **ricotta**, egg yolks, and fried lemon and orange peel. Can also include chocolate, dried chestnuts, sweet cocoa, candied fruit or cloves. (Calabria)

chiodino *kyo-dee-no* honey fungus – popular mushroom which must be cooked

chisció'i *ki-shi-o-i* flat cakes made with wholemeal flour and cheese, fried in oil or lard (Valtellina, Lombardia)

ciabatta *chah-baht-tah* crisp, flat and long bread

cialzons *chahlt-sons* **ravioli** stuffed with sultanas, spinach, chocolate and candied peel; they are seasoned with melted butter, sugar, cinnamon, smoked **ricotta** and grated cheese. They can also be stuffed with herbs such as basil, sage and marjoram, or with chicken. (Friuli)

ciambelle al mosto *chahm-be-le ahl mos-to* ring-shaped cakes made with flour, sugar, oil, yeast and grape must (Ascoli Piceno, Marche)

ciammotta *chah-mo-tah* mixed vegetable-fry prepared with potatoes, peppers, tomatoes, aubergines, onions, olives and, sometimes, scrambled eggs (Basilicata)

cianfotta *chan-fo-tah* stew prepared with peppers, aubergines, potatoes, onions, tomatoes, garlic and basil (Campania, Napoli)

ciaudedda *chah-oo-de-dah* dish prepared with artichokes, onions, and potatoes, stewed with olive oil (Basilicata)

ciavarro *chah-vah-ro* tasty spring soup made with cereals and legumes – chickpeas, beans, lentils and spelt (Ascoli Piceno, Marche)

C

cibreo *chi-bre-o* chicken livers and giblets with an egg yolk and lemon sauce (Toscana)

cibuddau *chi-boo-dah-u* onion-based dish where the onions are covered with oil and salt and cooked until they become golden brown (Sardegna)

cicala *chi-kah-lah* crustacean – can be a largish shrimp or a smallish lobster

ciccioli *chi-cho-lee* tasty pieces of crispy fat (*see* **strutto**)

cicerchiata *chi-cherk-yah-tah* ring-shaped cake prepared with little balls made of flour, eggs, yolks, butter and sugar. These are fried and then made into a cake with honey, orange peel and candied fruit. (Umbria)

ciceri e tria *chi-che-ree e tree-yah* dish prepared with boiled chickpeas and pasta, served with onions (Puglia)

cicirata *chee-chee-rah-tah* small sweet balls fried and covered with honey (Basilicata)

cicoria *chi-ko-ree-yah* chicory
–strascinata *strah-shee-nah-tah* chicory, boiled and sautéed with garlic, oil and small red spicy peppers. Sometimes with anchovies in oil. (Lazio)

cima *chee-mah* breast, normally veal
–alla genovese *ah-lah je-no-ve-ze* fillets of veal breast stuffed with minced veal, nuts, peas, vegetables, eggs, marjoram and breadcrumbs, boiled and served sliced (Liguria, Genoa)

cime di rapa *chee-me dee rah-pah* turnip tops – used as a green vegetable

cinghiale *ching-gyah-le* boar; also a dish of wild boar marinated in herbs, vinegar and wine, stewed with juniper berries, herbs and tomatoes – often served with polenta (Siena, Toscana)
–in agrodolce *in ah-gro-dol-che* boar, stewed with spices, sugar and vinegar and served with a sauce made of raisins, pine nuts, sour

black cherries, plums and lemon (Lazio)

Cinque Terre *ching-kwe te-re* dry white wine (Liguria)

Cinque Terre Sciacchetra *ching-kwe te-re sha-ke-tra* sweet dessert wine (Liguria)

cioccolata/o *cho-ko-lah-tah/to* chocolate
–fondente *fon-den-te* plain chocolate

cipollata *chi-po-lah-tah* dish prepared with pork, spare ribs, stale bread and a lot of white onion (Toscana)

cipolle *chee-po-le* onions
–ripiene *rip-ye-ne* halved onions stuffed with chopped onion pulp, parmesan, egg, butter, spices and **grappa, then** baked and eaten cold. Sometimes sausage and meat are used as stuffing. (Piedmont)
–selvatiche *sel-vah-tee-kah* wild onions (*see* **lampascioni**)

coccois *ko-ko-is* flat bread made with salty cheese and crackling (Sardegna)

cocomero *ko-ko-me-ro* watermelon

coda *ko-da* tail; also angler fish
–alla vaccinara *ah-lah vah-chi-nah-rah* beef tail and cheek stewed with lard, garlic, parsley, onion, carrots, celery and spices – in some recipes pine nuts, raisins and cocoa are added (Roma, Lazio)
–di rospo al rosmarino *ko-dah dee ros-po ahl roz-mah-ree-no* angler fish with oil, garlic, rosemary and chilli (Pescara, Abruzzo)

codino *ko-dee-no* pig's tail

coglioni di mulo *kol-yo-ne deemoo-lo* 'mules' balls' (*see* **mortadella di Campotosto**)

cognà *kon-yah* apple, pear, fig and grape sauce

coietas *ko-ye-tas* this word means 'quails', but the **coietas** are simple roulades made with savoy cabbage stuffed with meat sauce. They can

264

also be meatballs stuffed with lard, garlic and parsley. (Sardegna)

colapasta *ko-lah-pahs-ta* colander, strainer

colazione *ko-lah-tsyo-ne* breakfast

Colli Albani *ko-lee ahl-bah-nee* white wine with a straw-yellow colour, delicate characteristic aroma – well suited to fish and as an **aperitivo** (Lazio)

colomba/o *ko-lom-bah/o* dove, pigeon; also a type of cake
  –di Pavullo *dee pah-vu-lo* cake made with many layers of pastry, stuffed with apple and pear jam, raisins and pine nuts (Emilia-Romagna)
  –pasquale *pahs-kwah-le* traditional dove-shaped Easter cake, similar to **panettone**, sprinkled with chopped almonds and sugar (Lombardia)

coltello *kol-tel-o* knife

compreso *kom-pre-zo* included (in the price)

concentrato (di pomodoro) *kon-chen-trah-to (dee po-mo-do-ro)* (tomato) concentrate

conchiglie *kon-kil-ye* pasta shells

condiata *kon-dee-yah-tah* soup prepared with water, bacon, beaten eggs, and sheep's cheese (Abruzzo)

condimento *kon-dee-men-to* dressing

confetti *kon-fe-tee* sugar-coated almonds

coniglio *ko-nil-yo* rabbit
  –alla canavesana *ah-lah kah-nah-ve-zah-nah* rabbit cooked in meat stock, with potatoes and spices (Piedmont)
  –alla ligure *ah-lah li-goo-re* rabbit cooked with pine nuts and olives (Imperia, Liguria)
  –in porchetta *in por-ke-tah* rabbit stuffed with bacon, wild fennel, garlic, salt and pepper, then baked and sprinkled with red wine (Marche); also, baked boned rabbit stuffed with minced meat, eggs, breadcrumbs, wild fennel, garlic and lard (Marche)

conserva *kon-ser-vah* preserved
  –di pomodoro *dee po-mo-do-ro* traditional tomato sauce where the tomatoes are cut, salted and dried for two days (Campania)

contorni *kon-tor-nee* side dishes

coperto *ko-per-to* cover charge

coppa *ko-pah* cup, bowl; also cured pork
  –umbra *um-brah* salami prepared with pork, salt, pepper, spices and orange peel (Umbria)

coratella *ko-rah-tel-ah* lamb's pluck (lungs, heart and liver)
  –d'abbacchio con carciofi *dah-bah-kyo kon kahr-cho-fee* lamb's pluck with onion, rosemary, white wine and fried artichokes (Lazio)

cornetto *kor-ne-to* breakfast pastry

coscia *ko-shah* leg/haunch

cosciotto di capretto nel fieno maggengo *ko-sho-to dee kah-pre-to nel fee-ye-no mah-jen-go* kid's leg with herbs cooked with white wine

costata *kos-tah-tah* beef steak (rib)
  –alla napoletana *ah-lah nah-po-le-tah-nah* beef steak cooked with oil, tomato sauce, oregano, garlic and white wine (Napoli)
  –di manzo alla pizzaiola *dee mahn-zo ah-lah pit-sah-yo-lah* beef steak with garlic, oil, tomatoes, oregano (Lazio)

costine *kos-ti-ne* ribs
  –di maiale *dee mah-yah-le* pork spare ribs grilled on stone (Lombardia)

costoletta *kos-to-le-tah* veal cutlet
  –alla valdostana *ah-lah vahl-dos-tah-nah* fried veal cutlet stuffed with **fontina** and sometimes white truffle (Valle d'Aosta)

cotechinata *ko-te-kee-nah-tah* roulades made with pig rind stuffed with garlic, parsley and lard cooked with tomato sauce (Basilicata)

cotechino *ko-te-kee-no* boiled pork sausage (Emilia-Romagna)

–in galera *in gah-le-rah* 'cotechino in prison', meatloaf made with beef and ham, stuffed with a boiled **cotechino**. (Modena, Emilia-Romagna)

cotto *ko-to* cooked

cotto, ben *ko-to, ben* well done (cooked)

cotoletta *ko-to-le-tah* cutlet, normally veal and usually breaded and fried
–alla bolognese *ah-lah bo-lon-ye-ze* breaded veal cutlet sautéed with butter and baked with a slice of cured ham and a slice of fresh parmesan – tomato sauce or meat sauce can be added (Bologna, Emilia-Romagna)
–alla milanese *ah-lah mi-lah-ne-ze* loin veal steak breaded, then fried in butter (Milano, Lombardia)

cozze *kot-se* mussels

crauti acidi (sauerkraut) *krah-u-tee ah-chee-dee (zah-uer-kra-hut)* this German standard is also found in the north of Italy. Cabbages are pickled by being finely cut and arranged in layers in wooden tubs with salt, saffron and spices for around two months. It's usually served with pork or salami. (Trentino Alto-Adige)

crema *kre-mah* custard/cream

crema inglese *kre-mah in-gle-ze* custard

cren *kren* horseradish

crescia di Pasqua *kre-shah dee pahs-kwah* kind of pizza eaten at Easter. Made from flour, eggs, parmesan, lemon and orange peels, yeast, milk, lard, oil, nutmeg, salt and pepper. (Urbino, Marche)

crescenza *kre-shen-za* fresh soft cheese (Lombardia)

crespella *kres-pe-lah* thin fritters made with eggs, milk and flour

crespelle bagnate *kres-pe-le bahn-yah-te* pasta stuffed with grated cheese and served covered with chicken stock and other cheese (Teramo, Abruzzo)

crocchette *kro-ke-te* croquettes of mashed potatoes and various ingredients

crostacei *kros-tah-chay* crustacean

crostata *kros-tah* crust

crostata *kros-tah-tah* fruit tart
–di ricotta *dee ri-ko-tah* shortcrust pastry with a stuffing made with fresh **ricotta** and custard, yolks, sugar, cinnamon and candied fruit (Frosinone, Lazio)

crostini *kros-tee-nee* slices of bread baked with **mozzarella**, anchovies, tomato, salt and oregano (Calabria)
–al mosaico *ahl mo-zah-ee-ko* toast spread with a sauce prepared with truffles, pistachios, ham cubes, corned tongue and butter (Umbria)
–di provatura *dee pro-vah-too-rah* sliced cheese arranged in layers with slices of bread, butter and anchovies, then baked (Lazio)
–neri *ne-ri* little bits of toast spread with a sauce of calf's spleen, onion, pork liver, anchovies, capers, pepper and parsley (Siena, Toscana)

crostoi *kros-toy* little fritters made with **porcini**, garlic, parsley and butter (Trentino Alto-Adige)

crostoli *kros-to-li* sweet pastry fried and sprinkled with icing sugar; also small flat bread (Marche)

crucetta *kroo-che-tah* baked sweet made with figs stuffed with nuts, almonds and citron peel, arranged as a cross (Calabria)

cruda/o *kroo-dah/o* raw

crumiri *kru-mee-ri* dry biscuits made from flour, maize meal, eggs, sugar and vanilla (Casale Monferrato, Piedmont)

crusca *kroos-kah* bran

cucchiaio *ku-kyah-yo* spoon

cucchiaino *il ku-kyah-ee-no* teaspoon

cucina *koo-chee-nah* kitchen/cuisine

culatello (di Busseto) *kool-ah-te-lo (dee boo-set-o)* excellent and quite expensive ham made of salted and spiced pig's buttock, matured for about 12 months (Busseto, Emilia-Romagna)

culingiones *kool-in-jo-nes* kind of **ravioli** stuffed with potatoes or chards, sheep's cheese, garlic and mint (Sardegna)

culungiones *kool-oon-jo-nes* (see **culingiones**)

cuocere *kwo-che-re* to cook
–al dente *ahl den-te* cooking method where pasta, rice or vegetables are still quite hard after cooking
–a vapore *ah vah-po-re* to steam

cupeta *ko-pe-tah* thin almond nougat made with honey, minced nuts, pine nuts, sugar and white flour, stuffed between two wafers (Lombardia)

cuscus *koos-koos* couscous – can be served with seafood, lamb, or chicken and fried broccoli. A remnant of the Arabian influence in Sicilia.

cutturiddi *ku-tu-ri-dee* lamb stew with chilli, tomatoes, small onions and celery (Basilicata)

cutturo *ku-tu-ro* large copper pot

D

d'... *dah...* from ...

dadi *dah-dee* stock cubes

data di scadenza *dah-tah dee skah-den-za* use-by date

datteri *dah-te-ree* dates (fruit)
–di mare *di mah-re* type of mussel

degustare *de-goo-stah-re* to taste carefully

degustazione *de-goo-stah-zee-yo-ne* tasting

della casa *de-lah kah-zah* 'of the house', house specialty

denominazione d'origine controllata (e garantita) *de-no-mee-naht-syo-ne dee oree-gi-ne kon-tro-lah-tah (e gah-rahn-tee-tah)* (see **DOC**)

dentice *den-tee-che* sea bream

di ... *dee* ... 'from ...'

diavola, alla *dee-yah-vo-le, ah-lah* spicy dish

diavolicchio *dyah-vo-lik-yo* dynamite chilli that's almost always present in the recipes of Abruzzo

digestivo *dee-jes-tee-vo* bitter drink taken to aid digestion (see **amaro**)

ditali(ni) *dee-tah-lee(-nee)* small bits of pasta normally used in soups

DOC *dee oh chee* a government classification system certifying the origin of wines (and also other products)

DOCG *dee oh chee jee* (see **DOC**)

dolce *dol-che* sweet, dessert
–di granturco al cacao *dee grahn-toor-ko ahl kah-kah-o* baked sweet polenta cake (Cremona, Lombardia)

dolcelatte *dol-che-lah-te* soft mild blue cheese

dolcetti di pasta di mandorle *dol-che-ti dee pah-stah dee mahn-dor-le* traditional delicious sweets made with marzipan, sugar and egg whites (Sicilia)

dolci *dol-chee* sweets, desserts

doppio zero *dop-yo ze-ro* 'double zero' – (see **farina**)

duro *doo-ro* hard

E

ebraico *e-bray-ee-ko* Jewish (style)

enoteca *e-no-te-ka* wine shop; a collection of wines

erbazzone *er-baht-so-ne* baked pasta stuffed with boiled spinach, lard, spices, parmesan, eggs and parsley (Emilia-Romagna)

erbazzone dolce *er-baht-so-ne dol-che* sweet baked shortcrust pastry filled with boiled and chopped chards mixed with **ricotta**, sugar and almonds (Emilia-Romagna)

erbe *er-be* herbs; also grass

espresso *es-pres-so* short black coffee

etto *e-to* 100 gms

F

fagiano *fah-jah-no* pheasant

fagioli *fah-jo-lee* beans – usually dried legumes
 –all'uccelletto *ahl-ooch-e-le-to* white beans boiled and cooked with garlic, rosemary, sage and tomatoes, served with grilled pork sausages (Siena, Toscana)
 –borlotti *bor-lot-tee* borlotti beans – reddish speckled beans
 –cannellini *kah-ne-lee-ni* small white cannellini beans
 –con le cotiche *kon le ko-ti-ke* beans and pork rind boiled, then cooked with lard, garlic, parsley and tomato sauce (Lazio)
 –e castagne *e kahs-tahn-ye* soup prepared with beans and chestnuts cooked in water with oil, garlic, parsley, salt and white figs (Campania)

fagiolini *fah-jo-lee-nee* green beans

false salsicce *fahl-se sahl-sich-e* 'false sausages' – sausages made with lard and potatoes and coloured with beet (Valle d'Aosta)

faraona *fah-rah-o-nah* guinea-fowl

farcito *fahr-chee-to* stuffed (food)

fare *fah-re* to make
 –la passeggiata *lah pah-se-jah-tah* to go for a stroll/walk
 –la scarpetta *lah skahr-pe-tah* 'make a shoe' – common way of wiping your plate with bread
 –una prenotazione *u-nah pre-no-tahts-yo-ne* to make a reservation

farfalle *fahr-fah-le* butterfly (bow) shaped pasta

farina *fah-ree-nah* flour
 –00 *ze-ro ze-ro* finely ground flour
 –di castagne *dee kah-stah-nye* chestnut flour
 –integrale *in-te-grah-le* wholewheat flour

farinata *fah-ri-nah-tah* delicious starter – very thin and simple flat bread, prepared with chickpea flour

farro *fah-ro* spelt – an ancient grain

fasoi col muset *fah-zoy kol moo-zet* this dish is prepared with dried beans, sausage, pork rind and spices (Friuli)

fatto *fah-to* made
 –a mano *ah mah-no* made by hand
 –casa *fah-to in kah-za* home-made; made on the premises

favata *fah-vah-tah* rustic dish with dried broad beans cooked with pork rind and ribs, sausages, tomatoes, and herbs (Sardegna)

fave *fah-ve* broad beans
 –col guanciale *kol gwahn-chah-le* broad beans with the side part of a pork head, onions and broth (Lazio)

fegato *fe-gah-toh* liver
 –alla lodigiana *ah-lah lo-dee-jah-nah* fried pig's liver coarsely minced with fennel seeds (Lodi, Lombardia)
 –alla veneziana *ah-lah ve-nets-yah-nah* sliced calf's liver cooked with butter, oil and onions and covered with fresh parsley (Venezia, Veneto)

felino *fe-lee-no* type of salami (Parma, Emilia-Romagna)

ferri, ai *fe-ree, ay* grilled on an open fire

fesa *fe-zah* northern Italian word for veal (leg) used for cutlets, roasts or scaloppine

fetta *fe-tah* a slice of meat, cheese, etc
 –col cavolo *kol kah-vo-lo* winter dish where cauliflower is cooked and served on big slices of toasted bread sprinkled with garlic (Siena, Toscana)

fettuccine *fe-tu-chee-ne* long ribbon-shaped pasta

–alla romana *ah-lah ro-mahn-ah* Roman-style **fettuccine** served with meat sauce, mushrooms and sheep's cheese (Lazio)

fiadoni alla trentina *fyah-do-nee ah-lah tren-tee-nah* little sweets stuffed with almonds, honey, cinnamon and rum (Trentino Alto-Adige)

fiandolein *fyahn-dol-ayn* kind of **zabaglione**, that is, an 'egg flip' made with yolks, milk, sugar and lemon peel (Valle d'Aosta)

fico *fee-ko* fig
–d'India *din-dee-yah* prickly pear

filetto *fi-let-to* fillet

filoncino *fi-lon-chee-no* breadstick

finanziera *fi-nahnts-ye-rah* sweetbreads, mushrooms and chicken livers in a creamy sauce (Piedmont)

finocchio *fi-nok-yo* fennel

fior di latte *fee-yor dee lah-te* fresh and very soft cheese; also a **gelato** flavour

fiori *fyo-ree* flowers – some, especially zucchini flowers, are commonly eaten
–di zucca farciti *dee zoo-kah* zucchini or squash flowers stuffed with breadcrumbs, **mozzarella**, anchovies and parsley, battered and fried in olive oil (Lazio)

focaccia *fo-kahch-ah* flat bread – often stuffed with cheese, ham, vegetables and limitless other ingredients (Liguria)

foglia d'alloro *fol-yah dah-lo-ro* bay leaf

fondo *fon-do* stock

fondua *fon-doo-ah* **fontina** cheese melted in milk and butter and egg yolks. It's eaten hot, covered with thin slices of truffle, together with toast, fried in butter. (Piedmont)

fonduta *fon-doo-tah* similar to **fondua**, but without truffles (Valle d'Aosta)

fontal *fon-tahl* mild and less tasty **fontina** style cheese

fontina *fon-tee-nah* fatty, sweet and creamy cheese, similar to Gruyère (Valle d'Aosta)

forchetta *for-ke-tah* fork

formaggio *for-mah-jo* cheese

fornaio *for-nah-yo* bakery

fornello *for-ne-lo* stovetop/range

forno *for-no* oven
–a legno *ah len-yo* wood-fired oven

forno, al *for-no, al* can refer to anything cooked in an oven

fragole *frah-go-le* strawberries
–all'aceto *ah-lah-che-to* strawberries seasoned with white wine, vinegar and sugar (Lazio)

franciacorta rosso *frahn-chah-kor-tah ro-so* red wine with an intense and characteristic aroma (Lombardy)

frascarella *frahs-kah-re-lah* liquidy polenta flavoured with oil (Umbria)

Frascati *frahs-kah-tee* light white wine (Lazio)

freddo/a *fred-o/ah* cold (temperature)

fregnacce *fren-yah-che* thin rolled pancakes stuffed with meatballs, liver, chicken breast and cheese, and baked with meat sauce (Abruzzo); also triangles of pasta made with flour and water, served with cheese and tomato sauce. (Lazio)

fregola *fre-go-lah* type of couscous

fresca *fres-kah* fresh

friggere *fri-jere* fry

frisceu *fri-sheu* fritters with lettuce, whitebait, zucchini, liver, brain, dried salted cod, pumpkin, etc (Liguria)

friseddé *fri-ze-de* big toasted ring-shaped cakes made with flour and oil, boiled and baked. Dried, soaked in water and served with fresh tomatoes, olive oil, salt and origano. (Puglia)

fritole *free-to-le* sweets – fritters made with flour, sultanas, pine nuts, candied citron and liqueur (Veneto)

fritta/o *fri-tah-tah/to* fried

frittata *fri-tah-tah* thick omelette, with eggs and many other ingredients, served hot or cold

–di maccheroni *dee mah-ke-ro-ni* omelette, like a browned and crunchy pizza prepared with **maccheroni** and sauce, eggs, grated cheese, butter and oil (Campania)

–di pasta *dee pah-stah* omelette with **spaghetti** or **vermicelli**, eggs, sheep's cheese and chunks of sausage (Calabria)

–di patate *dee pahtahte* omelette with potatoes (Liguria)

frittatensuppe *fri-tah-ten-su-pe* thin omelettes of eggs, flour, milk & parsley, cut into strips and served with meat stock (Trentino Alto-Adige)

frittatine di farina al miele di fichi *fri-tah-tee-ne dee fah-ri-nah ahl mee-ye-le di fee-kee* pancakes made with flour, salt and water, folded and stuffed with fig honey (Calabria)

frittelle *fri-te-le* fritters

–di S.Giuseppe *dee sahn joo-ze-pe* rice-based, sweet fritters made only in February and early March (Siena, Toscana)

frittelloni *fri-te-lo-ni* **tortellini** stuffed with boiled spinach and sautéed with butter, sultanas and cheese, then fried in lard and served hot, sprinkled with sugar (Emilia-Romagna)

fritto *fri-to* fried

–di animelle e carciofi *dee ah-ni-me-le e kahr-cho-fee* lamb or veal sweetbreads, floured and fried with artichokes (Lazio)

–misto *mis-to* literally 'mixed fry-up' – in general, various ingredients, depending on the region and time of year, are fried in olive oil

–misto *mis-to* mix of entrails and vegetables (artichokes, courgettes, cauliflowers) fried in olive oil (Lazio)

–misto abruzzese *mis-to ah-broot-se-ze* perhaps the most common **fritto**

misto – diced artichokes and boiled fennel breaded and fried (Abruzzo)

–misto alla romana *mis-to ah-lah ro-mah-nah* liver, artichokes, brain, sweetbreads, apples, pears and slices of bread are soaked in milk and fried (Roma, Lazio)

frittura di pesce gatto *fri-too-rah dee pesh-e gah-to* catfish cut in pieces, floured and fried (Piacenza, Emilia-Romagna)

frizzante *frit-sahn-te* fizzy/sparkling

frullatore *froo-lah-to-re* mixing bowl

frumento *froo-men-to* wheat

frutta *froo-tah* fruit

–secca *se-kah* dried fruit

frutti di mare *froot-ti dee mah-re* sea food

fugazza *fu-gaht-sah* ancient, very rich, tasty sweet pastry (Venezia, Veneto)

funghi *fun-gee* mushrooms

fuoco *fwo-ko* fire

fusilli *fu-zi-li* corkscrew shaped pasta

–alla molisana *ah-lah mo-lee-zah-nah* home-made **fusilli** served with tomato sauce and chilli (Molise)

G

galani *gah-lah-ni* strips of pastry fried in lard, layered, and sprinkled with icing sugar (Venezia, Veneto)

gallina *gah-lee-nah* chicken/hen

gamberetti *gahm-be-re-tee* little prawn

gambero *gahm-be-ro* prawn, shrimp

gamberoni *gahm-be-ro-ni* prawns

gambon *gahm-bon* pig's leg, boned, pressed and matured – it's served boiled with different sauces (Piacenza, Emilia-Romagna)

garagoli *gah-rah-go-li* shellfish – similar to periwinkles

–in porchetta *in por-ke-tah* **garagoli** cooked with spices, herbs, wild fennel, and white wine (Marche) garganelli *gahr-gah-ne-li* small square pasta served with meat sauce and peas (Emilia-Romagna)

gassato *gah-sah-to* carbonated, gassy

gastronomia *gah-stro-no-mee-ya* gastronomy

gattò di patate e salsiccia *gah-to dee pah-tah-te e sahl-see-chah* baked meatloaf made with mashed potatoes, eggs, ham, **mozzarella**, **provolone** and parmesan (Napoli, Campania)

Gavi *gah-vee* popular white wine (Piemonte)

gelato *je-lah-to* traditional Sicilian ice-cream

gelateria *je-lah-te-ree-yah* ice-cream shop

genepy *je-ne-pee* herbal based liqueur used as a **digestivo** (Valle d'Aosta)

genovese, alla *je-no-ve-ze, ah-lah* sauce, including olive oil, garlic and herbs

gerstensuppe *ger-sten-su-pe* barley-soup with onions, parsley, spices and **speck** (Trentino Alto-Adige)

ghiotta *gyo-tah* dripping pan; also a sauce made from dripping
 –di peperoni arrostiti *dee pe-pe-ro-ni ah-ros-ti-ti* baked vegetable-based dish, with chunks of peppers, potatoes, tomatoes, courgettes and other vegetables (Abruzzo)

gianchetti *jahn-ke-tee* (*see* cecenielli)

gianduiotto *gyahn-du-yo-to* soft chocolate paste made with soft plain chocolate, hazelnut cream, vanilla and sugar (Torino, Piedmont)

giardineria *jahr-dee-ne-ree-ya* pickled vegetables

girello *ji-re-lo* round cut of meat

gnocarei *nyo-kah-rey* chicken with polenta and eggs (Brescia, Lombardia)

gnocchi *nyo-ki* small dumplings – the most common being the ubiquitous potato dumplings

 –alla bava *ah-lah bah-vah* **gnocchi** baked with fresh tomato and **fontina** cubes, thick boiling cream and truffles (Piedmont)
 –alla comasca *ah-lah ko-mah-skah* batter thrown in spoonfuls into boiling water and seasoned with cheese, tomato or meat sauce (Lombardia)
 –alla fontina *ah-lah fon-tee-nah* **gnocchi** baked with little knobs of butter and **fontina** cubes (Valle d'Aosta)
 –alla romana *ah-lah ro-mah-nah* small round dumplings made with semolina and cooked with milk, cheese and egg yolks, baked with butter and parmesan

gnocchetti *nyo-ke-tee* small shell-shaped pasta

gnocco di pane *nyo-ko dee pah-ne* stale pieces of bread fried in butter, mixed with eggs, milk, flour and minced ham, steamed and served sprinkled with grated cheese (Friuli)

gnummerieddí *nyu-mer-ye-dee* roulades prepared with lamb's giblets or liver, fresh sausage and chicken, baked, grilled or cooked in a pan with potatoes (Puglia)

goregone *go-re-go-ne* freshwater lake fish

gorgonzola *gor-gon-zo-lah* very popular spicy, sweet, aromatic and very creamy blue vein cow's milk cheese (Lombardia and Piedmonte)

gó'stl *ger-stel* boiled meat, cut into little cubes and sautéed with potatoes and spices (Trentino Alto-Adige)

gran fritto alla piemontese *grahn fri-to ah-lah pye-mon-te-ze* very rich and heavy fried dish. Many ingredients (including brain, sweetbread, chicken fillets, sausages, liver, heart, vegetables, croquettes, macaroons, courgettes, artichokes, mushrooms, fruit and fresh-water fish) are dipped in batter and fried in heart-stopping amounts of butter. (Piedmont)

grana (padano) *grah-na (pah-dah-no)* hard cheese, very similar to parmesan

granceola *grahn-che-o-la* spider crab

granchio *grahn-kyo* crab

granita *grah-nee-tah* very refreshing flavoured finely crushed ice (Sicilia)

granseola *grahnseolah* spider crab; also the name of a starter in which spider crab is boiled, seasoned and stuffed back into the shell (Venezia, Veneto)
  –alla triestina *ah-lah tri-yes-tee-nah* spider crab, whose pulp is extracted and baked with oil, garlic, lemon, breadcrumbs and parsley and stuffed back into the shell (Trieste, Friuli)

grano *grah-no* wheat

granoturco *grah-no toor-ko* corn

granturco *grahn toor-ko* corn

grappa *grah-pah* distilled grape must (the stalks and grapes left over after the wine making process). A strong drink, it's usually drunk straight or in coffee (see **caffé corretto**).

grassa/o *grah-sah/o* fat

graticola *grah-tee-ko-lah* barbeque grill

Greco di Tufo *gre-ko dee too-fo* dry white wine (Campania)

grembiule *grem-byoo-le* apron

griglia *gril-yah* a grill

Grignolino d'Asti *grin-yo-lee-no dah-stee* red wine with a lightly bitter taste (Piedmontese)

grissini *gri-see-nee* breadsticks

guanciale *gwahn-chah-le* cheek, usually pig's; also cured pig's cheek
  –di manzo al vino rosso *-dee mahn-zo ahl vee-no ross-o* cheek served with polenta (Cremona, Lombardia)

guasto *gwah-sto* 'off' food – gone bad

gubana *goo-bah-nah* sweet pastry (Friuli)

H

hirn–profesen *hirn-pro-fe-zen* fried bread (Trentino Alto-Adige)

I

il/i *il/i* the (sg/pl – masculine)

impanadas *im-pah-nah-dahs* stuffed pastry (Sardegna)

in *in* in

indivio *in-dee-vee-yo* chicory

infarinata *in-fah-ri-nah-tah* liquid polenta with beans, black cabbage, pork rinds, garlic, lard and spices (Toscana)

insalata *in-sah-lah-tah* salad
  –caprese *kah-pre-ze* salad with **mozzarella**, tomato and basil
  –di carne cruda *dee kahr-ne kroo-dah* salad in which minced meat is served with dressing and garnished with parsley, lemon slices, anchovies and pickled gherkins (Piedmont)

interiora *in-ter-yo-rah* giblets

involtini *in-vol-tee-nee* stuffed rolls of meat or fish
  –di carne *dee kahr-ne* small veal slices, rolled-up and stuffed with breadcrumbs, oil, parmesan, parsley and garlic, pierced on kebabs and baked or grilled (Calabria)
  –siciliani *si-chil-yah-nee* meat rolled in breadcrumbs, stuffed with egg, ham and cheese (Sicilia)

ippoglosso *ip-o-gloss-o* turbot (fish)

J

jota *yo-tah* soup with beans, milk, turnips and polenta flour; also soup with beans, potatoes, sauerkraut and smoked pork rinds (Friuli)

K

kiwi *ki-wi* kiwifruit

L

l' *l'* the – the contraction of **la**

la/le *lah/le* the (sg/pl – feminine)

laganelle e fagioli *lah-gah-ne-le e fah-jo-lee* hand-made sheets of pasta served with a bean soup (Molise)

Lambrusco *lahm-broo-sko* naturally sparkling rich red wine (Emilia-Romagna)

lampascioni *lahm-pah-sho-ni* small, bitter onions – often wild (Puglia)

lamponi *lahm-po-nee* raspberries

lasagne *lah-zahn-ye* rectangular and flat sheets of egg pasta
  –alla bolognese *ah-lah bo-lon-ye-ze* baked **lasagne** arranged in layers with meat sauce, bechamel and parmesan (Bologna, Emilia-Romagna)

latte *lah-te* milk

lattina *laht-tee-nah* can (tin)

lattughe *lah-too-ge* lettuce
  –ripiene *rip-ye-ne* lettuce stuffed with meat, served in meat stock (Liguria)

lauro *lah-oo-ro* bay (*see* **alloro**)

lavandino *lah-vahn-dee-no* sink

lavapiatti *lah-vah-pee-yah-tee* dishwasher

lavare *lah-vah-re* to wash

lavarelli *lah-vah-re-li* fresh water whitefish
  –al vino bianco *ahl vee-no byahn-ko* whitefish cooked with butter, parsley and white wine (Lombardia)

lecca–lecca *le-kah-le-kah* lollipop

lenticchie *len-tik-ye* lentils
  –nere *ne-re* brown lentils
  –rosse *ross-e* red lentils
  –verdi *ver-dee* green lentils

lepre *le-pre* hare

lesso *le-so* boiled

lianeddè *lyah-ne-de* noodles made with fresh dough and served with chickpeas or rabbit sauce (Puglia)

lievito *lye-vee-to* yeast

limone *limone* lemon
  –al piatto *ahl pee-yah-to* salad prepared with cubed peeled lemons, mint, garlic, chilli, olive, oil and salt (Campania)

lingua *ling-wah* tongue
  –di bue *dee-boo-e* large mushroom

linguina *lin-gwee-nah* (*see* **trenette**)

linguine *lin-gwee-ne* long thin ribbons of pasta

liquore *li-kwo-re* liqueur

lisci *li-shee* smooth – used to describe pasta with a smooth surface

lista *lees-tah* menu

litro *lee-tro* litre

lo *lo* the

Locorotondo *lo-ko-ro-ton-do* light white wine (Puglia)

lonzo *lon-zo* loin; also a salami

luccio *loo-cho* pike

luganega *lu-gah-ne-gah* pork sausage (Monza, Lombardia)
  –veneta *ve-ne-tah* pork neck and cheek sausage (Treviso, Veneto)

luganiga di verze *lu-gah-nee-gah dee ver-ze* cabbage sausage stuffed with minced veal, cheese, eggs, and breadcrumbs (Trentino Alto-Adige)

lumache *loo-mah-ke* snails
  –al barbera *ahl bahr-be-rah* friedsnails slowly cooked with **Barbera**, served with ground nuts (Piedmont)
  –alla piemontese *ah-lah pye-mon-te-ze* baked snails with onion, tomato sauce, broth, nuts, anchovies, parsley, salt and pepper (Cuneo, Piedmont)
  –di Bobbio *dee bob-yo* snails browned in oil with leeks, then stewed with wine, water and herbs

luppoli *lu-po-lee* hops

M

maccaruni di casa con ragù *mah-kah-roo-ni dee kah-zah kon rah-goo* home-made pasta, shaped like small hollow cylinders, served with tomato and meat sauce (Calabria)

maccheroni *mah-ke-ro-ni* can refer to any pasta in general

–alla chitarra *ah-lah ki-tah-rah* square spaghetti made with flour and eggs and passed through a frame called a 'guitar' – generally served with meat sauce and peppers or a meat sauce prepared with meatballs (Abruzzo)

–con la nana *kon lah nah-nah* pasta with a duck sauce (Siena, Toscana)

–con la ricotta *kon lah ri-kot-ah* pasta served with ricotta, sheep's cheese and sometimes also parmesan (Lazio)

–con le noci *kon le no-chi* an Etruscan dish now prepared for Christmas Eve – boiled home-made pasta, flavoured with sugar, cinnamon, chopped nuts, breadcrumbs, cocoa, honey and lemon peel (Umbria)

macelleria *mah-che-le-ree-ya* butcher shop

macinapepe *mah-chee-nah-pe-pe* pepper mill

maggiorana *mah-jo-rah-nah* marjoram

magro *mah-gro* thin/lean/meatless

maiale *may-ah-le* pork

mais *mah-iz* maize

malfatti *mahl-fah-ti* dumplings made with spinach, eggs, ricotta, flour, bread and egg yolk, baked with butter and parmesan (Lombardia)

malloreddus *mah-lo-re-doos* dumplings made with flour and saffron, served with meat sauce (Sardegna)

maltagliati *mahl-tahl-yah-tee* odd shapes of pasta

Malvasia *mahl-vah-zee-yah* type of grape, made into many varieties of white or red wine

mammella *mah-mel-lah* breast

mandarino *mahn-dah-ree-no* mandarine

mandorle *mahn-dor-le* almonds

mangiare *mahn-jah-re* to eat

manteca *mahn-te-kah* fresh cheese, usually scamorza, rolled in a ball and stuffed with butter

mantecato *mahn-te-kah-to* any ingredients pounded to a paste

manzo *mahn-zo* beef

maraschino *mah-rah-skee-no* cherry liqueur

marcetto *mahr-che-to* very spicy cheese paste (Abruzzo)

mare *mah-re* sea

margarina *mahr-gah-ree-nah* margarine

marille *mah-ri-le* crazily shaped pasta designed by an engineer to retain the maximum amount of sauce

marinara, alla *mah-ree-nah-rah, ah-lah* sauce – mainly includes tomato, oil, garlic and herbs

maritozzi *mah-ri-tot-si* small soft sweet cakes stuffed with pine nuts, sultanas, orange peel and candied fruit (Lazio)

marmellata *mahr-me-lah-tah* jam; marmalade

–di lampascioni *dee lahm-pah-sho-ni* mashed lampascioni eaten with bread – also served on pizzas (Basilicata)

marrone *mah-ro-ne* large chestnut

marsala *mahr-sah-lah* fortified wine (Sicilia)

marubini *mah-ru-bee-nee* round pasta stuffed with toasted and milled bread, parmesan, marrow and eggs, usually eaten in meat stock (Cremona)

mascarpone *mahs-kahr-po-ne* very soft and creamy cheese (Lombardia)

matura *mah-too-rah* ripe

mazzafegato *maht-sah-fe-gah-to* matured dry-cured pork sausage, made with liver and lung minced with other kinds of meat and spices (Marche) mela *me-lah* apple

melagrana *me-lah-grah-nah* pomegranate

melanzanata di Lecce *me-lahn-zahn-ah-tah dee le-che* sliced fried eggplant, baked with tomatoes, onion, basil and sheep's cheese (Lecce, Puglia)

melanzane *me-lahn-zah-ne* eggplant – common throughout Italy but especially popular in southern Italy
  –al cioccolato *ahl cho-ko-lah-to* eggplants stuffed with their pulp, chocolate, **ricotta**, eggs, toasted almonds and citrus, baked and sprinkled with icing sugar and cinnamon (Napoli, Campania)
  –ripiene *rip-ye-ne* eggplant stuffed with their pulp, beaten eggs, cheese, marjoram, garlic, salt, olive oil and bread and baked – can be served either hot or cold (Liguria)
  –violette *vee-yo-le-te* purple eggplant

melone *me-lo-ne* melon

menta *men-tah* mint

menu *me-noo* menu
  –fisso *fee-so* set-price
  –turistico *too-rees-tee-ko* set-price

mercato *me-kah-to* market

merenda, (ora di) *me-ren-dah, (o-rah dee)* snack (time)

meringa *me-rin-gah* meringue

merlano *mer-lah-no* whiting

merluzzo *mer-loo-zo* cod

mescolare *me-sko-lah-re* to mix

mesta e fasoi *mes-tah e fah-zoy* polenta cooked with beans (Friuli)

mestolo *mes-to-lo* ladle

metà *me-tah* half

mettere sott'aceto *met-e-re sot-ah-che-to* to pickle

mezzo *med-zo* half

miele *mee-ye-le* honey

migliaccio 'e cigule *mil-yah-cho e chi-goo-le* baked polenta with pork,

sausages, sheep's cheese and pepper (Campania, Napoli)

milanese, alla *mi-lah-ne-ze, ah-lah* can mean any sauce associated with Milano – normally includes butter

millecosedde *mi-le-ko-ze-de* hearty and rich soup prepared with vegetables, legumes and short pasta (Calabria)

minestra *mi-nes-trah* general word for soup
  –alla pignata *ah-lah pin-yah-tah* traditional soup with beans, pork and vegetables (Ciociaria, Lazio)
  –cò i cece *ko ee che-che* soup with chickpeas and pasta (Umbria)
  –di broccoli in brodo di arzilla *dee bro-ko-li in bro-do dee ard-si-lah* soup of skate broth and **broccoletti**, with either small pasta or thin spaghetti broken into small pieces (Lazio)
  –di farro *dee fah-ro* spelt soup with grated cheese
  –di lardo *dee lahr-do* simple but tasty lard soup (Brianza, Lombardia)
  –di pane *dee pah-ne* soup with beans and vegetables served covered with slices of bread (Siena, Toscana)
  –di riso alla valdostana *dee ri-zo ah-lah vahl-dos-tah-nah* rice and turnip soup (Valle d'Aosta)
  –di riso, latte e castagne *dee ri-zo, lah-te e kahs-tahn-ye* chestnut and rice soup (Valle d'Aosta)
  –di trippa alla trentina *dee tri-pah ah-lah tren-tee-nah* light soup of boiled tripe, vegetables and toasted bread cubes (Trentino Alto-Adige)
  –marinara *mah-ree-nah-rah* rich fish soup, prepared with many kinds of fish and herbs (Teramo, Abruzzo)
  –maritata *mah-ree-tah-tah* meat soup with broccoli

minestrone *mi-nes-tro-ne* traditional soup prepared in many different ways but usually including tomatoes, peas, beans, zucchini, potatoes, onion, basil, parsley, sage and garlic with or without pasta or rice, sometimes with bacon cubes and, sometimes, pork rinds. In summer it can be served cold. (Milano, Lombardia)

missoltit *mis-ol-tit* dried and preserved freshwater fish

mista/o *mis-tah/o* mixed

misticanza *mees-tik-ahnt-sah* salad with mixed lettuce (Roma, Lazio)

moleche *mo-le-ke* the name given to crabs when they change their shells
–col pien *kol pyen* live crabs dipped in batter and fried in oil – served hot and crunchy (Venezia, Veneto)

molluscho *mol-loos-ko* mollusc

moncoi *mon-koy* baked polenta with **speck**, cheese and butter (Trentino Alto-Adige)

montasio *mon-tah-zee-yo* hard cheese (Friuli)

Montepulciano d'Abruzzo *mon-te-pul-chah-no dah-broot-so* popular dry red wine (Abruzzo)

morbido *mor-bi-do* soft

mortadella (di Bologna) *mor-tah-de-lah (dee bo-lon-yah)* salami made with minced pork, kneaded with lard and flavoured with black pepper – the best ones are tagged with an 'S' (Bologna, Emilia-Romagna)
–di Campotosto *dee kahm-po-tos-to* this salami is completely different to other **mortadella**. A small oval salami made with minced lean pork and lard. (Campotosto, Abruzzo)

Moscadello di Montalcino *mos-kah-de-lo dee Mon-tahl-chee-no* sweet dessert wine (Toscana)

Moscato *mos-kah-to* grape made into sweet, dry or sparkling wines

mostaccioli *mos-tah-cho-lee* small sweet chocolate-covered biscuits (Abruzzo)

mostarda *mos-tahr-dah* dessert made with grape must and flour or fig juice (Sicilia)
–di Cremona *dee kre-mo-nah* spicy seasoning prepared with whole, chopped, or candied fruit, honey, white wine, mustard and spices (Cremona, Lombardia)

mostardelle *mos-tahr-de-le* sausage prepared with pork, liver, heart, knuckles and lungs, sometimes pig's ears, a mixture of garlic, leeks, chilli, herbs, red wine and pig's blood (Piedmont)

motzetta *mot-se-tah* salami made with haunch of mountain-goat or chamois, salted and dried like **prosciutto** (Valle d'Aosta)

mozzarella *mot-sah-re-lah* soft fresh white cheese traditionally made from cow's milk and produced in many southern regions – it can be shaped like hazelnuts, cherries, plaits, etc, but the traditional shape is round
–di bufala *mot-sah-re-lah dee boo-fah-lah* the best! – delicious and rich **mozzarella** made from buffalo's milk
–in carrozza *in kah-rot-sah* slices of bread stuffed with **mozzarella**, battered and fried (Campania)

'mpanada *m-pah-nah-dah* savoury tart made with flaky pastry stuffed with vegetables and many kinds of meat and fish (Sicilia)

'mpepata di cozze *m-pe-pah-tah dee kot-se* fish-based dish prepared with mussels, lemon and oil (Calabria)

mucca *moo-kah* cow

muffa *moo-fah* mould

muggine *moo-jee-ne* mullet

mulette *mu-le-te* similar to **coppa** and **capocollo** except that a lot of chilli is used rather than pepper (Molise)

murseddu *mor-se-doo* tripe and giblets fried with red wine, tomatoes, chilli and herbs (Calabria)

N

napoletana, alla *nah-po-le-tah-nah, ah-lah* from Napoli, or in the style of – usually includes tomatoes and garlic

nasello *nah-ze-lo* hake

Natale *nah-tah-le* Christmas

'ndugghia *n-doo-gyah* dry-cured pork and fennel seed sausage (Calabria)

Nebbiolo *neb-yo-lo* popular grape – the main grape used in **barolo**

Nebbiolo d'Alba *neb-yo-lo dahl-bah* red wine which goes well with grilled meats and truffles (Piemonte)

neonati *ne-yo-nah-tee* (see **bianchetti**)

nero *ne-ro* black
  –**di seppia/calamaro** *dee sep-yah/kah-lah-mah-ro* squid/calamari ink – used to add a striking black colour to various dishes

nervetti con fagioli *ner-ve-ti kon fahj-yo-lee* calves' cartilages boiled and served with beans – normally served cold (Lombardia)

nocciola *no-cho-lah* hazelnut

noce *no-che* nuts; also walnut
  –**di cocco** *dee kok-ko* coconut
  –**moscata** *mos-kah-tah* nutmeg

nocino *no-chee-no* walnut liqueur

non troppo cotta/o *non trop-o kot-ah/o* medium rare

norma, alla *nor-mah, ah-lah* pasta sauce with fried eggplant and tomato (Sicilia)

nostrano *nos-trah-no* hard cheese; also refers to local, homemade or domestic produce

O

oca *o-kah* goose

offelle *off-e-le* round stuffed pasta made with flour and potato
  –**in minestra** *in mi-nes-trah* **offelle** stuffed with minced meat, sausage and spinach, served in broth (Trieste, Friuli)

olio *ol-yo* oil – almost always olive oil
  –**d'oliva** *do-lee-vah* olive oil (see the **Olive Oil** section in the **Staples** chapter for more details)

olive *o-li-ve* olives
  –**ascolane** *ahs-ko-lah-ne* breaded and fried olives stuffed with roast chicken, pork or veal mixed with eggs, cheese and spices (Ascoli Piceno, Marche)

olivo *o-li-vo* olive tree

ombrichelli *om-bri-ke-lee* sweets made with flour, water, hazelnuts and chestnut honey (Lazio)

opinus *o-pee-noos* pine-cone-shaped biscuits sprinkled with melted sugar and egg whites (Sardegna)

ora dello spuntino *o-rah de-lo spun-tee-no* snack time

ora di merenda *o-rah dee me-ren-dah* snack time

orata *or-ah-tah* bream/gilthead

orecchiette *o-rek-ye-te* shell-shaped hand-made pasta, served with vegetables and olive oil or a rich meat sauce
  –**con cime di rapa** *kon chee-me dee rah-pah* **orecchiette** with turnip tops and anchovies (Puglia)

origano *o-ree-gah-no* oregano

ortiche *or-tee-ke* nettles

Orvieto *or-vee-ye-to* usually a dry white wine but can sometimes be sweet

orzo *or-zo* barley
  –**e fagioli** *e fah-jo-lee* thick barley and bean broth

ossa *os-ah* bones

ossi di morti *os-ah dey mor-ti* very hard crunchy biscuits (Lombardia)

ossobuco *os-o-boo-ko* veal shanks
  –**milanese** *mi-lahn-e-ze* veal shanks cut into small pieces cooked with butter, oil and tomato sauce and a sauce prepared with chopped lemon peel, garlic, rosemary, sage and parsley (Milano, Lombardia)

P

osteria *os-ter-ee-yah* cheap restaurants that offer simple local dishes and generally cater for locals

ostriche *os-tri-ke* oysters

ovolo *o-vo-lo* delicate rare Caesar's mushroom
–in fricassea *in fri-kah-see-ah* **ovoli** fried in oil, served with beaten eggs and lemon juice are added (Calabria)

P

padella *pah-del-ah* frying pan

padella, in *pah-del-ah, in* sauté

paesana, alla *pah-ye-sah-nah, ah-lah* country style – hearty/rustic

Pagadebit (di Romagna) *pah-gah-de-bit (dee rom-ahn-yah)* white grape variety and **DOC** zone

pagliata *pahl-yah-tah* small intestine of milk-fed calves

pagnottella *pahn-yo-te-lah* bread roll

pajata *pah-yah-tah* small intestine of milk-fed calves

palle *pah-le* balls
–del nonno *del no-no* 'grandpa's balls' – sweet fried **ricotta** balls; also crinkly pork sausages
–di riso *dee ri-zo* rice croquettes stuffed with bacon, and vegetables breaded and fried (Campania)

palombaccio *pah-lom-bah-chee* squab, wood pigeon
–alla ghiotta *ah-lah gyo-tah* squab roasted on a spit and served with a red wine sauce, often accompanied by black olives (Umbria)

palombo *pah-lom-bo* dove, pigeon; also a delicious fish related to sharks
–alla todina *ah-lah to-dee-nah* roasted pigeon (Umbria)

pan biscotto condito *pahn bis-kot-o kon-dee-to* toasted bread served with oil, tomatoes and herbs (Calabria)

pan de mej *pahn de may* sweet, round, crunchy flat corn bread prepared for Saint George's Feast (Milano, Lombardia)

pan speziale *pahn spets-yah-le* tasty bread made with honey, almonds, hazelnuts, raisins, chocolate, pine nuts, candied fruit and cinnamon (Emilia-Romagna)

panadas *pahn-dahs* pastry filled with flattened meatballs made with minced pork and veal, cheese, dried tomatoes, parsley and saffron (Sardegna)

pancetta *pahn-che-tah* salt-cured bacon

pancotto *pahn-kot-o* soup made with boiled bread, oil or butter, cheese and eggs or fresh tomatoes (Lombardia)

pandolce di Natale *pahn-dol-che dee nah-tah-le* Christmas cake made with candied fruit, sultanas, pine nuts, pistachios and **Marsala** (Liguria)

pandoro di Verona *pahn-do-ro dee ve-ro-nah* traditional star-shaped Christmas cake (Verona, Veneto)

pane *pah-ne* bread – each region tends to have its own style of bread and they're all simply called **pane**.
–all'olio *ahl ol-yo* oil bread
–aromatico *ah-ro-mah-tee-ko* herb or vegetable bread
–carasau *kah-rah-sah-oo* long-lasting bread used by isolated shepherds (Sardegna)
–casereccio *kah-ze-rech-o* firm, floury loaf
–col mosto *kol mos-to* bread made with nuts, anise, almonds, raisins, sugar and must (Urbino, Marche)
–di segale *dee se-gah-le* rye bread
–frattau *frah-tah-oo* very thin slices of bread sprinkled with grated sheep's cheese, tomato or meat sauce, boiling broth and poached eggs (Sardegna)
–fresa *fre-zah* flat crispy bread (Sardegna)
–integrale *in-te-grah-le* wholemeal bread

ITALIAN CULINARY DICTIONARY

–pugliese *pul-ye-ze* large crusty loaf

–salato *sah-lah-to* salty bread

–toscano *to-skah-no* crumbly, unsalted bread (Toscana)

–unto *oon-to* slices of bread toasted, sprinkled with fresh garlic and seasoned with abundant olive oil, salt and pepper (Toscana, Siena)

panelle *pah-ne-le* fried chickpea fritters

panetteria *pah-net-ter-yah* bakery

panettone (di Milano) *pah-ne-to-ne (dee mi-lah-no)* traditional sweet Christmas cake (Milano, Lombardia)

panetun magher *pah-ne-toon mah-ger* (see **biscio'la**)

panforte (senese) *pahn-for-te (se-ne-ze)* hard cake made with almonds, candied fruit and spices (Toscana, Siena)

panino *pah-nee-no* bread roll

paniscia novarese *pah-nee-shah no-vah-re-ze* rice-based dish with onion, sausage and a rich vegetable soup (Novara, Piedmont)

panna *pah-nah* cream

panna cotta *pahn-ah kot-ah* thick creamy dessert (Piedmont)

panon *pah-non* (see **biscio'la**)

panotti *pah-no-tee* large grilled meatballs prepared with maize meal, sausage and potatoes (Liguria)

panpepato *pahm-pe-pah-to* ring-shaped sweet cake (Ferrara, Emilia-Romagna)

pansotti in salsa di noci *pahn-so-ti in sahl-sah dee no-chi* pasta stuffed with **preboggion** and served with a nut-based sauce (Liguria)

panzanella *pahnt-sah-ne-lah* starter – stale Tuscan bread served with tomato sauce, onion, lettuce, anchovies, basil, olive oil, vinegar and salt (Siena, Toscana)

panzerotti *pahn-ze-ro-tee* half-moon pastries, either fried or baked, stuffed with savoury fillings

–dolci *dol-chi* sweet **panzerotti** stuffed with boiled chickpeas, sugar, cinnamon and chocolate sprinkled with icing sugar or honey (Basilicata)

paparot *pah-pah-rot* spinach and corn soup (Istria, Friuli)

papassinas *pah-pah-si-nahs* small sweet cone-shaped cakes (Nuoro, Sardegna)

pappa *pahp-pah* babyfood

–pomodoro *kol po-mo-do-ro* soup made with thin slices of stale bread, tomatoes, basil, garlic, olive oil, cloves and pepper (Siena, Toscana)

pappardelle *pah-pahr-de-le* wide flat pasta ribbons

–alla lepre *ah-lah le-pre* with a stewed hare, red wine and tomato sauce (Toscana)

pardulas *pahr-doo-lahs* (see **casadinas**)

parmigiana, alla *pahr-mee-jah-nah, ah-lah* could be any type of cheesy sauce

parmigiana di melanzane *pahr-mee-jah-nah dee me-lant-sah-ne* fried eggplant layered with hard-boiled eggs, basil, **mozzarella**, tomato sauce and onion, and baked (Campania)

parmigiano (reggiano) *pahr-mee-jah-no (rej-ah-no)* parmesan cheese – made from cow's milk, it's matured for at least one year. Often simply called **grana**, it's used extensively as a grating cheese but is also delicious to eat on its own. (Emilia-Romagna)

parrozzo *pah-rot-so* home-made, sweet chocolate-covered bread (Pescara, Abruzzo)

partenopeo *pahr-ten-o-pay-o* from Napoli

passatelli *pah-sah-te-li* small dumplings made with eggs, breadcrumbs, parmesan, ox marrow and nutmeg, cooked and served in meat stock (Emilia-Romagna)

–all'urbinate *ahl-or-bee-nah-te* small dumplings made of pasta and other ingredients such as breadcrumbs, grated parmesan, sheep's cheese, lemon peel, nutmeg and eggs, cooked in meat stock, strained and served with white truffles (Urbino, Marche)

passeggiata *pah-se-jah-tah* a stroll/walk

pasta *pah-stah* general name for the numerous types of pasta shapes – mainly made with durham wheat; also dough

–'**ncasciata** *n-kah-shah-tah* baked pie made with small pasta, meat sauce, meatballs, hard-boiled eggs, fried eggplant, cheese, peas, dry-cured pork sausage and **caciocavallo** (Sicilia)

–**a la jonica** *ah-lah yo-nee-kah* pasta (usually **penne** or **ziti**) baked with anchovies, cheese, breadcrumbs, salt and fennel (Calabria)

–**col bianchetto** *kol byahn-ke-to* spaghetti with a whitebait, tomato, garlic, and chilli sauce (Calabria)

–**cresciuta** *kre-shoo-tah* anchovy or courgette flower fritters (Campania)

–**degli agnoli** *del-yi ahn-yo-lee* fresh pasta made with eggs and a mixture of normal and buckwheat flour (Turin, Piedmont)

–**e alici** *e ah-lee-chi* pasta with anchovies sprinkled with bread crumbs and sheep's cheese (Calabria)

–**e ceci** *e che-chee* meatless soup with chickpeas and short pasta (Lazio)

–**e fagioli** *e fah-jo-lee* bean soup with pasta

–**fresca** *fres-kah* general term for freshly made pasta

–**lardiata** *lahrd-yah-tah* rarely seen dish in which pasta is served with a sauce made with lard, onion, tomatoes, salt and basil (Campania)

pastasciutta *pah-stah-shoo-tah* odd term which means dry pasta, that is, drained pasta not served in broth

pasticceria *pah-stee-che-ree-yah* pastry shop

pasticcio di maccheroni *pah-sti-cho dee mah-ke-ro-ni* baked sweet pastry

stuffed with pasta and a squab sauce (Trento, Trentino Alto-Adige)

pastiera napoletana *pahst-ye-rah nah-po-le-tah-nah* Easter cake – flaky pastry stuffed with fresh **ricotta** (Napoli, Campania)

pastizzada *pah-stit-sah-dah* stew prepared with beef or horse meat, celery, carrots and parsley (Verona, Veneto)

patata/e *pah-tah-tah/te* potato/es

pecora *pe-ko-rah* sheep

pecorino (romano) *pe-ko-ree-no (ro-mah-no)* hard and spicy cheese made from ewe's milk (Roma, Lazio)

–**sardo** *sahr-do* nutty ewe's milk cheese (Sardegna)

penne *pen-ne* short and tubular pasta

–**all'arrabbiata** *ah-lah rahb-yah-tah* 'angry style', **penne** served with a spicy tomato, browned pig's cheek and mushroom sauce (Lazio)

pentola *pen-to-lah* pot or pan

–**a pressione** *ah pres-yo-ne* pressure cooker

peperonata *pe-pe-ro-nah-tah* pepper, onion and tomato stew

peperoncini *pe-pe-ron-chee-nee* hot chili

peperoni *pe-pe-ro-nee* pepperoni/capsicum

–**di Pontecorvo ripieni** *dee pon-te-kor-vo rip-ye-nee* red and yellow capsicum stuffed with stale bread, cooked must, pine nuts, nuts and raisins (Ciociaria, Lazio)

pera/e *pe-rah/re* pear/s

–**imbottite** *im-bot-ee-te* baked stuffed pears (Campania)

persico *per-see-ko* perch

pesca *pes-kah* peach

pesce *pesh-e* fish

–**gatto** *gah-to* catfish

–**San Pietro** *sahn pee-ye-tro* John Dory – expensive but popular fish

–**sciabola** *shah-bo-lah* sabre fish – very long and bony

pescespada *pesh-e-spah-dah* swordfish
–a ghiotta *ah gyo-tah* swordfish roulades (Sicilia)

pescestocco *pesh-e-sto-ko (see* **stoccafisso**)
–con patate *kon pah-tah-te* stoccafisso cooked with onion, tomato, chilli, potatoes and capers, garnished with green olives & parsley (Calabria)

pesto *pe-sto* one of the most famous Italian sauces – prepared with fresh basil, pine nuts (or, sometimes, walnuts), olive oil, garlic, cheese, sheep's cheese, parmesan and salt (Liguria, Genoa)

petrale *pe-trah-le* traditional Christmas cake made with shortcrust pastry filled with dried figs, almonds, nuts, mandarin peel, cocoa, cloves and cinnamon (Calabria)

petto *pet-to* breast

pettole *pet-o-le* home-made long thin ribbons of pasta (Campania)
–e fagioli sfritti *e fahj-yo-lee sfri-ti* served with beans, garlic and chilli (Campania)

piadina *pyah-dee-nah* flat round bread

piatto *pee-yah-to* plate, course

piccagge *pik-ah-je* long ribbon pasta served with **pesto** or an artichoke and dry mushroom sauce (Liguria)

piccante *pi-kahn-te* spicy (hot); also piquant, sharp tasting

piccata *pi-kah-tah* veal with a thick lemon and **Marsala** sauce

picchi pacchiu *pik-yi pahk-yoo* pasta sauce with tomato and chilli

pici *pee-chee* fresh pasta, like thick spaghetti (Siena, Toscana)
–all'aglione *ahl-ahl-yo-ne* served with a tomato, garlic, and chilli sauce (Siena, Toscana)

piccione *pi-cho-ne* squab/pigeon

picula ad caval *pi-koo-lah ahd kah-vahl* horse meat stew (Piacenza, Emilia-Romagna)

pignato grasso *pin-yah-to grah-so (see* **minestra maritata**)

pignolata *pin-yo-lah-tah* striking Christmas cakes – baked balls of pastry arranged as a pine cone (Messina, Sicilia)

pinoccate *pi-no-kah-te* small Christmas cakes wrapped up in coloured paper (Perugia, Umbria)

pinoli *pi-no-lee* pine nuts

pinza padovana *pin-zah pah-do-vah-nah* sweet pastry (Padova, Veneto)

pinzimonio *pin-zi-mo-nee-yo* seasoned virgin olive oil used for dipping raw vegetables *(see also* **cazzimperio**)

piopparello *pyo-pah-re-lo* common flat mushroom

pisarei e fasó *pi-zah-rey e fah-zo* small dumplings made with breadcrumbs, flour and milk, boiled and flavoured with tomato sauce, bacon and boiled beans (Piacenza, Emilia-Romagna)

piscial'Andrea *pish-al ahn-dre-ah* a cake which looks like a pizza, garnished with tomatoes, olives, pickles and anchovies (Imperia, Liguria)

piselli *pi-ze-lee* green peas
–col guanciale *kol gwahn-chah-le* green peas, cooked with the side portion of a pig's head and broth (Lazio)

pistum *pees-toom* sweet-and-sour first course – dumplings of breadcrumbs, sugar, eggs, herbs and sultanas, boiled and served with pork stock (Friuli)

pitta *pit-ah* soft and flat loaf of bread (Calabria)

pitte *pit-e* big circle or a ring-shaped cake flavoured with fried tomatoes, oil and chilli. It can also be covered with another disk of dough and stuffed with **ricotta**, hard-boiled eggs, **provola**, sausage and chilli. (Calabria)

pizza *pit-sah* there are more than 50 kinds of pizza, but the basic ingredient is always the same – dough cooked in a very hot wood-burning oven (Campania)

–a(l) taglio *ah(l) tahl-yo* slice of **pizza**

–di Pasqua *dee pahs-kwah* studded with fresh and mature sheep's cheese, eggs and olive oil, usually served with local dry-cured pork sausage and hard-boiled eggs (Umbria)

–dolce *dol-che* sponge cake with rum, chocolate and almonds (Abruzzo)

–Margherita *mahr-ge-ree-tah* pizza with simple ingredients such as oil, tomato, slices of **mozzarella**, basil and oregano (Napoli, Campania)

–rustica *roo-stik-ah* pizza stuffed with ham, hard-boiled egg, cheese, sausage, and cinnamon (Abruzzo)

pizzaiola, alla *pits-ah-yo-lah, ah-lah* loosely, a tomato and oil sauce

pizzaiolo *pits-ah-yo-lo* pizza maker

pizzeria *pit-sree-yah* pizza restaurant

pizzoccheri *pit-so-ke-ree* short buckwheat pasta with savoy cabbage and potatoes (Valtellina, Lombardia)

poco cotto *po-ko kot-o* rare (cooked)

polenta *po-len-tah* corn meal porridge staple of northern Italy served with myriad sauces. Traditionally slowly cooked in a copper pot and continually stirred, but instant varieties are now popular. Can be served soft, but is often left to cool and sliced, deep-fried or grilled.

–al ragù *ahl rah-goo* **polenta** served with a pork, tomato and chilli sauce

–concia *kon-chah* fresh, soft **polenta** flavoured with **fontina** cubes; also can be baked sliced **polenta** arranged in layers with **fontina** (Valle d'Aosta)

–e osei *e o-zey* there are two completely different versions of this dish: **polenta** with **stuffed** sparrows, thrushes or larks (Lombardia and Veneto); also a sponge cake with jam (usually apricot), covered with yellow icing topped with small chocolate birds and jam (Bergamo, Lombardia)

–pasticciata *pah-sti-chah-tah* **polenta** baked with meat sauce, butter and cheese. Sometimes bechamel, mushroom sauce or thin slices of truffle are added. (Lombardia)

–sulla spianatoria *su-lah spee-yahn-ah-tor-yah* communal dish where polenta with sausages, tomato and sheep's cheese is served from a **spianatoria** (pastry board) placed in the middle of the table (Umbria)

–Taragna *tah-rahn-yah* buckwheat **polenta** with lots of butter and cheese (Valtellina, Lombardia)

polipo *po-lee-po* octopus *(see **polpi**)*

–alla luciana *ah-lah loo-chah-nah* sliced octopus with oil, garlic, parsley, and lemon (Campania, Napoli)

pollame *po-lah-me* poultry

pollo *po-lo* chicken

–alla diavola *ah-lah dee-yah-vo-lah* grilled chicken with oil, red pepper (or chilli) and lemon juice (Toscana)

–alla marengo *ah-lah mah-ren-go* chicken with white wine, tomatoes and mushrooms (Piedmont)

–alla trentina *ah-lah tren-tee-nah* chicken stuffed with pine nuts, liver, egg and bread (Trentino Alto-Adige)

–con peperoni e patate al coccio *kon pe-pe-ro-nee e pah-tah-te ahl ko-cho* free-range chicken slowly cooked in a terracotta pot with sage, potatoes and capsicum (Ciociaria, Lazio)

polpette *pol-pe-te* meatballs

polpettine *pol-pe-tee-ne* small meatballs

–di carne con salsa di pomodoro *dee kahr-ne kon sahl-sah dee po-mo-do-ro* very small meatballs crumbed, fried and served with tomato sauce and parmesan (Cremona, Lombardia)

polpettone *pol-pe-to-ne* meatloaf – there are many versions of this, but they generally include meat, cheese and breadcrumbs

–di tacchino *dee tah-kee-no* rolled turkey breast fillets filled with minced veal and spices (Reggio Emilia, Emilia-Romagna)

polpi *pol-pi* octopus (see **polipo**)

–in purgatorio *in pur-gah-tor-yo* stewed octopus with tomato, parsley, chilli and garlic (Abruzzo)

pomià *pom-yah* slices of rye bread covered with a vegetable and bean soup (Brianza, Lombardia)

pomodoro/i *po-mo-do-ro/ri* tomato/es

–e peperoni ripieni *e pe-pe-ro-ni rip-ye-ni* capsicum and tomatoes stuffed with capers, basil, green olives and anchovies (Calabria)

–secchi *po-mo-do-ri se-kee* sun-dried tomatoes

pomodorini *po-mo-do-ree-nee* sun-dried tomatoes

pompelmo *pom-pel-mo* grapefruit

porchetta *por-ke-tah* suckling pig stuffed with wild fennel, rosemary, white wine, salt and pepper and baked in a wood-fired oven (Marche)

–infinocchiata *in-fee-nok-yah-tah* roast suckling pig stuffed with a mixture of heart, liver, lungs, fennel seed, pepper, garlic and salt (Umbria)

porcini *por-chee-nee* ceps – most popular mushrooms in Italy. Eaten fresh but also often dried.

porco *por-ko* pig

potizza *po-tit-sah* soft cake prepared with leavened pastry (Friuli)

pranzo *prahn-zo* lunch

prataiolo *prah-tah-yo-lo* popular button mushroom

preboggion *pre-bo-jon* mixture of wild herbs (Liguria)

prebugiun *pre-boo-joon* (see **preboggion**)

preivi *pray-vee* vegetables (mainly cabbage leaves) stuffed with cheese, eggs, garlic and parsley (Liguria)

prenotare *pre-no-tah-re* to book

prenotazione *pre-no-tat-syo-ne* reservation

presnitz *pres-nits* Easter fruit cake (Friuli, Trieste)

pressione, pentola a *pres-yo-ne, pen-to-ah* pressure cooker

prezzo *pret-so* price

prima colazione *pree-mah ko-lah-tsyo-ne* breakfast

primo *pree-mo* first course, although **antipasto** usually comes before it

prosciutto *pro-shoo-to* basic name for many types of ham and, sometimes, salami

–affumicato *ah-foo-mi-kah-to* smoked salami (Molise and Abruzzo)

–aretino *ah-re-tee-no* lean, salty ham (Arezzo, Toscana)

–cotto *ko-to* cooked ham

–crudo (di Parma) *kroo-do (dee pahr-mah)* excellent air-dried and salt-cured ham – the best known and best Italian ham (Parma)

–di Montefeltro *dee mon-te-fel-tro* salted and smoked ham (Marche)

–San Daniele *sahn dahn-ye-le* sweet and delicate ham (Friuli)

Prosecco *pro-se-ko* type of white grape; also a delicious sparkling white, (though sometimes not sparkling)

provola *pro-vo-lah* semi-hard cheese made from buffalo and cow's milk (Campania)

provolette *pro-vo-le-te* similar to **provolone**

provolone *pro-vo-lo-ne* rich medium hard cheese made from cow's milk. The less mature cheese has a sweet and buttery taste while the mature is spicy and salty. Originally from the south but now made all over Italy.

puttanesca, alla *poo-tah-nes-kah, ah-lah* 'whore's style' – tomato, chilli and black olive pasta sauce (Lazio)

Q

quaglie *kwal-ye* quails

quartirolo *kwahr-tee-ro-lo* sweet and delicate soft cheese (Lombardia)

quattro formaggi *kwah-tro for-mah-jee* pasta sauce with four different cheeses

quattro stagioni *kwah-tro stah-jo-nee* pizza with different toppings on each quarter

R

rabarbaro *rah-bahr-bah-ro* rhubarb

raccolto *rah-kol-to* harvest

radicchio *rah-dik-yo* chicory
   –rosso *ross-o* slightly bitter vegetable with long leaves (Treviso, Veneto)

rafano tedesco *rah-fah-no te-desk-o* horseradish

ragù *rah-goo* generally a meat sauce but sometimes vegetarian
   –alla bolognese *ah-lah bo-lon-ye-ze* meat sauce, prepared with minced veal or pork, liver, onion, ham, carrots, celery, tomatoes, lemon peel and nutmeg (Bologna, Emilia-Romagna)
   –alla napoletana *ah-lah nah-po-le-tah-nah* sauce made with chunks of meat (pork and veal), vegetables and red wine (Napoli, Campania)
   –di maiale e vitello *dee mah-yah-le e vi-te-lo* sauce prepared with pork, veal, wine and tomatoes (Calabria)
   –napoletano *nah-po-le-tah-no* slow-cooked sauce of tomato, minced veal, ham, salted bacon, parsley and wine (Napoli, Campania)

ramaiolo *rah-mah-yo-lo* ladle

rambasicci *rahm-bah-zee-chi* stuffed cabbage leaves (Friuli)

rane *rah-ne* frogs
   –in guazzetto *in gwah-ze-to* frogs cooked in butter, white wine and broth (Pavia, Lombardia)

rapa *rah-pah* turnip

rapa, cime di *rah-pah, chee-me dee* turnip tops – used as a vegetable

ravioli *rah-vee-o-lee* stuffed pasta squares – can be stuffed with meat, fish or vegetables
   –di magro *dee mah-gro* stuffed with fish, potatoes or artichokes and other vegetables (Liguria)
   –di Potenza *dee po-ten-zah* stuffed with cured ham, parsley, eggs and **ricotta**, served with meat sauce and **ricotta** or sheep's cheese (Basilicata)
   –liguri *li-gu-ree* stuffed with meat, breadcrumbs and served with parmesan and sauce (Liguria)

raviolini *rah-vee-o-lee-nee* small **ravioli**

ravioloni *rah-vee-o-lo-nee* large **ravioli**

razza *raht-sah* skate

regione *rej-yo-ne* region

resto *res-to* change (coins)

ri in cagnon *ree in kahn-yon* boiled rice sautéd in a saucepan with melted butter and cubed soft cheese (Piedmont); also prepared with boiled rice flavoured with parmesan, melted butter, garlic and sage (Lombardia)

ribes nero *ri-bes ne-ro* blackcurrant

ribes rosso *ri-bes ross-o* redcurrant

ribollita *ri-bo-lee-tah* vegetable soup reheated and thickened with bread, usually includes cabbage (Toscana)

ricciarelli *ri-chah-re-li* delicious almond biscuits (Siena, Toscana)

ricci di mare *ri-chee dee mah-re* sea urchins

ricetta *ri-che-tah* recipe

ricotta *ri-ko-tah* soft cheese
   –affumicata *ah-foo-mi-kah-tah* smoked

–infornata *in-for-nah-tah* oven baked

–romana *ro-mah-nah* sheep's milk **ricotta**

ridurre *ri-doo-re* to reduce

rigaglie *ri-gahl-ye* giblets

rigati *ri-gah-tee* ridged – used to describe ridged pasta

rigatoni *ree-gah-to-nee* short fat tubes of pasta

–con la pagliata *kon lah pahl-yah-tah* served with **pagliata** cooked in white wine, tomatoes and spices (Lazio)

ripieno *rip-ye-no* stuffed

riservare *ri-ser-vah-re* to book

risi e bisi *ri-zi e bi-zi* thick rice-based soup prepared with peas and a delicate pea pod broth (Venezia, Veneto)

risi e bruscandoli *ri-zi e brus-kahn-do-lee* bitter hop sprouts cooked in broth with rice, salt and pepper served with parmesan and butter (Veneto)

riso *ri-zo* rice – there are around 50 varieties grown in Italy separated into different grades:

–comune *ko-moo-ne* lowest quality, small grained rice usually used in soups

–fino *fee-no* good quality with large grains

–semifino *se-mee fee-no* slightly better quality than **comune**, with larger grains – varieties include vialane nano and rubino

–superfino *soo-per-fee-no* best quality rice used in **risotto** – varieties include arborio and carnaroli

riso al salto *ri-zo ahl sahl-to* half-cooked rice cooked again to form a crusty pie (Lombardia)

risotto *ri-zo-to* rice dish slowly cooked to a creamy consistency with the rice absorbing broth so that is **al dente**. Often served with meat dishes.

–alla milanese *ah-lah mi-lah-ne-ze* rice with ox marrow, meat stock, and saffron (Milano, Lombardia)

–alla monzese *ah-lah mon-ze-ze* rice with sausage and red wine (Monza, Lombardia)

–alla piemontese *ah-lah pye-mon-te-ze* white **risotto** cooked with white wine and truffles. There's a 'red' version with tomato sauce. (Piedmont)

–alla sbirraglia *ah-lah sbi-rahl-yah* rice cooked in broth with chicken breasts (Treviso, Veneto)

–alla trevisana *ah-lah tre-vi-zah-nah* rice cooked with onion, celery and sausage (Treviso, Veneto)

–allo zafferano *ah-lo zah-fe-rah-no* (see **risotto alla milanese**)

–con filetti di pesce persico *kon fi-le-ti dee pesh-e per-see-ko* white **risotto** with perch fillets (Lombardia)

–con le rane *kon le rah-ne* rice with frog legs, garlic, herbs, and frog broth (Pavia, Lombardia)

–nero *ne-ro* black **risotto** with chards, onion, cuttlefish & their ink (Toscana)

–polesano *po-le-zahn-o* rice with eel, grey mullet and bass, white wine and fish broth (Venezia, Veneto)

ristorante *ri-sto-rahn-te* restaurant

ristretto *ree-stre-to* very short black coffee

robiola *rob-yo-lah* cheese made mainly from cow's milk with some sheep and goat's milk. Soft, compact, delicate and a little sour. There's a more mature spicy version. (Piedmont)

romana, alla *ro-mah-nah, ah-lah* sauce, usually tomato based

romagnolo, alla *ro-mahn-yo-lo, ah-lah* (see **romana, alla**)

rombo *rom-bo* turbot

rosada *ro-zah-dah* (see **budino del prete**)

rosbif *roz-bif* roast beef

rosmarino *roz-mah-ree-no* rosemary

rosolata *ro-zo-lah-tah* sauté

rospo *ross-po* angler fish

rosso *ro-so* red

rosticceria *ros-ti-che-ree-ya* restaurant that specialises in grilled meat and is often takeaway only

rosumada *ro-soo-mah-dah* very energy-giving egg-nog with beaten yolks and good red wine (Lombardia)

rotolo *ro-to-lo* large folded sheet of pasta stuffed with spinach, **ricotta** or meat, usually served with tomato sauce

rotondo *ro-ton-do* semi-dry/full (wine)

rubinetto *ru-bi-ne-to* tap/fawcett

ruchetta *roo-ke-tah* rocket

rucola *roo-ko-lah* rocket

rum–babà *room bah-bah* **babà** sprinkled with rum and sugar

rustica *roo-sti-kah* rustic

ruta *roo-ta* rue – bitter herb, sometimes used to flavour **grappa**

S

sa fregula *sah fre-goo-lah* soup – small balls of flour and saffron cooked in broth, served with cheese (Sardegna)

sagne chine *sahn-ye kee-ne* baked pasta with small meatballs, hard-boiled eggs and cheese (Calabria)

salama da sugo ferrarese *sah-lah-mah dah soo-go fe-rah-re-ze* pork sausage matured for a year. It's usually stewed and served with mashed potatoes or pumpkin. (Ferrara, Emilia-Romagna)

salame *sah-lah-me* (see **salami**)

salame di Felino *sah-lah-me dee fe-lee-no* excellent dry-cured pork sausage (Felino, Emilia-Romagna)

salami *sah-lah-mee* generally any type of sausage – usually pork

salamino *sah-lah-mee-no* small salami

salumeria *sah-loo-me-ree-yah* salami shop

salato/a *sah-lah-to/ah* salty

sale *sah-le* salt

salmì *sahl-mee* marinade prepared with spices and sometimes wine – usually used with game (Lombardia)

salmone *sahl-mo-ne* salmon

salsa *sahl-sah* sauce
  –alfredo *ahl-fre-do* sauce with butter, cream, parmesan and parsley
  –alla checca *ah-lah ke-kah* cold sauce with tomatoes, olives, basil, capers and oregano (Roma, Lazio)
  –alla pizzaiola *ah-lah pit-sah-yo-lah* pizza-style sauce (with tomatoes and red capsicum)
  –di cren *dee kren* sauce with grated radish and apples, onion, broth and white wine, usually served with boiled meat (Trentino Alto-Adige)
  –di pomodoro al tonno e funghi *dee po-mo-do-ro ahl to-no e foon-gi* tuna and mushroom in tomato and cream
  –di pomodoro alla siciliana *dee po-mo-do-ro ah-lah si-chil-yah-nah* sauce with eggplant, anchovies, olives, capers, tomato and garlic (Sicilia)
  –verde *ver-de* green sauce with basil, parsley, capers, olives, egg yolks, pine nuts, anchovies, breadcrumbs, garlic and vinegar (Emilia-Romagna)

salsicce all'uva *sahl-si-che ahl-oo-vah* sausage and grape casserole (Umbria)

salsiccia *sahl-si-chah* sausage
  –di sangue *dee sahng-gwe* blood sausage, made with pig's blood, parsley, breadcrumbs, garlic and celery (Trentino Alto-Adige)

saltare *sahl-tah-re* to sauté

saltimbocca *sahl-tim-bo-kah* 'jump into the mouth', bite-sized
  –alla romana *ah-lah ro-mah-nah* slices of very tender veal with ham and sage leaves, cooked in butter and white wine (Roma, Lazio)

salume *sah-loo-me* salami

salumeria *sah-loo-me-ree-yah* smallgood shop specialising in salami

Salute! *sah-loo-te* Cheers!

salvia *sahl-vee-yah* sage
  –fritta *fri-tah* a variety of sage with large leaves battered and fried. Served hot and crunchy – often an anchovy is added. (Toscana, Siena)

sambuca *sahm-boo-kah* anise liqueur

Sangiovese *sahn-jo-ve-ze* red grape – mainly used in **Chianti**

sangue *sahng-we* blood

sangue, al *sahng-we, ahl* rare (cooked)

sanguinaccio *sahng-gwi-nah-cho* black pudding made with pig's blood, olives and cocoa (Lazio)

saor, in *sah-or* sweet and sour vinegar-based marinade for fish

saorina *sah-or-ee-na* wine-based sauce (see **tortelli sguazzarotti**)

sapore *sah-po-re* taste (flavour)

sarago *sah-rah-go* white bream

sarde *sahr-de* sardines
  –a beccafico ripiene *ah be-kah-fee-ko rip-ye-ne* baked sardines with bread crumbs, anchovies, pine nuts, cinnamon, raisins and lemon juice (Sicilia)
  –a scapece *ah skah-pe-che* fried sardines (Calabria)
  –alla marchigiana *ah-lah mahr-ki-jah-nah* sardines marinated in oil, salt and rosemary, sprinkled with grated cheese and baked (Marche)

sardele in saor *sahr-de-le in sa-hor* dish prepared with fried pilchards marinated in onions, vinegar, sugar, pine nuts and sultanas (Venezia, Veneto)

sartù 'e riso *sahr-too e ri-zo* savoury rice dish with meatballs, sausage, chicken giblets, **mozzarella**, peas, mushrooms, hard-boiled eggs and meat sauce (Napoli, Campania)

sas corrias *sahs ko-ree-ahs* (see **pane carasau**)

sas melicheddas *sahs me-li-ke-dahs* marzipan cakes sprinkled with sugar (Sardegna)

sassolino *sah-so-lee-no* salami boiled and served with mashed potatoes (Modena, Emilia-Romagna); also an aniseed liqueur

sausa d'avie *sauw-sah dah-vee-ye* honey, nut and mustard sauce

savoiardi *sah-voy-ahr-dee* ladyfinger biscuits, eaten at breakfast and often used in desserts

sbrofadej *zbro-fah-day* thin pasta (Lombardia)
  –in brodo *in bro-do* **sbrofadej** served in broth (Lombardia)

scagliuozzoli *skahl-yu-ots-o-li* fried **polenta** stuffed with **provolone** (Campania)

scaloppine *skah-lo-pee-ne* thin cutlets, usually veal but often pork or turkey
  –al marsala *ahl mahr-sah-lah* lean veal cutlet with **marsala** (Lombardia)

scamorza *skah-mort-sa* white soft cheese, similar to **mozzarella** and often smoked

scampi *skahm-pee* a small type of delicious lobster

scapece *skah-pe-che* vinegar-based marinade usually used for fish
  –di Vasto *dee vahs-to* Vasto is a town famous for its big fish market – this dish is prepared with sliced and fried fish, preserved in a marinade of garlic, onion, vinegar and saffron (Abruzzo)

scarole *skah-ro-le* bitter leafy vegetable
  –farzite *fahr-chee-te* stewed stuffed-**scarole** served with garlic and salted anchovies (Napoli, Campania)

scarpetta *skahr-pe-tah* (see **fare la scarpetta**)

scatola *skah-to-lah* can (tin)

scatola, in *skah-to-la, in* canned

scatoletta *skah-to-le-tah* tin (can)

scelta *shel-ta* choice

schiaffettuni chini *skyah-fe-too-ni ki-ni* rectangular stuffed pasta served with tomato sauce and cheese (Calabria)

schiuma *skee-yoo-mah* foam/froth

schmorbraten *shmor-brah-ten* veal marinated and cooked in wine and tomato sauce (Trentino Alto-Adige)

sciatt *shahtt* soft round fritters made with buckwheat pastry, cheese and **grappa** (Valtellina, Lombardia)

scimù'd *shim-ood* skim milk cheese – lightly salted and spicy (Valtellina, Lombardia)

sciroppo *shi-ro-po* syrup

scivateddi *shi-vah-te-dee* home-made big spaghetti served with meat sauce (usually pork) and salted and smoked **ricotta** (Catanzaro, Calabria)

scottiglia *sko-teel-yah* very rich stew, prepared with tomatoes and many kinds of meat (Toscana)

scrippelle 'mbusse *skri-pe-le m-boo-se* (see **crespelle bagnate**)

sebadas *se-bah-dahs* big round sweet **ravioli** stuffed with sheep's cheese, fried and covered with honey (Nuoro, Sardegna)

seccia 'mbuttunata *se-chah m-boo-too-nah-tah* stuffed cuttlefish stewed with tomato sauce (Napoli, Campania)

secco *se-ko* dry

secondo *se-kon-do* second course

selvaggina *sel-vah-jee-nah* game

selvatico *sel-vah-tee-ko* wild

semifreddo *se-mi-fre-do* can refer to many cold creamy desserts
—al torrone *ahl to-ro-ne* rich dessert with milk, vanilla, eggs and almond nougat (Lombardia, Cremona)

semola *se-mo-lah* bran

semolino *se-mo-lee-no* semolina

senapa *se-nah-pa* mustard

seno *se-no* breast

seppia *sep-yah kon* cuttlefish
—col nero alla veneziana *kol ne-ro ah-lah ve-nets-yah-nah* striking dish of cuttlefish cooked in their ink, served with white polenta (Venezia, Veneto)
—con piselli *kon pi-ze-lee* cuttlefish, cooked with tomato sauce, anchovies and green peas (Lazio)

serpe *ser-pe* cake made with marzipan and almonds sprinkled with icing sugar or covered with chocolate (Marche, Macerata)

servizio *ser-vit-see-yo* service

sfoglia *sfol-yah* sheet (of pastry)

sfogliatelle *sfol-yah-te-le* rich cake prepared with layers of deep-fried crunchy flaky pastry; also a simple flaky pastry. Both are stuffed with **ricotta**, cinnamon, candied fruit and vanilla. (Napoli, Campania)

sformato *sfor-mah-to* flan
—di spinaci con cibreo al vinsanto *dee spee-nah-chee kon chi-bre-o ahl vin sahn-to* flan with spinach, milk, and nutmeg, served with liver (Toscana)

sgombro *sgom-bro* mackerel

sinistra *si-nis-trah* left (not right)

sogliola *sol-yo-lah* sole

sopa còada *so-pah ko-ah-dah* soup of meat stock, stewed pigeon, cheese and bread (Treviso, Veneto)

soppressa *so-pre-sah* pork sausage (Veneto)

soppressata *so-pre-sah-tah* matured raw salami made with minced pig's tongue, lean pork and spices (Basilicata); also a big, soft salami made with pork and lard (Veneto)
—molisana *so-pre-sah-tah mo-lee-zah-nah* large pork sausage, made with minced meat and lard (Molise)

sorbetto *sor-be-to* sorbet

sott'aceti *sot-ah-che-ti* pickles

sott'olio *sot-ol-ee-yo* preserved in oil

spacatto *spah-kah-to* split

spaghetti *spah-ge-ti* ubiquitous long thin strands of pasta

–ajo e oio *ah-yo e o-yo*
spaghetti flavoured with hot oil, garlic and sometimes chilli (Lazio)

–alla amatriciana *ah-lah ah-mah-tree-chah-nah* spaghetti with a sauce made with pig's cheek, lard, white wine, tomato, chilli and sheep's cheese (Rieti, Lazio)

–alla bolognese *ah-lah bo-lon-ye-ze* (*see* **ragù alla bolognese**)

–alla carbonara *ah-lah kahr-bo-nah-rah* spaghetti with bacon, butter, cheese, beaten eggs and sheep's cheese (sometimes parmesan) (Lazio)

–alla partenopea *ah-lah pahr-te-no-pe-ah* spaghetti with a **mozzarella**, tomato, bread crust, capers, olive, anchovies, basil, oil, chilli and salt sauce (Campania)

–alla pescatora *ah-lah pes-kah-to-rah* spaghetti with a fish, tomato and sweet herb sauce (Lazio)

–alla pommarola *ah-lah po-mah-ro-lah* spaghetti with a simple tomato sauce (Campania)

–alla puttanesca *ah-lah poo-tah-nes-kah* spaghetti with a garlic, anchovy, black olive, caper, tomato sauce, oil, chilli and butter sauce (Campania)

–cacio e pepe *kah-cho e pe-pe* spaghetti seasoned with black pepper and a lot of sheep's cheese (Lazio)

–con il tonno *kon il to-no* spaghetti with tomato, tuna and chilli (Lazio)

–con le vongole *kon le von-go-le* spaghetti with tomato and clam sauce, at times strongly peppered. It can also be served without tomatoes. (Lazio)

–con tartufo di Norcia *kon tahr-too-fo dee nor-chah* spaghetti served with a sauce prepared with black truffle, garlic, oil and anchovies (Umbria)

spá'tzle *spet-sle* little dumplings made with flour and eggs, boiled and then baked with melted butter and parmesan. They can also be served in broth. (Trentino Alto-Adige)

speck *spek* smoked ham, made with pork, flavoured with salt, bay leaf, pepper and grappa, smoked and matured for about three months. (Trentino Alto-Adige)

spezie *spet-see-ye* spices

spianatoria *spee-yah-nah-tor-ee-yah* pastry board

spiccioli *speech-o-lee* change (coins)

spiedino *spee-ye-dee-no* skewer

spiedo *spee-ye-do* skewer

spiedo, allo *spee-ye-do, ah-lo* roasted on a spit

spigola *spee-go-lah* sea bass

spina/e *spi-nah/e* fish bone

spinaci *spi-na-chee* spinach

spongada *spon-gah-tah* shortcrust pastry filled with honey, fruit mustard, breadcrumbs, walnuts, pine nuts, cinnamon, candied peel and spices (Emilia-Romagna)

spongarda *spon-gahr-dah* shortcrust pastry filled with honey, hazelnuts, candied citron, sultanas and spices (Crema, Lombardia)

spremuta *spre-moo-tah* fruit juice

spugnola *spoon-yo-lah* morel, sponge-like mushroom

spuma *spoo-mah* froth

Spumante *spoo-mahn-tee* sparkling sweet white wine

spuntino, (ora dello) *spun-tee-no, (o-rah de-lo)* snack (time)

stagionato *stah-jo-nah-to* aged

stecchi *ste-ki* sticks/kebabs

–alla ligure *ah-lah li-goo-re* kebabs with veal, chicken, sweetbread, marjoram, eggs, mushrooms, artichokes and spices (Chiavari, Liguria)

stecco *ste-ko/ki* stick/kebab

stiacciata *stee-yah-chah-tah* flat bread

–di berlingaccio *dee ber-lin-gah-cho* small sweet cakes (Firenze, Toscana)

stinchetti di pasta di mandorle *stin-ke-ti dee pahs-tah dee mahn-dor-le* little marzipan cakes prepared in November for All Souls' Day (November 2nd) – bone-shaped and covered with meringue (Umbria)

stinco *stin-ko* shank

stoccafisso *sto-kah-fee-so* stockfish – small air-dried cod
–a brandacujun *ah brahn-dah-koo-yoon* creamy dish made with potatoes and **stoccafisso** (Liguria)
–accomodato *ah-ko-mo-dah-to* **stoccafisso** cooked in a casserole with anchovies, served with olives, pine nuts and potatoes (Liguria)

stracchino *strah-kee-no* soft and delicate cheese (Lombardia)

stracciatella *strah-chah-te-lah* broth with whipped egg and parmesan

stracotto *strah-ko-to* 'cooked for a long time'; also beef cooked with oil, red wine, tomato and spices (Toscana)

strangolapreti *strahn-go-lah-pre-ti* shell-shaped pasta made with eggs, flour, and lemon peel, then fried (Basilicata) – however, there are as many versions of this dish as there are regions in Italy

strangozzi *strahn-got-see* (see **stringozzi**)

stravecchio *strah-vek-yo* very old, aged for a long time

strega *stre-gah* strong yellow herb liqueur used as a **digestivo**

stringozzi *strin-got-see* short pasta made with flour and water and served with tomato or meat sauce (Umbria)

strinù *stri-noo* tasty sausage made with pork or beef, usually grilled (Brescia, Lombardia)

stroscia di Pietrabruna *stro-shah dee pye-trah-broo-nah* sweet cake (Liguria)

strozzapreti *strot-sah-pre-ti* long strips of pasta usually served with a vegetable sauce (Emilia-Romagna); also dumplings made with spinach, chards and **ricotta** (Toscana)

strudel *stroo-del* pastry with a rich stuffing including apples, sultanas, pine nuts and breadcrumbs (Trentino Alto-Adige)

strutto *stroo-to* melted and strained pork fat eaten with bread or polenta

stufatino *stu-fah-tee-no* lean veal, cut and stewed with oil, garlic, rosemary, red wine and tomatoes (Toscana)

stuzzicadenti *stoot-si-kah-den-tee* toothpicks

stuzzichini *stu-tsi-kee-nee* snacks

subrics *soo-briks* (see **crocchette**)

succo *suk-ko* juice
–fresco *fres-ko* fresh juice

sugna *soon-yah* (see **strutto**)

sugo *soo-go* sauce/juice (usually tomato)

supa barbetta *soo-pah bahr-be-tah* rich stock prepared with chicken, pork, pig's bones, carrots, celery, leek and herbs, served with slices of stale bread and breadsticks (Piedmont)

suppa *soo-pah* soup
–a sbira *ah sbee-rah* tripe soup (Liguria)
–cuatta *koo-ah-tah* baked dish prepared with bread, cheese, meat stock, and lard (Sardegna)

supplì *su-plee* fried rice balls (similar to **crocchettes**)
–al telefono *ahl te-le-fo-no* fried rice balls stuffed with meat sauce, **mozzarella** cubes and mushrooms (Lazio)

surgelati *sur-je-lah-tee* frozen foods

suricitti *su-ri-chi-tee* dumplings made with polenta flavoured with sausage fat and fried in oil and lard (Macerata, Marche)

susamelli *su-zah-me-li* s-shaped biscuits prepared with sugar, honey, sesame and candied fruit (Campania)

susina *su-zee-nah* plum

sventrare *sven-trah-re* to gut

T

tacchino *tah-kee-no* turkey
–alla gosutta *ah-lah go-zu-tah* casseroled turkey with wild fennel and broth (Urbino, Marche)
–con sugo di melagrana *kon soo-go dee me-lah-grah-nah* turkey with pomegranate sauce (Venezia, Veneto)
–ripieno *rip-ye-no* stuffed turkey, served with potatoes, spinach and raisins (Lombardia)

tagliare *tahl-yah-re* to cut

tagliatelle *tahl-yah-te-le* long ribbon-shaped pasta (Emilia-Romagna)
–alla salsa di noci *ah-lah sahl-sah dee no-chee* with nuts, oil, butter, **ricotta** and parmesan (Emilia-Romagna)
–con finocchio selvatico *kon fi-nok-yo sel-vah-tee-ko* served with a fennel, bacon and parsley sauce (Calabria)

tagliere *tal-ye-re* cutting board

taglierini *tahl-ye-ree-nee* thin strips of pasta (Marche)
–al ragù *ahl rah-goo* served with meat sauce (Marche)

tagliolini (blò blò) *tahl-yo-lee-ni (blo blo)* thin strips of pasta in broth, with grated sheep's cheese (Umbria)

tajarin *tah-yah-rin* thin pasta usually served with meat sauce, but also with truffles or liver (Piemonte)

taleggio *tah-lej-yo* sweet, soft and fatty cheese with a soft rind which, traditionally, is matured for 40 days in caves (Lombardia)

taralli *tah-rah-lee* boiled and baked pretzel-like biscuits

tartufo/i *tahr-too-fo/fee* truffle – very expensive kind of fungus with an intense and unique aroma. Found underground, they are a basic ingredient for excellent **risotto**, omelettes and other dishes; also a rich chocolate ice-cream

–d'Alba/bianco *dahl-bah/bee-yahn-ko* white truffle – the rarest and most expensive
–arrostiti *ah-ro-stee-tee* slices of black truffle wrapped in slices of bacon, baked or cooked in ash (Umbria)
–di mare *dee mah-re* sea truffle – a type of mollusc (not fungus)
–di Norcia/nero *dee nor-chee-ya/ne-ro* black truffle

taverna *tahvernah* small rustic restaurant, though not always cheap

tavola *tah-vo-lah* table
–calda *kahl-dah* restaurants that offer cheap self-service with a selection of hot dishes

tavola, da *tah-vo-lah, dah* of table wine or cheese

tazza *taht-sah* cup

tazzina *taht-see-nah* little cup

tè *te* tea

tegamata di maiale *te-gah-mah-tah dee mah-yah-le* traditional dish where sweetbread, pieces of fat and lean meat are cooked for hours with tomatoes and fennel seed (Siena, Toscana)

tegame *te-gah-me* frying pan

tegame, in *te-gah-me, in* fried/braised

tegole d'Aosta *te-go-le dah-os-tah* almond biscuits, sometimes covered with chocolate (Valle d'Aosta)

tenero *te-ne-ro* tender

testa *tes-tah* head (of an animal)

testaió' *tes-tah-yo* squares of pasta served with **pesto** and parmesan, or just olive oil (Liguria)

testaroli *test-ah-ro-lee* discs of pasta, like pancakes
–al pesto *ahl pes-to* **testaroli** served with pesto sauce (Liguria)

testina *tes-tee-nah* calf's head
–alla carniola *ah-lah kahrn-yo-lah* calf's head boiled, sliced and seasoned with a sauce prepared with brain, garlic, vinegar and horseradish (Friuli)

tiella *tee-ye-lah* baked vegetables with oil, garlic and spices. There are two other versions of this dish: one with rice, potatoes and mussels and another one prepared with lamb, giblets, **lampascioni** and potatoes. (Puglia)

–di Gaeta *dee gah-e-tah* pasta stuffed with tomato, vegetables, anchovies, squid and olives (Lazio)

tigelle modenesi *ti-je-le mo-de-ne-zee* little round flat bread served hot with lard, rosemary, garlic and parmesan (Modena, Emilia-Romagna)

timballo *tim-bah-lo* baked pie which can come in many forms and can be made with pastry or **lasagne**

–abruzzese *ah-broot-se-ze* baked crepes with layers of meatballs, meat, **scamorza**, tomato sauce, parmesan and chicken giblets (Abruzzo)

–di piccione *dee pi-cho-ne* stewed pigeon with pasta baked in short-crust pastry (Cremona, Lombardia)

timo *tee-mo* thyme

timpano 'e maccaruni *tim-pah-no e mah-kah-roo-ni* shortcrust pastry filled with cooked pasta, peas, mushrooms, black truffle, **mozzarella**, meat sauce and grated cheese (Napoli, Campania)

tipo 00 *tee-po ze-ro ze-ro* (see **farina**)

tiramisù *ti-rah-mi-soo* delicious dessert prepared with sponge cake or **savoiardi** soaked in coffee and arranged in layers with **mascarpone** cheese, then sprinkled with cocoa (Veneto)

toc de purcit *tok de poor-chit* pork and liver stew served with polenta (Friuli)

tòcco di carne *to-ko dee kahr-ne* veal sauce prepared for pasta, polenta or rice-based dishes (Liguria)

toma *to-mah* firm cow or sheep's cheese

–piemontese *pee-ye-mon-te-ze* there are two types of this cheese: soft and medium hard (Piedmont)

tomaxelle *to-mah-kse-le* veal roulades in wine and broth, usually served with mashed potatoes (Liguria)

tomino *to-mee-no* small fresh cheese

tonno *to-no* tuna

torciarelli al tartufo *tor-chah-re-li ahl tahr-too-fo* pasta served with a sauce prepared with extra-virgin olive oil, red onion, minced lean pork and veal, thyme, rosemary, mushrooms, truffles and cheese (Ciociaria, Lazio)

torcinelli *tor-chi-ne-li* lamb or kid entrails stewed with white wine or tomato sauce (Abruzzo)

Torcolati *tor-ko-lah-tee* sweet dessert wine

torcolo di San Costanzo *tor-ko-lo dee sahn kos-tahnt-so* ring-shaped cake (Perugia, Umbria)

torresani *to-re-sah-ni* tasty pigeon kebabs (Vicenza, Veneto)

torrone *to-ro-ne* nougat

–al cioccolato *ahl cho-ko-lah-to* very soft nougat (L'Aquila, Abruzzo)

–di Chieti *dee kee-ye-ti* nougat made with dried figs, chocolate and almonds (Chieti, Abruzzo)

–gelato *je-lah-to* mix of oranges, mandarins, candied fruit, almonds covered with chocolate (Calabria)

torroni di semi di sesamo (cupeta) *to-ro-ni dee se-mi dee se-zah-mo (koo-pe-tah)* crunchy little sweets made with honey, toasted almonds and sesame seeds (Catanzaro, Calabria)

torta *tor-tah* cake/tart/pie

–baciocca *bah-cho-kah* savoury tart prepared with potatoes, parmesan, beaten eggs and parsley (Liguria)

–di castagne *dee kahs-than-ye* chestnut cake covered with whipped cream (Trentino Alto-Adige)

–di fave *dee fah-ve* omelette with peeled broad beans, eggs, bread-crumbs and sugar (Sardegna)

–di formaggio *dee for-mah-jo* cheese tart (Basilicata)

–di Orvieto *dee or-vee-ye-to* bread/cake with sultanas, candied fruit and cherries – normally prepared for Easter (Umbria)

–di patate *dee pah-tah-te* savoury pie made with mashed potatoes, parmesan, eggs and minced veal (Piacenza, Emilia-Romagna)

–fregolotti *fre-go-lo-ti* very dry and crumbly almond cake (Trentino Alto-Adige)

–nera *ne-rah* sweet almond, coffee and cocoa pie (Modena, Emilia-Romagna)

–paradiso *pah-rah-dee-zo* very soft cake often served with **mascarpone** (Pavia, Lombardia)

–pasqualina *pahs-kwah-lee-nah* savoury cake prepared for Easter – made with 33 pastry sheets and **ricotta**, parmesan and chards (Liguria)

–sbrisolona *sbree-zo-lo-nah* very dry almond cake usually crumbled because it's difficult to slice (Mantua, Lombardia)

–tradizionale valdese alla crema *trah-dits-yo-nah-le vahl-de-ze ah-lah kre-mah* simple cream cake prepared on feasts (Turin, Piedmont)

tortelli *tor-te-lee* fat stuffed pasta

–di ricotta *dee ri-ko-tah* stuffed with **ricotta and** parmesan, served with tomato sauce (Piacenza, Emilia-Romagna)

–di San Leo *dee sahn le-o* stuffed with spinach, lemon peel, parmesan, **ricotta** and other kinds of cheese, usually served with meat sauce (Marche)

–di zucca *dee tsoo-kah* stuffed with pumpkin, almond biscuits, eggs, parmesan and apple – served with parmesan (Mantua, Lombardia)

–sguazzarotti *sgwaht-sah-ro-tee* **tortelli** stuffed with boiled beans, wine, pumpkin, orange peel, nuts and spices, served with **saorina** (Mantua, Lombardia)

tortellini *tor-te-lee-nee* pasta stuffed with pork, cured ham, turkey breast, parmesan and eggs. They look like very small rings and are served in meat stock or with meat sauce. (Bologna, Emilia-Romagna)

tortelloni *tor-te-lo-nee* large **tortellini**

tosella *to-ze-lah* fresh cheese sliced and fried in butter and served with polenta (Trentino Alto-Adige)

totano *to-tah-no* type of squid

tramezzino *trah-met-see-no* sandwich

trattoria *trah-tor-ee-yah* cheap restaurants offering simple dishes, generally catering for locals rather than tourists

Trebbiano *treb-yah-no* white grape found throughout Italy

trenette *tre-ne-te* a long and flat pasta

–al pesto *ahl pes-to* with potatoes, French beans and **pesto** (Liguria)

–avvantaggiae *ah-vahn-ta-ja-he* wholemeal **trenette** (Liguria)

Treviso radicchio *tre-vee-zo rah-dik-yo* popular type of chicory

trifola *tri-fo-lah* white truffle

trifolato *tri-fo-lah-to* cooking method which involves thinly slicing and cooking vegetables and meat with oil, garlic and parsley

triglia *tril-yah* red mullet

trippa *tri-pah* tripe

–alla trasteverina *ah-lah trahs-te-ve-ree-nah* tripe stewed in a sauce made with veal gravy, fresh mint leaves, wine and tomato sauce (Roma, Lazio)

–senese *se-ne-ze* boiled tripe cut into strips, cooked with tomato (Siena, Toscana)

–ù suffritto *oo soo-fri-to* boiled tripe cooked with tomato sauce, onion, oil, chilli and salt (Calabria) tritacarne *tri-tah-kahr-ne* mincer (meat)

tritare *tree-tah-re* to mince

tritaverdura *tri-tah-ver-doo-rah* mincer (vegetables)

trofie al pesto *tro-fee-ye ahl pes-to* thin and long pasta dumplings served with pesto sauce and sometimes boiled white beans (Genoa, Liguria)

trota *tro-tah* trout

tubetti *too-be-tee* short pasta tubes usually served in soups

turcinelli arrostiti *toor-chi-ne-li ah-ros-tee-ti* lamb offal stewed with oil, lard, white wine and tomato sauce, served with mature sheep's cheese (Molise)

U

uardi e fasoi *wahr-dee e fah-zoy* soup prepared with beans, barley, ham bone and spices (Friuli)

ubriaco/a *oo-bree-ah-ko/kah* drunk (m/f)

uccelletti *oo-che-le-tee* little birds

uccello *oo-che-lo* bird

umbricelli *oom-bree-che-lee* (see **umbrici**)

umbrici *oom-bree-chee* hand-made thick spaghetti (Umbria)
  –al tartufo *ahl tahr-too-fo* served with a truffle sauce

umido, in *oo-mee-do, in* cooked in liquid

una/o *oo-nah/no* one

ungere *oon-je-re* to baste

uova *wo-vah* eggs

uva *oo-vah* grapes
  –bianca *bee-yahn-ka* green grapes
  –nera *ne-rah* red grapes
  –passa *pah-sah* raisins
  –secca *se-kah* raisins

V

vacca *vah-kah* cow

Valpolicella Amarone *vahl-po-lee-che-lah ah-mah-ro-ne* red wine with an intense aroma – excellent with roast meats or ripe cheeses (Veneto)

Valtellina Sfursat *vahl-po-lee-che-lah sfoor-saht* red wine with an intense and spicy aroma, excellent with game, meat or ripe cheeses (Lombardia)

vaniglia *vah-nil-yah* vanilla

vapore *vah-po-re* steam

vapore, cuocere a *vah-po-re, kwo-che-re ah* to steam

vecchio *vek-yo* old/aged

ventresca di tonno *ven-tres-kah dee to-no* the belly of tuna – best and most expensive cut of tuna

verde *ver-de* green

Verdicchio dei Castelli di Jesi *ver-deek-yo dey kahs-te-lee dee ye-zee* delicate dry white wine – excellent with fish soups, shellfish or poultry (Marche)

verdura/e *ver-doo-rah/re* vegetable/s

vermouth *ver-moot* herbal fortified wine – used in martinis

Vernaccia di Oristano *ver-na-chah dee o-ris-tah-nah* white wine but sometimes a dessert wine (Sardegna)

Vernaccia di San Gimignano *ver-na-chah dee sahn jim-in-yah-no* very dry white wine (Toscana)

verza *ver-za* savoy cabbage

vialone nano *vee-yah-lo-ne nah-no* short grain rice ideal for **risotto**

Vigilia di Natale *vi-jee-lyah dee nah-tah-le* Christmas Eve – often celebrated more than Christmas Day

vigna *vin-yah* vineyard

Vin Santo *vin sahn-to* deliciously sweet dessert wine

vincisgrassi *vin-chiz-grah-see* rich baked dish with offal, bechamel, grated cheese and, sometimes, truffles (Macerata, Marche)

vino *vee-no* wine (see the **Wine** section in the **Drinks** chapter for details)
  –bianco *byahn-ko* white wine

–cotto *ko-to* wine obtained from cooking the must – it's normally made with grapes, but also with figs, and is widely used to prepare cakes

–da tavola *dah tah-vo-lah* table wine – these wines are generally of a lower standard although some can be of excellent quality and great value

–della casa *de-lah kah-zah* house wine

–rosso *ross-o* red wine

Vino Nobile di Montepulciano *vee-no no-bee-le dee mon-te-pool-chah-no* robust red wine which ages wonderfully (Toscana)

viscidu *vi-shi-doo* dry, salty and sour cheese, sliced and pickled (Sardegna)

vite *vee-te* vine

vitello *vi-te-lo* veal – very popular meat

–tonnato *to-nah-to* thin round slices of veal covered with a tuna, capers and anchovy sauce (Piedmonte)

vongole *von-go-le* clams

W

wurstel *voor-stel* frankfurter

Z

zabaglione *zah-bahl-yo-ne* creamy mix of beaten egg, **marsala**, and sugar, srved in a bowl in which dry biscuits can be dunked. It can also be used in sponge cakes. (Piedmont)

zabaione *zah-bah-yo-ne* (see **zabaglione**)

zafferano *zah-fe-rah-no* saffron

zampetto *zahm-pe-to* calf, lamb or pig trotter

zampone di Modena *zahm-po-ne dee mo-de-nah* stewed stuffed boned pig's trotter. Typical Christmas dish, usually served with lentils, mashed potatoes, stewed beans and spinach. (Modena, Emilia-Romagna)

zelten *zel-ten* rich Christmas cake made with rye flour, dried figs, sultanas, dates and pine nuts (Trentino Alto-Adige)

zenzero *zen-ze-ro* ginger

zeppule 'e cicenielli *ze-poo-le e chee-chen-ye-li* fritters made with flour, eggs, chopped parsley, grated cheese and anchovies (Napoli, Campania)

zeppule 'e San Giuseppe *ze-poo-le e sahn joo-ze-pe* small fried ring-shaped cakes sprinkled with icing sugar and cinnamon (Napoli, Campania)

zimin *zi-min* soup with haricot beans, pork and chards (Imperia, Liguria)

ziti *zee-tee* long fat hollow pasta

zona *zo-nah* zone/area

zucca *zoo-kah* pumpkin

–gialla in agrodolce *jah-lah in ah-gro-dol-che* fried pumpkin served with oil, vinegar, capers, garlic, mint and breadcrumbs (Calabria)

–ripiena *rip-ye-nah* green pumpkin stuffed with meat, cheese and spices, stewed with tomato sauce (Cosenza, Calabria)

zucchero *zu-kero* sugar

–a vela *ah ve-lah* icing sugar

–di canna *dee kah-na* cane sugar

zucchini *zoo-kee-nee* zucchini/courgette

zuccotto fiorentino *zoo-ko-to fyo-ren-tee-no* sponge cake with liqueur, custard, chocolate and whipped cream (Firenze, Toscana)

zuf *zoof* hot polenta served with cold milk (Friuli)

zuppa *zoo-pah* soup, usually thick – (see **minestra**)

–alla canavesana *ah-lah kahn-ah-ve-zah-nah* nourishing thick soup prepared with bread, boiled cabbage, broth, meat sauce, lard, onions, garlic and sausage (Piedmont)

–alla valpellentze *ah-lah vahl-pe-li-nent-se* soup made with bread, cabbage, **fontina** and stock (Valle d'Aosta)

–di cavolo nero lucchese *dee kah-vo-lo ne-ro lu-ke-ze* soup prepared with beans, black cabbage, savoy cabbage, chards, tomato, potato, zucchini and carrots (Lucca, Toscana)

–di ceci *dee che-chee* rich chickpea soup (Cuneo, Piedmont)

–di pesce alla marinara *dee pe-she ah-lah mah-ree-nah-rah* fish soup (Napoli, Campania)

–di scarola e fagioli *dee skah-ro-lah e fahj-yo-lee* rich soup prepared with beans, prickly lettuce, garlic, chilli and toasted bread (Ciociaria, Lazio)

–di soffritto *dee so-free-to (see* **zuppa 'e zuffritto**)

–di trippe *dee tri-pe* tripe soup

–'e zuffritto *e tsu-free-to* not a soup as such, but a sauce prepared with pig's offal cooked in red wine and tomato sauce. It's traditionally served on slices of toasted bread or as a sauce for spaghetti. (Campania, Napoli)

–inglese *in-gle-ze* 'English soup', dessert prepared with layers of sponge cake, custard and chocolate cream. (Emilia-Romagna)

–lombarda *lom-bahr-dah* cannellini bean soup (Siena, Toscana)

–pavese *pah-ve-ze* soup with bread, butter, chicken broth and fresh eggs (Pavia, Lombardia)

Photo Credits

Alan Benson Front cover, p1, p5, p8, p9 top right, p12, p13, p14, p16, p19, p20, p21, p22, p23, p24, p26, p27, p29, p34, p36, p40, p41, p42, p43, p44, p45, p46, p47, p48, p49, p50, p55, p56, p58, p59, p60, p61, p64, p65, p66, p67, p69, p70, p71, p73, p75, p76, p78, p80, p81, p82, p87, p90, p92, p94, p96, p98, p100, p101, p102, p103, p105, p107, p109 top right, bottom, p111, p112, p114, p117, p118, p119, p120, p122, p123, p125, p127, p128, p129, p130, p132, p133, p134, p135, p136, p137, p139, p141, p145, p146, p148, p153, p156, p157, p158, p159, p161, p164, p165, p167, p169, p170, p172, p173, p174, p175, p176, p180, p182, p183 left, p184, p186, p187, p189, p190, p192, p193, p194, p195, p196, p197, top right, left, p199, p202, p207, p208, p209, p212, p214, p215 left, p216, p218, p219, p221.

Jon Davidson Back cover, p9 top left, bottom right, p150, p215 bottom right.

Simon Rowe p203.

Damien Simonis p9 bottom left, p109 top left.

Teresa Gaudio p183 right.

Christopher Groenhout p142 & 143, p197 bottom right.

Greg Elms p178.

Juliet Coombe p38, p160, p205.

Oliver Strewe p63.

The Lonely Planet Story

Lonely Planet published its first book in 1973 in response to the numerous 'How did you do it?' questions Maureen and Tony Wheeler were asked after driving, bussing, hitching, sailing and railing their way from England to Australia. Written at a kitchen table and hand collated, trimmed and stapled, *Across Asia on the Cheap* became an instant local bestseller.

Eighteen months in South-East Asia resulted in their second guide, *South-East Asia on a Shoestring*, which they put together in a backstreet Chinese hotel in Singapore in 1975. The 'yellow bible', as it quickly became known to backpackers around the world, soon became the guide to the region. It has sold well over ¾ million copies and is now in its 10th edition, still retaining its familiar yellow cover.

Today there are over 400 titles, including travel guides, walking guides, language kits & phrasebooks, travel atlases & maps, diving guides, restaurant guides, first time travel guides, condensed guides, illustrated pictorials and travel literature. The company is the largest independent travel publisher in the world.

The emphasis continues to be on travel for independent travellers. Tony and Maureen still travel for several months of each year and play an active part in the writing, updating and quality control of Lonely Planet's guides.

They have been joined by over 120 authors and over 400 staff at our offices in Melbourne (Australia), Oakland (USA), London (UK) and Paris (France). Travellers themselves also make a valuable contribution to the guides through the feedback we receive in thousands of letters each year and on our web site.

The people at Lonely Planet strongly believe that travellers can make a positive contribution to the countries they visit, both through their appreciation of the countries' culture, wildlife and natural features, and through the money they spend. In addition, the company makes a direct contribution to the countries and regions it covers. Since 1986 a percentage of the income from each book has been donated to ventures such as famine relief in Africa; aid projects in India; agricultural projects in Central America; Greenpeace's efforts to halt French nuclear testing in the Pacific.

Lonely Planet Offices

Australia
PO Box 617, Hawthorn, Victoria 3122
☎ 03-9819 1877
fax 03-9819 6459
email:talk2us@lonelyplanet.com.au

USA
150 Linden St, Oakland, CA 94607
☎ 510-893 8555 TOLL FREE: 800 275 8555
fax 510-893 8572
email: info@lonelyplanet.com

UK
10a Spring Place, London NW5 3BH
☎ 020-7428 4800
fax 020-7428 4828
email: go@lonelyplanet.co.uk

France
1 rue du Dahomey, 75011 Paris
☎ 01 55 25 33 00
fax 01 55 25 33 01
email: bip@lonelyplanet.fr